THE VICTORIAN NOVEL OF ADULTHOOD

Series in Victorian Studies
Joseph McLaughlin, series editor

Katherine D. Harris, *Forget Me Not: The Rise of the British Literary Annual, 1823–1835*

Rebecca Rainof, *The Victorian Novel of Adulthood: Plot and Purgatory in Fictions of Maturity*

The Victorian Novel of Adulthood

PLOT AND PURGATORY IN FICTIONS OF MATURITY

Rebecca Rainof

OHIO UNIVERSITY PRESS • ATHENS, OHIO

Ohio University Press, Athens, Ohio 45701
ohioswallow.com
© 2015 by Ohio University Press
All rights reserved

To obtain permission to quote, reprint, or otherwise reproduce or distribute material from Ohio University Press publications, please contact our rights and permissions department at (740) 593-1154 or (740) 593-4536 (fax).

Printed in the United States of America
Ohio University Press books are printed on acid-free paper ∞ ™

25 24 23 22 21 20 19 18 17 16 15   5 4 3 2 1

Library of Congress Cataloging-in-Publication Data
Rainof, Rebecca Elise, 1979–
The Victorian novel of adulthood : plot and purgatory in fictions of maturity / Rebecca Rainof.
  pages cm. — (Series in Victorian studies)
Includes bibliographical references and index.
ISBN 978-0-8214-2178-9 (hc : alk. paper) — ISBN 978-0-8214-4538-9 (pdf)
1. Adulthood in literature. 2. Middle age in literature. 3. English fiction—19th century—History and criticism. 4. English fiction—20th century—History and criticism. I. Title.
PR878.A375R35 2015
823'.809354—dc23
                    2015022080

This book is dedicated to my family with love.

Contents

List of Illustrations ix

Acknowledgments xi

INTRODUCTION
    The Belly of Sheol
      1

CHAPTER ONE
    "Strange Introversions"
    Newman, Mature Conversion, and the Poetics of Purgatory
      23

CHAPTER TWO
    George Eliot's Winter Tales
      59

CHAPTER THREE
    The Bachelor's Purgatory
    Arrested Development and the Progress of Shades
      116

CHAPTER FOUR
    Odd Women and Eccentric Plotting
    Maturity, Modernism, and Woolf's Victorian Retrospection
      156

CODA
    Descent and Tradition
      188

Notes 195

Bibliography 229

Index 245

Illustrations

FIGURE 2.1
"La Pia of Siena," Canto V, *Le Purgatoire*, Gustave Doré, 1868
99

FIGURE 2.2
"The Earthly Garden of Bliss," Canto XXVIII, *Le Purgatoire*, Gustave Doré, 1868
101

FIGURE 2.3
"The Late-Repenters," Canto IV, *Le Purgatoire*, Gustave Doré, 1868
102

FIGURE 2.4
La Pia de' Tolomei, Dante Gabriel Rossetti, 1868–80
103

Acknowledgments

I am delighted to thank the many people who fostered this book's maturation. I thank Deborah Nord and Maria DiBattista of Princeton University for their generous insight and inspiring kindness. They helped support this book and its author at every turn. This book also benefitted from the kind comments and guidance of Susan Stewart, Jeff Nunokawa, Uli Knoepflmacher, Bill Gleason, Diana Fuss, Esther Schor, and many other members of the Princeton Department of English over the years.

To my colleagues at the Catholic University of America I owe special thanks. Ernest Suarez, Taryn Okuma, Daniel Gibbons, Tobias Gregory, Christopher Wheatley, Steven Wright, Pamela Ward, Joseph Sendry, Gregory Baker, Lilla Kopar, and the whole English Department—thank you for helping this book grow and for sharing your wit and wonderful company. I am lucky to have such fine colleagues and good friends.

Numerous institutions and individuals further supported this book's development and completion. The Catholic University of America gave crucial research support in the form of grants. Early work on this manuscript was funded by the Graduate School of Arts and Sciences at Princeton University and the Josephine de Kármán Foundation. Librarians at Princeton's Firestone Library and Marquand Art Library and at the Library of Congress in Washington, DC, invaluably aided this book from beginning to end. The members of the Birmingham Oratory in Birmingham, England, provided archival assistance and the most generous hospitality. It has been a great pleasure to work with everyone at Ohio University Press, and I thank the editors and two anonymous readers whose comments provided essential guidance. Jacky Shin lent her expertise as a friend and scholar. Rosalind Parry was an excellent research assistant.

I would also like to acknowledge the publishers who have given me permission to reprint parts of this book. An earlier version of chapter 1 first appeared as "Victorians in Purgatory: Newman's Poetics of Conciliation and the Afterlife of the Oxford Movement," *Victorian Poetry* 51, no. 2 (Summer 2013): 227–47. A version of chapter 2 first appeared as "George Eliot's Screaming Statues, *Laocoon*, and the Pre-Raphaelites," *SEL: Studies in English Literature 1500–1900* 54, no. 4 (Autumn 2014): 875–99.

After all these years, it is my great pleasure to include in these thanks dear friends: Sonia Velázquez, J. K. Barret, Briallen Hopper, Jacky Shin, Mary Noble, Roger Bellin, Wendy Lee, Kerry Chun, and Elizabeth Ferrell. Your friendship means the world to me. To my extended family, the Mas-Silbersteins, the Ferrells, and the Merolas, your presence in our lives during the period of this book's writing has been a tremendous blessing.

Finally, this book is dedicated to my family:

To my father and mother, Alexandre and Alice Rainof, who taught my sister, Mila, and me about the importance of magic, including a love of literature and writing. You are the best teachers I know. To my daughters, Anya and Clara, who brought sweetness and sparkle to the years of this book's completion. Your hugs and kisses are pure magic. To Alex Mas, who made this book and all the goodness of our lives together possible, I send my biggest thanks with love. And to Mila Rainof, my brilliant and beautiful sister, this book is dedicated with fierce and abiding affection. You promised to be always by my side. You are.

INTRODUCTION

The Belly of Sheol

Swallowed whole and trapped in the leviathan's belly, Jonah spends three days underwater before surfacing to accept his role as God's prophet. The biblical story of Jonah's descent has become a favorite example for several literary critics interested in theorizing narrative lulls, for they take the prophet's most memorable turning point—his three days spent inside a fish—as emblematic of the uneventful in literature, a climax that is itself an anticlimax.

George Orwell's interpretation of the story insists that this aquatic journey to the interior "is a very comfortable, cosy, homelike thought," and he imagines the leviathan's stomach as a "womb big enough for an adult," if ultimately as an unproductive space of gestation. "Short of being dead," he writes, "it is the final, unsurpassable stage of irresponsibility."[1] Yet Orwell misses a crucial detail when he states that Jonah's marine reckoning stops short of death. The lesson Jonah learns inside the whale, like other famed trips to the realm of shadows—Odysseus's visit to Hades, Saint Patrick's quest through purgatory, Dante's journey from hell to paradise—involves an immersion not solely in viscera but in the realm of death itself: in Sheol.[2] As the prophet's prayer proclaims,

> I called to the Lord out of my distress,
> and he answered me;
> out of the belly of Sheol I cried for help,
> and you heard my voice.[3]

Addressing novels that resist plot, Robert Caserio usefully seizes upon Orwell's "Inside the Whale" as providing a model for describing narrative inaction in nineteenth- and twentieth-century literature.[4] He finds that to be "inside the whale" is to be immersed in a plot lull or, in his reading of Orwell's essay, to be the author of works that tend toward these troughs.[5] The ethical significance of becoming Jonah in the guise of author, character, or reader comes immediately into question in such studies that probe a discomfort with places of seeming lassitude in novels. Do these passages bear witness to contemplation and introspection or to an avoidance of action in the face of an urgent call? This question has characterized the work of scholars such as Anne-Lise François, who interestingly reframes narrative lulls in terms of recessive action rather than passivity, and Stefanie Markovits, who asks, "Can thinking ever be doing?"[6] Markovits follows in Caserio's steps in rightly drawing our attention to the "suspect" nature of refusing or failing to act, but in her study "inaction" and "inward action" can be considered jointly, thereby making it difficult to discuss thinking that amounts to doing separately from mental states in which this may not be the case. These less-active mental states could include apathy, complacency, boredom, idleness, and other forms of passivity that figure centrally in Orwell's "Inside the Whale."

A survey of Jonah's literary-critical fate reveals that when critics invoke this biblical story to discuss narrative lulls another submerged concern also surfaces: how to represent the hidden workings of adult conversion and unseen maturation in novels. The tendency has been to interpret these subtle changes in terms of inaction, stasis, or even regression. Nowhere is this affiliation between lulls and arrested development made clearer than in Orwell's depiction of Jonah in utero, a grown man crawling back into the womb. But if Jonah's story gives us a model of narrative lulls, as I contend, it is certainly a more productive one than has previously been set forth by literary critics. To uncover a more productive, and less parodic and static, account of mature conversion requires new attention to the varieties of plots offered by stories of adult growth and development. Instead of framing representations of adult conversion in terms of inaction or passivity, then, this study focuses on a temporal concern: on radical gradualism in Victorian stories of adulthood and midlife.

Taking another trip "inside the whale," and into the afterlife that waits there, provides a useful first step in thinking through the ways that authors capture an extreme gradualism that belies the apparent lack of plot in narratives about maturity. To return to the prophet's example, what exactly can be said to *happen* to Jonah inside the whale? In invoking Jonah, critics often overlook the reference to Sheol as well as the curious detail that Jonah makes *two* "descents" (*yarad*) in rapid succession.[7] Fleeing from God's commandment that he preach repentance in Nineveh, Jonah sets sail in the opposite direction, toward Tarshish. En route, he performs his first descent, hiding deep in the ship's hull and falling asleep, leaving the crew above to struggle against God's wrath without having knowledge of its source. Eventually, through the casting of lots, Jonah is brought forth, at which point he insists that he be thrown into the sea, where a portable afterlife awaits within the leviathan. He then makes his second descent, this one into the "belly of Sheol." The difference between Jonah's two descents provides a crucial turn in his narrative, illustrating his transition from a type of inaction to inward action, his time in Sheol being devoted to prayer and reflection. It becomes a place where the Aristotelian categories of "character" and "action" become difficult to pry apart and where an internalized form of action, not simply inaction, produces a transformed prophet.[8]

This submerged storytelling model found in Jonah's narrative is not one readily identified with the bildungsroman, the novel of momentous first transgressions and the transition from youth to adulthood. Instead, the trip to the underworld and into the whale has proven to be one particularly suited to *mature* protagonists—to travelers resembling Odysseus more than Telemachus. *The Victorian Novel of Adulthood* considers how many novels diagnosed with a lack of plot by contemporary literary scholars appear to be written against the bildungsroman tradition, extending past the coming-of-age story into the realm of *having come of age*. This is a time when marriage plots may have run their course or when stories of vocational pursuit have petered out, leaving characters in a midlife lull that Henry James labeled, with some irony, "the country of the general lost freshness."[9] Yet as common as such accounts are in Victorian literature, these times of mature struggling and introspection have been largely neglected in literary critical studies. Instead, we tend to think of novels about adulthood and midlife as an eccentric species in the nineteenth century, an aging relative to the more nimble and popular bildungsroman.[10] This account of the bildungsroman's dominance is bolstered by scholarship that upholds the coming-of-age story as the quintessential expression of Victorian nation building, a narrative of historical progression grafted onto a story of individual growth. Our attraction to the bildungsroman has proven so potent that a body of literature devoted to adulthood has been relegated to the sidelines, framed as a marginal subgenre, and ultimately absented from literary critical studies of the Victorian period as well as narrative and novel theories that discuss plot more broadly.

Challenging a longstanding critical love affair with stories of youth, *The Victorian Novel of Adulthood* proposes that novels about adulthood and midlife demonstrate a model of plot distinct from that of the bildungsroman and, as such, deserve separate consideration in studies of the novel. My goal, however, in discussing fictions of maturity is not simply to define this novelistic subgenre against the bildungsroman as a more dominant genre or to argue over the boundary lines for definitions of the bildungsroman. Numerous studies already exist to those ends.[11] Instead, I examine how our emphasis on the novel of youthful formation has shaped and, in many important ways, limited our understanding of, first, the range of experience captured in Victorian fiction and, second, the distinctly gradual plots these fictions exhibit. In shifting our angle of perception and looking at the development of the Victorian novel through another subgenre of literature (namely, works dealing with midlife and adulthood), we can address an alternative, comparatively uneventful kind of storytelling than the one that has been commonly accepted and used as a model for novel studies. This approach requires that we rethink the way that we have framed the bildungsroman in scholarship on Victorian novels as the masterplot for the period and that we instead recognize the widespread representations of adulthood, midlife, and maturity.

This new awareness of the centrality of mature fictions in the nineteenth century, in turn, necessitates a reconsideration of the development of the English novel and the genealogy of Victorian historical consciousness. More than simply addressing the features that compose such fictions, this book argues for an alternative understanding of the development of the British novel that includes the many novels about midlife, showing how they equally constitute our sense of the novel's growth and defining features: its periods of suspension and its fascination with interiority, its wealth of accumulated daily detail, and its ability to render these details into a progressive, if at times uneventful, whole.

In representing barely perceptible development that unfolds slowly in adulthood, many of the works in this study are well-known for the biting criticism they inspire: Henry James's accusation that *Daniel Deronda* is more like a lake than a river in terms of its narrative flow; George Gissing's diagnosis of *Little Dorrit*'s "prevalent air of gloom" (a sign that "the hand of the master is plainly weary"); H. G. Wells's frustration with the way James's "vast paragraphs sweat and struggle" in "tales of nothingness" about cautious bachelors "going delicately" through life.[12] These novels, and many others accused of similar crimes against plot, have something in common: mature protagonists. Rather than depict the tumults of first love, loss, and transgression, they illustrate an adult-onset "arrested development." As a result, their authors face the unique challenge of accommodating the prolonged inactivity of protagonists in a novel form that demands progression. Subtle narrative developments like these are truly "arrested developments," as they come to fruition when a character, and potentially a plotline, seems to stop moving. This paradoxical development within stasis is, upon inspection, a vision of the most extremely gradual and inward change imaginable, change that eludes surface recognition, requiring the powers of fictional insight to be uncovered.[13]

Despite the lack of critical attention given to midlife in Victorian fiction, these gradualist plots of maturity are surprisingly common. For example, a classic bildungsroman by Dickens, *David Copperfield*, is as much about maturity as it is about youth, for it reveals a process of disillusionment born of adulthood. As the protagonist reflects after his first marriage and success as a writer, "I was happy; but the happiness I had vaguely anticipated, once, was not the happiness I enjoyed. . . . What I missed, I still regarded—I always regarded—as something that had been a dream of my youthful fancy; that was incapable of realization; that I was now discovering to be so, with some natural pain, as all men did."[14] Another archetypal bildungsroman, *Jane Eyre*, comes to rest in contemplative doldrums as vast and deceptively uniform as the space of the moors where Jane wanders. These suspended stretches on the moors follow the revolutionary rush of first experience, allowing the heroine to perform the work of maturity. Likewise, Ellen Wood's sensation novel *East Lynne*, which enthralled nineteenth-century readers with its illicit twists, mires itself for long periods in the complexities of married life and second unions, depicting motherhood and female aging as central concerns.[15] And *Vanity Fair*, a novel driven at the relentless pace of Becky Sharp's ambition, surpasses the boundaries of the bildungsroman early in its story arc, moving from the school days of Becky, Amelia, Dobbin, and George into accounts of failed marriages and widowhood, visions of second marriages, and an intergenerational chronicle of parental shortcomings. As Dobbin thinks back on the ten years that make up this portion of the novel, he observes, "Long years had passed. . . . He had now passed into the stage of old-fellow-hood. His hair was grizzled, and many a passion and feeling of his youth had grown grey in that interval."[16] The "interval" of graying includes the entire middle of the novel up to its end, and while it occasions some of Thackeray's sharpest satire, it also includes his greatest overtures toward compassion for his aging central characters.

A Love Affair with the Bildungsroman: Novel Studies and Forgotten Narratives of Midlife

Beginning in the mid-twentieth century, novels dealing with maturity were increasingly considered under a rubric that gives precedence to the coming-of-age story as "the 'symbolic form' of modernity," to quote Franco Moretti's influential assertion.[17] Works as varied as *Great Expectations* and *Little Dorrit* have been considered alike in scholarship that not only prioritizes the bildungsroman as a plot model but also goes so far as to cast the genre's "rise" and "development" as a bildungsroman narrative itself. For example, Mikhail Bakhtin frames the novel's history as an intergenerational conflict between rebellious youths and staid elders. The novel, presented as a scrappy pugilist, is "the leading hero in the drama of literary development," and it "fights for its own hegemony in literature; wherever it triumphs, the other older genres go into decline."[18] Georg Lukács likewise casts the novel as a protagonist in a story of formation, saying that the novel expresses the modern dissonance between the individual and his environment or, rather, between a "youthful confidence" and an "outside world ... [that] will never speak to us in a voice that will clearly tell us our way and determine our goal."[19] In these foundational works of literary theory, the novel comes to occupy a role very similar to that of Pip in *Great Expectations* or Julien Sorel in *The Red and the Black:* the position of an upstart, of questionable class distinction, ascending the ranks.

This bias toward the bildungsroman in literary criticism continues today, and a new group of scholars including Jed Esty interestingly extend Moretti's account of the bildungsroman to address the genre's colonial, even colonizing reach.[20] Indeed, the term *bildungsroman* has been applied so expansively in recent years as to include novels that imagine, more fully, second chances, second marriages, and the trials and tribulations of adult life. Moretti may claim *Middlemarch* as an example of the female coming-of-age story, but Virginia Woolf applauded this "mature" work for being "one of the few English novels written for grown-up people."[21] Woolf's assertion can be taken as an alternative starting point for uncovering a vast counter-tradition to the bildungsroman, one that centers on Victorian literature about "grown-up people" and their gradual plots of development.

To begin thinking about these mature plots requires reexamining our critical bias toward the bildungsroman and identifying how our most gradual models of plotting fell out of current critical discussions. Our existing studies more easily follow what Marianne Hirsch has called the picaresque strain in her discussion of the bildungsroman's overwhelming appeal in "Defining Bildungsroman as a Genre."[22] For this reason, many critics, notably Peter Brooks, struggle to encompass the introversion that Hirsch links with confessional narratives, instead consigning interiority to the static or suspended aspects of fiction. In discussing E. M. Forster's *Aspects of the Novel*, Brooks challenges Forster's dismissal of plot in favor of character, countering that if characters' "'secret lives' are to be narratable, they must in some sense be plotted, display a design and logic."[23] Brooks's opening volley would seem to suggest an ensuing discussion of plot's hidden, inward workings, but the quieter parts of characters' "secret" lives go largely unaccounted for in his study as well. He poses "desire" as a subject through which to discuss internalized action—or rather, those sequential movements that make character "narratable"—though, as his following chapters soon reveal, his real focus is on ambition that manifests itself in observable action. Many of his central case studies in *Reading for the Plot* are the "desiring machines" (41) of nineteenth-century literature: Pip, Julien Sorel, and Lucien from *Lost Illusions*, in other words, bildungsroman protagonists. Characters who find themselves less outwardly active or unable to translate desire into visible acts—those hampered by factors including age, temperament, and gender—are less easily discussed in Brooks's model of plot based on engines, male arousal, and the Freudian death drive. His difficulty in accounting for what he terms the "female" narratives of desire reveals how his larger concept of plot strains to include an array of domestic, middle-aged, or otherwise less overtly "active" fictions. In this sense, his definition of plot does not vary deeply from the one he identifies as problematic in Forster's earlier work, for both his study and Forster's rely on a similarly eventful model of plot extrapolated from the bildungsroman—a model that effectively consigns periods of suspension and contemplation to fiction's other, less temporally focused "aspects," including character, style, and description.

How, then, should we regard lulls in which introspection displaces outward action? Are scenes of inward growth active or passive? Do they represent a cessation of plot or its most urgent turning points? This question of the relationship between interiority and plot has become a source of some critical impasse. Caserio has noted the challenge of trying to theorize introspective action at all. Invoking D. H. Lawrence's assertion that George Eliot "started putting all the action inside," Caserio writes that "[w]e find a novelist like D. H. Lawrence, for example, pointing to George Eliot as the major revisionist of the senses of plot and action because she *internalizes* action. . . . It is perhaps by the internalization of action, a step that ultimately makes action imponderable or makes it at best an arbitrary and unfixed sign in an unending series of metonymies, that George Eliot most undermines Dickens's sense of plot" (95). But must action "brought inside" really become "imponderable" in terms of plot?

These places of unseen, inward conversion are often overlooked in studies of plot even as they have been widely accepted as a central feature of realism. Ian Watt long ago noted that realism follows a "more minutely discriminating time-scale," asserting that before its advent "much of man's life had tended to be almost unavailable to literary representation merely as a result of its slowness."[24] This ability to capture slow processes is, in Watt's assessment of temporality in the realist novel, the genre's hallmark and vital innovation. But in thinking about plot, we find a basic contradiction at work, apparent in George Levine's later gloss on Thackeray that "plot . . . is not an essential element for realism."[25] This view is echoed, in perhaps less stark terms, by Caserio and Markovits, who turn to character and inaction as central terms for discussing the "slow" parts of realist fiction—posing these stretches of text as comparatively static and devoid of plot. Examination of recent criticism reveals that an understated type of narrative momentum has been overlooked precisely because it has been absorbed into considerations of the plot's antitheses: character, discourse, style, description, and lyrical suspension, or in other words, aspects of narrative that fall under Gérard Genette's heading of "discourse," loosely defined as everything counterposed to "story" in a novel. Amanpal Garcha has tried to reclaim features of "discourse," notably style and description, as central to perceiving the pleasures of reading the "plotless" parts of fiction, but there is still a need to address what occurs during fallow places in novels.[26] As Garcha notes, other pleasures attend reading than the ones identified by latter-day structuralists such as Brooks, but he claims these pleasures for reading style and description alone. He therefore focuses on narrative features that arise when plot, as he defines it, ceases its machinations. One might ask whether plot really stops in this manner, giving way clearly to descriptive or discursive passages. It would seem that, on the contrary, it is during these apparent lulls in "story" that a gradual form of narrative progression is often most rigorously at work.

The question remains: what it is we read for when dramatic plotting subsides into an understated form of narrative development? To address these places of seeming quietude, some of the ground recently ceded to character and discourse might be more usefully discussed in terms of plot. Therefore, rather than eschew "plot" as a central term through which to understand lulls, it is time to consider *what kind* of plot is at work in many of the uneventful stretches that compose Victorian novels about adulthood and midlife.

Defining Novels of Midlife: Events, Epochs, and "Turning Stretches"

Beginning with the smallest unit of plot, the event, one might ask, what do these gradual plots of adult development look like in terms of events?[27] Many of the changes that compose novels of maturity tend toward lengthy representation and are hard to define in our existing critical rhetoric; they evade the tight narrative unit of the "turning point" and, more confoundingly, do not conform to larger attempts at excerption, such as the episode or the chapter. If anything, the drawn-out events in these novels are best captured by a phrase of George Eliot's in *Daniel Deronda* when she refers to them as "epochs" within a novel. Looking back on Gwendolen Harleth's adult maturation over the course of a year, the narrator of *Daniel Deronda* reflects that there are "differences" that "are manifest in the variable intensity which we call human experience, from the revolutionary rush of change which makes a new inner and outer life, to that quiet recurrence of the familiar, which has no other epochs than those of hunger and the heavens."[28] These swaths of time in which the "quiet recurrence of the familiar" can itself make a "new inner and outer life" offer an entry point for understanding what might be termed the "turning stretches" that compose novels of adult development.

One such example of an "epoch" of slow change can be found, over the span of hundreds of pages, in *Middlemarch*, a work in which Eliot resists a hasty return to the marriage plot. After Casaubon dies, Dorothea is left to consider his "shining rows of note-books" that stand as "the mute memorial of a forgotten faith."[29]

> At first she walked into every room, questioning the eighteen months of her married life, and carrying on her thoughts as if they were a speech to be heard by her husband. Then, she lingered in the library, and could not be at rest till she had carefully ranged all the note-books as she imagined that he would wish to see them, in orderly sequence. The pity which had been the restraining compelling motive in her life with

him still clung about his image, even while she remonstrated with him in indignant thought and told him that he was unjust. (304)

Despite the less than riveting pace of Dorothea rearranging Casaubon's books, this is not an entirely uneventful passage. In this moment of dutiful remembrance mixed with "indignant thought," Eliot reveals an internal turn of events for Dorothea, a move from duty to rebellion bound up in her decisive act of writing a note scribbled inside an envelope left for her by Casaubon. "*Do you not see now that I could not submit my soul to yours, by working hopelessly at what I have no belief in?—Dorothea?*" (304). This note turns the posthumous decree of Casaubon's will into a correspondence, a dialogue with the dead. Nevertheless, although this rebellious act of writing marks Dorothea's changing inward course, her plot remains as devoid of outward action as before. Time passes and readers encounter her many months later still "seated with her hands folded on her lap, looking out along the avenue of limes to the distant fields. Every leaf was at rest in the sunshine, the familiar scene was changeless, and seemed to represent the prospect of her life, full of motiveless ease—motiveless, if her own energy could not seek out reasons for ardent action" (335). Casaubon's death might be expected to return Dorothea to the plot of youthful possibility, but Eliot resists this convention to prioritize a different and much less eventful development for her heroine. In a departure from the typical progression of the bildungsroman, Eliot downplays the idea of the momentous first romance, both by presenting the desiccated figure of Casaubon as the initial leading man and, subsequently, by giving this failed first marriage so little space in the larger story of second chances. In this period between Dorothea's marriages, the prolonged uneventfulness of her central plotline achieves another kind of development, giving readers a view of her continued maturation after she has already come of age.

Such interludes appear throughout this study in novels and short stories about a cast of middle-aged types in Victorian and early twentieth-century fiction, figures including the miser, the widow, the bachelor, and the spinster. These character types pervade Victorian novels but are often thought of as "ficelles" to the youthful heroes and their plots of adventure. They stand on the margins of the bildungsroman in the same way that, in Austenian ball scenes, characters like Miss Bates, Sir William Lucas, and Mr. Knightley ring the dance floor observing the youthful dancers and helping their courtship plots along, rarely being pulled onto the floor themselves—and then, to memorable effect. They may appear resigned that their participation in the ball is over, but as self-consciously sidelined as these characters may be, their marginal position often becomes the fixation, the very center, of novels that imagine life after the marriage plot. This cast of characters is represented in the central protagonists studied in this book: Silas Marner, who undergoes a period of isolation and hoarding as a miser; Gwendolen Harleth, who experiences penitence as a young widow; Arthur Clennam, with his midlife homecoming and sojourn in the Marshalsea prison; James's "poor sensitive gentlemen"[30] who hesitate their way through hundreds of pages; and the unmarried middle-aged women of modernist fiction, these twentieth-century protagonists offering a more distanced reflection on the Victorian era and its waning marriage plots. The novels that contain these protagonists have been chosen as case studies because they each tend, in exemplary ways, to the "epochs" of slow change that characterize novels of maturity more generally. Although these works are exceptional for their uneventful plotting, they also stand as widely representative of a larger focus in Victorian literature on the imagined lives and emotional growth of middle-aged characters. For every Silas Marner there is a host of Victorian Scrooges and Boffins whose pattern of accretion matches the novel's own accumulative ends. Gwendolen has an array of sister widows, whose courtship plots range from the demure Eleanor Bold's remarriage to Madame Madeline Neroni's more brazen, if prone, flirtations in Anthony Trollope's *Barchester Towers*. On his own, Henry James peoples English literature with morose middle-aged bachelors, but his Marchers and Strethers find themselves in the good company of John Jarndyce and a league of avuncular wallflowers. The "old maid," that varied staple of British and American fiction, at once includes the kindly Miss Bates and the more dynamic and iconoclastic Miss Wade and Rhoda Nunn, appearing in the late nineteenth and early twentieth centuries as one of fiction's most flexible and surprising character types, a vehicle for both narrative experimentation and visions of larger social transformation, as Woolf's fiction demonstrates. Giving closer study to these protagonists and their fictions of maturity makes it possible to chart a correspondence between middle age and "narrative middles," uncovering a fuller range of lived experience in nineteenth- and early twentieth-century fiction.

Historical Context and Contents

Why did plots of maturity become more common in the early to mid-nineteenth century? Looking back on an era fascinated by development, G. K. Chesterton questioned why, in the nineteenth century, the "most important event in English history was the event that never happened at all—the English Revolution on the lines of the French Revolution."[31] J. S. Mill framed the period in slightly different terms in *The Spirit of the Age*, conceiving of his own time in terms of process rather than inaction: "The first of the leading peculiarities of the present age is, that it is an age of transition. Mankind have outgrown old institutions and old doctrines, and have not yet acquired new ones."[32] He concludes, "A man may not be either better or happier at six-and-twenty, than he was at six years of age: but the same jacket which fitted him then, will not fit him now" (53). The metaphor of having "outgrown" the vestments of youth is telling, for it speaks to an emerging national self-conception of being an era past the age of revolutionary fervor, engaged instead in searching for alternative models of change—models that, in novels as in political discourse, attended to newfound maturity as a vital part of British self-identity.

In many ways, the nineteenth-century obsession with conceptualizing gradualism across disciplines emerged just when British subjects began viewing themselves in more-distanced relation to the French

Revolution. This new national self-identity coincided with the emergence of middle age as a modern concept in the Victorian period.[33] It was an era when, as Walter Pater objected, "the idea of development" seemed to be "invading one by one . . . all the products of the mind."[34] A generation earlier, a sense of youthful revolution infused Wordsworth's retrospective insistence that to be "alive" at the time of the French Revolution was "bliss" but to be "young" was "very heaven,"[35] but discourse in the Victorian period increasingly yielded to a new set of guiding tropes oriented around maturation and uneventful development—economic growth, evolution, geological accretion and erosion, and, in theology, spiritual progress in the afterlife.

Modern critics, however, follow Gillian Beer and George Levine to focus overwhelmingly on only Darwinian evolution and geology as the main culturally available models of radically slow change.[36] Yet more than any other discourse, theology offered writers a narrative template for understanding and representing extremely slow development in later life. In contrast to a large body of scholarship focused on Darwinian and geological models of development in Victorian fiction, this study uncovers the presence of another, as yet underexamined, inspiriting zeitgeist that appeared frequently as a metaphor for midlife development: debates about redefining purgatory initiated by Tractarians in Tract 90.

Beginning historically with the start of the Oxford Movement, *The Victorian Novel of Adulthood* seeks to ground aesthetic claims about plots of maturity in their historical and intellectual contexts. A new focus on mature protagonists in the mid-nineteenth century and early twentieth century corresponds with a period in which redefining the afterlife became a national obsession and source of ongoing controversy. The afterlife was a subject of the highest importance to Victorians, with discussions about purgatory occupying a central position in religious discussions initiated by the Oxford Movement. As Geoffrey Rowell states, eschatology was "discussed more publicly, and perhaps with more vehemence, than in any previous age."[37] If Jonah's unfolding is obscured by curtains of flesh and the elliptical style of biblical narration, Victorian theologians' writing on the afterlife sought to illuminate the epistemological gap at his story's center: the problem of how we can understand and represent inward change. In the Bible, Jonah's conversion remains hidden, for in the style noted by Erich Auerbach, he enters and exits the leviathan with little intervening text to explain what happens there.[38] The transition from man to prophet occurs with a rapidity that verges on simultaneity; the development is implied but not shown. In contrast, theologians during the Victorian period produced hundreds of pages of sermons, poetry, and tracts that attempted to describe the change souls undergo in the afterlife. Judgment became the center for many of these theological works, for it is the only realm in the afterlife to have change as its fundamental condition, as opposed to either heavenly or hellish stasis.

The debate over reconceiving Judgment reached its most fevered pitch in the 1830s and 1840s, when theologians following John Henry Newman began to reconceive purgatory as a kinder, gentler—and much less eventful—state of growth, rather than as a place for a punitive trial by fire. The British public was especially transfixed and outraged when Newman published Tract 90 in 1841, the document in which he suggested that purgatory could exist for all Christians, not just Catholics. In this tract, Newman altered the popular conception of purgatory to frame the afterlife in terms of gentle maturation. He urged that a period of Judgment could offer souls "a time of maturing that fruit of grace, but partly formed in them in this life,—a schooltime of contemplation."[39] This emphasis on growth and development provided Newman with a way of constructing a productive narrative of spiritual eventfulness, and as a testimony to his success, maturation remained a feature of eschatology well into the twentieth century, particularly after World War I, when the idea of a progressive state after death offered the consolation of future maturation for the many young men who died fighting. In the Victorian period, his model of the afterlife may have initially drawn fire for all its proposed extinguishing of "Romish" flames, but as these developments evidence, it also seeped into popular religion and culture.

Indeed, the model of Judgment that Newman proposed increasingly found its way into literature that used purgatory as a metaphor for the gradual work of adult *Bildung:* in *Daniel Deronda,* Gwendolen Harleth's arduous grasping after self-knowledge, described at length as her "purgatory . . . on the green earth" (669); in *Little Dorrit,* the narrator's repeated references to Judgment that accompany Arthur Clennam's penitential growth in the Marshalsea prison; in *Villette,* Lucy Snowe's desperate search for consolation that leads her to dabble in Catholic practices including confession and to consider the "unspeakable solace . . . of purgatory."[40] Whereas Gwendolen's and Arthur's stories unfold with purgatorial pacing, Lucy's unresolved ending maintains the novel in an ongoing narrative middle, a purgatorial state of midlife suspension. Thus, although this book addresses a range of cultural forms that authors invoke to create a sense of the gradually unfolding in literature, this study recurs to purgatory as a central modality that authors used to think about narrativity. In these "purgatorial plots," Dante emerges at key points, his imagined journey to purgatory functioning as a metaphorical quest story for mature protagonists. For writers ranging from George Eliot to Virginia Woolf, the *Divine Comedy* provides a source through which to envision the gradual transformation of characters who find themselves, like Dante in the beginning of the *Inferno,* "Nel mezzo del cammin di nostra vita," midway through life's journey.[41] However, even when citing Dante in these novels of adulthood, the writers in this study invoke a distinctly modern model of eschatology devoted to slow growth and not the Florentine poet's strenuous and clearly plotted trip up Mount Purgatory.

Tracing the evolution of purgatory as a theological concept and as a literary metaphor, this book offers a new critical understanding of the ways that religious and intellectual concepts from the Oxford Movement were inflected and engaged in Victorian fiction. Early chapters reveal how the methods employed by theologians came to influence fiction writers, notably Dickens and George Eliot, who sought to capture subtle maturation in the novel form. Later chapters show how this lineage of purgatorial plotting continued into the nineteenth and early twentieth centuries in works by writers, in particular Woolf, who portrayed the Victorian era as purgatorial while emulating Victorian methods for showing maturation and historical change.

On a formal level, each chapter reveals how specific methods borrowed and adapted from discourses including primarily theology but also visual art, lyric poetry, botany, economics, and folklore appear in a variety of literary approaches to remaining indefinitely in medias res. These methods and techniques include establishing closure while gesturing at its impossibility, spinning counterfactual "shadow" stories that absorb the main action from a central storyline, extending the "sense of a middle" by concealing the beginning of a given action or event, and destabilizing the "moment" as the unit for measuring events. In its broadest scope, then, *The Victorian Novel of Adulthood* engages questions about how historical influences shaped literary form to understand why a gradualist approach to plot arose as a common feature of Victorian novels of adulthood. Uncovering a vital connection between gradual plots in theology and those in fictions starring mature protagonists, it addresses a critical intersection between religious studies, intellectual history, and novel studies to reveal how the form of Victorian fiction evolved both alongside and through changes in religious philosophy.

In seeking to give context for literary developments, the book's first chapter, "'Strange Introversions': Newman, Mature Conversion, and the Poetics of Purgatory," probes the historical and theological origin for many accounts of gradual maturation in Oxford Movement controversies through twentieth-century conversations about purgatorial maturation. After defining purgatory and discussing how it became the epicenter for Victorian controversies about redefining the afterlife, the chapter turns toward considering purgatory as a narrative model, using Newman's essay on Aristotle's *Poetics* and *The Dream of Gerontius* as central examples to understand his complex ideas about action, character, and plot. These works foreground the conundrums and paradoxes that come with capturing a "state of change," the kind of action that purgatorial quest stories demand and delimit, exemplifying the innovations employed by theologians such as Newman to approach these kinds of representational challenges. On a larger historical scale, Newman's gentler model of purgatory offered Victorians a model for converting their own animosities about the Oxford Movement into a productive narrative of change. The chapter ends with a consideration of how Newman's eschatology continued to haunt late nineteenth- and early twentieth-century religious fictions and works of theology, his model of Judgment as a maturational state experiencing a great resurgence after World War I in offering the grieving the consolation that the youths who died in battle could mature in the afterlife.

Chapters that follow show how purgatory and other related metaphors for gradual transformation began to appear in secular Victorian novels that capture adult *bildung*. Taken together, these works make manifest a cultural pattern of gradualist thinking; in their use of metaphors at once scientific, economic, art historical, and theological, they comment self-reflexively upon their own gradualist storytelling mode as it unfolds. In terms of organization, each chapter centers on a figure who strongly embodies this method of purgatorial plotting, beginning with the miser and continuing on to the widow, the bachelor, and the "old maid."

Building on the historical and religious context from chapter 1, chapter 2, "George Eliot's Winter Tales," explores Eliot's fictions of maturity, beginning with her slimmest novel, *Silas Marner*, in which she portrays her protagonist's purgatorial development during his sixteen years as a miser. For all its apparent stasis, this period allows Silas to undergo a process of "collecting himself" (among many other things) that recalls the "school-time of contemplation" and "time for maturing that fruit of grace" that Newman presented as the nature of accretive change occurring in purgatory ("Intermediate State," 377). The uneventful interlude that characterizes Silas's miserly years subsequently appears in the lives of Eliot's young widows as well, and the second part of the chapter discusses Gwendolen Harleth's struggles with maturity as a young widow, a time described explicitly as her "purgatory . . . on the green earth," rendered in images from Dante's

Purgatorio. *Daniel Deronda* proves to be Eliot's most extended vision of purgatory, but in alluding to Dante's tragic female penitent, Madonna Pia—a favorite subject of Pre-Raphaelite painters—Eliot rewrites the role of the tragic waiting woman as a figure of inward action rather than of inaction.

From misers and widows, the third chapter, "The Bachelor's Purgatory: Arrested Development and the Progress of Shades," passes onto another recurring figure of stalled adult malaise: the "poor, sensitive gentleman," as Henry James termed his favored protagonist, a figure who rears his downcast head in numerous Jamesian fictions. Chapter 3 traces the prehistory of the sensitive bachelor as a mature protagonist, focusing primarily on Arthur Clennam's anxious homecoming at age forty in *Little Dorrit*, and shows how Dickens uses folkloric and purgatorial imagery to portray Clennam's adult "arrested development." It examines a previously overlooked source for the novel in revealing how Amy Dorrit's curiously static "fairy story" is a rewriting of the Peter Schlemihl folktale of the man who sold his shadow. This folkloric source resonates throughout the novel as Dickens blends shadow folklore with images of the purgatorial progress of shades. These shadow folktales provide a model for how a longer form (like the Victorian novel) can function to absorb a protagonist's lengthy inactivity, for the action in many shadow folktales is displaced into a counterfactual realm embodied by a shadow or "No-body" figure—as demonstrated in the novel by Clennam's thus-named alter ego, "Nobody." Cast as a No-body, Clennam becomes akin to a Victorian shade, undergoing the trials of waiting and sensory deprivation that are common to conceptions of purgatory. In Dickens's secular novel, these extended trials are transposed to an earthly place for penitence—the purgatory of the Marshalsea penitentiary. I conclude the chapter by briefly tracing how James, following in the steps of his predecessor, uses counterfactual techniques that strongly resemble Dickens's approach in *Little Dorrit*. As with Clennam's midlife odyssey, James imagines alter egos for his sedentary bachelors in his short works including "The Beast in the Jungle," "The Altar of the Dead," and "The Jolly Corner." However, it is in *The Ambassadors* that James truly takes uneventful plotting to new extremes to capture his hero's midlife renaissance, extending techniques for remaining in medias res that can be found in his earlier short fiction.

In my final chapter, "Odd Women and Eccentric Plotting: Maturity, Modernism, and Woolf's Victorian Retrospection," I follow purgatorial plotting into the terrain of the modernist novel to explore the "odd woman" as a figure through whom Woolf—and several other authors who bridge the late Victorian period and early twentieth century—frame their accounts of mature retrospection. My contention in this chapter is that the middle-aged unmarried woman plays a crucial focalizing role in decentered modernist plots, or as I call them, "eccentric plots" of maturity, and I focus on Woolf's *The Years* as an interlude dually shaped by Dante and Victorian literature. In writing *The Years*, Woolf openly emulated Victorian novelists for their ability to capture prosaic life, and the novel exemplifies Woolf's desire to descend into a literary past, for she modeled her vision of Eleanor Pargiter's midlife quest for greater understanding on the *Purgatorio* as well as on Victorian descents into the lulls of daily existence. In finding continuity between Woolf's vision of midlife development and Victorian encounters with the prosaic, I chart how the visit to Hades recurs as the metaphorical journey of maturity, an allegorical descent that is part of a rich tradition from *The Odyssey* to *Ulysses*. This conclusion gestures toward a larger understanding of how a purgatorial approach to plotting comes to characterize a fundamentally modern philosophy about storytelling, one more commonly ascribed to modernists and postmodernists in their "resistance to plot" but which, upon investigation, has its origin in the uneventful fictions of Victorian novelists who sought to represent maturity.

The book ends with a coda, "Descent and Tradition," that further explores how myths of descent function as the archetypal quest story of adulthood, appearing in each of the novels in this study as they reveal the transformations that result from an immersion in the past. This story of mature renovation through preservation provides another way of thinking about the overarching history of the novel in the period between Newman and Woolf, for each story of descent builds on previous ones to form a continuous tradition of recounting the challenges and adventures of maturity.

CHAPTER ONE

"Strange Introversions"

Newman, Mature Conversion, and the Poetics of Purgatory

Conversion, for Newman, was a process well suited to middle age. Although his novelistic depiction of a young man's call to Catholicism, *Loss and Gain*, takes the form of a bildungsroman, his own conversion was a decidedly adult affair. In the *Apologia Pro Vita Sua*, first published in 1864, Newman recounts a long period of adult probation, contrasting his middle-aged decision to become a Catholic with his youthful adoption of Evangelical Christianity at age fifteen: "When I was fifteen (in the autumn of 1816) a great change of thought took place in me. I fell under the influences of a definite creed. . . . I received it at once, and . . . retained it till the age of twenty-one."[1] His first conversion is presented as a coming-of-age story par excellence, a sharp revolution in perception that occurred "at once" but, for all its force, "faded away" after a few years. In contrast, in describing his conversion to Catholicism thirty years later, Newman stresses the measured unfolding of his beliefs: "I was not conscious to myself, on my conversion, of any difference of thought or of temper from what

I had before.... I had not more fervour; but it was like coming into port after a rough sea; and my happiness on that score remains to this day without interruption" (184). Juxtaposing the calmness of his adult conversion with the *sturm* and *drang* of his earlier spiritual *bildung*, Newman turns away from the nostalgic form of the revolutionary epiphany ("to be young was very heaven") to devote his autobiography to a new, and distinctly Victorian, story of midlife revelation.[2]

This story, for Newman, is necessarily a gradual one. Capturing the slow pace of his spiritual awakening proved to be not simply an issue of philosophical importance but also one of political necessity. As he relates, the pace of his conversion became a source of constant rebuke: "it was made a subject of reproach to me at the time, and is at this day, that I did not leave the Anglican Church sooner" (147). Indeed, Newman's pacing in leaving the Church of England has become one of the most notable features of his conversion story. Stephen Prickett writes, "His movement towards Rome was agonizingly slow.... Even the Bishop of Oxford's condemnation of the Tract in his charge of May 1842 did not speed the death-throes of Newman's Anglican existence"; and George Levine asserts that in "Newman's world, as the history of his own conversion testifies, nothing that happens suddenly is trustworthy."[3] Perhaps the most notorious "reproach" of Newman's timing in converting came from Charles Kingsley, causing the infamous skirmish that prompted Newman to write the *Apologia* in the first place. Kingsley's accusation amounted to a charge that Newman had been disseminating Roman Catholic ideology from inside the Anglican Church all along, an argument based on the assumption that his conversion had to have occurred more quickly than had been disclosed. It becomes clear that Kingsley and Newman not only clashed over larger questions of religious doctrine, they also clashed over their understandings of conversion as a narrative. Kingsley presupposed a model in which religious calling arrives like a bolt from the blue, as in descriptions of Paul's conversion on the road to Damascus. Newman countered with what might be described as an anti-Pauline model of conversion, one that could be understood as prosaic in its unfolding, deliberate, and less the product of youthful zeal than of middle-aged reflection.

The surprise was that many Victorians accepted Newman's account of his mature conversion as compelling and authentic, spurning Kingsley's claims even though he was a readier source of mainstream religious affiliation. This sympathetic reception of Newman's work amounted to a complete about-face in public perception, brought about in no small part by his ability to capture conversion convincingly as a gradual process instead of an epiphany. As "agonizingly slow" as his conversion seemed, it was this quality of uneventful development that won Newman sympathizers across religious denominations. The success of Newman's autobiography also revealed a wider interest among Victorian readers for accounts of mature transition, middle age being a category of self-identity that was emerging contemporaneously in the nineteenth century.[4]

On the whole then, the *Apologia* can be said to have accomplished many purposes, serving not simply as an effective defense against detractors but also as an introduction for readers to the gradualist vision that pervades Newman's theological and poetical work more broadly. As Cardinal Nicholas Wiseman said of *Loss and Gain*, "to call the work before us a novel, or even a story, would be a misapplication of the terms. It pretends to no plot. . . . [T]he object of this beautiful work is to trace the gradual working of Grace upon a mind."[5] This process is more fully elaborated in the *Apologia*, an account not only autobiographical in nature but also devoted to illustrating a mature, not youthful, conversion. The vision of gradualism found in these works reaches a new extreme in Newman's depictions of the ultimate mature "conversion": the transition between life and the afterlife. In sermons, tracts, and religious poetry, Newman transposes the model of slow progression on display in the *Apologia* and *Loss and Gain* to the afterlife, taking his earthly ideas about incrementally slow conversion to their furthest conceptual limit by imagining Judgment as a state of maturation. For Newman, this middle realm of the afterlife becomes "a time of maturing," "a school-time of contemplation," and an experience characterized by "strange introversion."[6] This emphasis on maturing as a central process differs markedly from earlier visions, like Dante's, in which this middle realm of the afterlife is imagined as a mountain with ascending trials conveyed as physical torments. Instead, Newman envisioned purgatory as a state for imperceptible and inward change that takes place over an immeasurable duration, a seeming infinitude that ends when a soul ascends to heaven. Newman's fascination with portraying Judgment as a gentler state for improvement proved to be a constant throughout his career as both an Anglican and a Catholic, surfacing in his earliest unpublished Anglican sermons dating back to 1825, his most inflammatory work, Tract 90 (1841), and later in his widely read Catholic devotional poem *The Dream of Gerontius* (1865). The mystery is that Victorian readers who were outraged by the Anglican purgatory he proposed in Tract 90 found consolation in an almost identical model of purgation offered twenty years later, this time in poetic form in *The Dream*.

The question remains today of why *The Dream of Gerontius* was so popular with mainstream Victorian audiences. Our ingrained historicist instincts tell us that this should not have been the case. After all, Newman was the one who made purgatory a subject of national ire in the first place. When Newman first published Tract 90, his suggestion that Anglicans could believe in a non-Catholic version of purgatory stirred considerable controversy that lasted for decades after its publication. To understand the uproar that Newman caused, and subsequently calmed, requires entering into one of the mysteries of religious history in the Victorian period. Historians of religion have ventured their own theories to explain how Newman found an unexpected degree of public reacceptance a generation after the Oxford Movement, but few of these explanations take into account the surprisingly unchanging nature of Newman's ideas about purgatory, the topic of some of his most popular and *un*popular published works. For example, studies of the aftermath of the Oxford Movement tend to fold reconciliation into the rise of modern concepts of liberal tolerance and accounts of the turn toward ritualism in poetry, approaches that smooth over the startling inflexibility of Newman's ideas about the afterlife over the years and across a major conversion.[7] The most common explanation for the poem's success is that Newman redeemed himself in publishing his *Apologia Pro Vita Sua* to wide acclaim in 1864, a year before *The Dream*. Not only did this autobiography help him trump Kingsley's charges of his being a Catholic in disguise all along, it won him general acceptance and paved the way for the success of his future writing with wider audiences. There is additional evidence that a shift occurred in anti-Catholic sentiment in the early 1860s and that this movement had begun waning by the time Newman published both the *Apologia* and *The Dream*.[8] These theories partly explain Newman's reacceptance by the British public in the 1860s, but they do not explain how purgatory became palatable too—and a model of purgatory strongly resembling the one from Tract 90.

Given the outcry that he inspired, it seems impossible that his devotional poem on the subject should be warmly embraced, and not just hotly disputed. And yet, embraced it was. The *Dream* became one of the best-known and, moreover, best-loved Victorian consolation poems about death. Some scholars place it second to Tennyson's *In Memoriam*.[9] By 1888, the poem's twenty-four published editions had made their way into numerous Victorian households. General Gordon carried it with him on his campaign in Egypt prior to his death in Khartoum, and Edward Elgar turned it into a successful choral opera. Poets and professors alike bestowed their stamp of approval. Algernon Charles Swinburne praised its "genuine lyric note,"[10] and Francis Hastings Doyle, Oxford Professor of Poetry, devoted a lecture to the poem in which he said it deserved "high commendation."[11] Taking his commendation a step further, he urged the Oxford community to stop being "envenomed" by "the spirit of these religious differences" (123). The pièce de résistance is that no one better gratified Doyle's wish than Newman's old nemesis, Kingsley, who wrote in a private letter that he "read the *Dream* with awe and admiration. However utterly I may differ from the *entourage* in which Dr. Newman's present creed surrounds the central idea, I must feel that that central idea is as true as it is noble."[12] These statements came from the same man who had proclaimed Newman "worse than dead to Englishmen" in *Fraser's Magazine* a few years earlier.[13] Although Kingsley later tempered his praise with poison in a public review of the poem, he still backhandedly admired "the wonderful beauty of its poetry," thereby initiating a reviewer tradition of separating the poem's "poetry" from its overt Catholic theology.[14]

Although it is no longer the critical favorite that it was in the nineteenth century, *The Dream of Gerontius* remains of vital relevance in illuminating a crucial shift in the Victorian era, a turn toward embracing maturity and gradualism over youthful fervor as a central trope for historical change.[15] As a literary work, *The Dream* went beyond simply garnering praise from unlikely sources; more broadly, it had an unprecedented ability to convert individual consolation into larger public conciliation, successfully redirecting Oxford Movement animosities for public consumption twenty years later. The anger that had brewed over the *Tracts for the Times* and Newman's subsequent conversion found a soothing balm in his writing in the 1860s, most especially in his popular and comforting work of death consolation literature, *The Dream*. Consolation, a quality often presented as the modest legacy of Tractarian devotional poets such as John Keble and Isaac Williams, proved central to Newman's understated method of framing his writing for an increasingly divided readership in the 1860s.[16] This soothing quality, which G. B. Tennyson has identified as the limited accomplishment of Tractarian poetry, has been framed as part of *The Dream*'s initial success. Yet it is important to recognize that Newman used the form of death consolation poetry in *The Dream* to accomplish broader goals that resonated beyond individual comfort. His poem moved readers from private solace toward a larger easing of public tensions, and it did so largely by promulgating a gradualist mode of maturation, presenting inconceivably slow development as the means to achieve profound change. This brand of gradualism appealed to those seeking comfort and counsel in facing death but also to men including

Doyle who sought to move past the pains of the Oxford Movement toward a reconciliation effected first on literary grounds.

It was ultimately on these literary grounds that Newman would prove most influential in mainstream Victorian culture, for as I show in subsequent chapters, the ideal of a gentler purgatory oriented around maturation, which Newman and other Victorian theologians increasingly espoused, served as a recurring metaphor in novels that capture the gradual, introspective trials of adult life. One example, which offers an introductory insight into the presence of mid-Victorian eschatology in fiction of the period, appears in *Villette*, a novel published in 1853, well after Newman's publication of Tract 90. In *Villette*, Brontë depicts a staunchly Protestant heroine, Lucy Snowe, storm-blown and seeking refuge in Catholic confession as well as in reading a Catholic theological book for "comfort," a word that she repeats multiple times in discussing her heroine's wary attraction to Catholicism. As Lucy recounts, the small theological work "possessed its own spell, and bound [her] attention at once. It preached Romanism; it persuaded to conversion. . . . The Protestant was to turn Papist, not so much in fear of the heretic's hell as on account of the comfort, the indulgence, the tenderness holy Church offered."[17] The book sparks an immediate commentary on purgatory as the source of this sense of "tenderness" and "comfort," for Lucy discusses how "the Catholic who had lost dear friends by death could enjoy the unspeakable solace of praying them out of purgatory" (413). This *comforting* model is clearly not Dante's series of painful punishments but instead a uniquely Victorian conception of purgatory shaped by popular discussions of the afterlife midcentury, these discussions having been fostered by Newman and other vocal theologians of the period. And although Lucy treats these "indulgences" with suspicion, immediately bolstering her disavowal of Catholicism, the gradual model of purgatory that religious leaders like Newman advocated exerts a strange undercurrent in this secular novel, emerging at a time when Lucy seeks solace and undergoes strenuous introspection.

To trace the cultural pattern that I identify of purgatorial plotting in secular literary works, I begin by giving the religious-historical context for literary developments of the nineteenth and twentieth centuries, showing how Victorian ideas about the afterlife—many of which were shaped in crucial ways by Newman and the Oxford Movement—pervaded the culture more broadly, appearing not only in theological works but also in fiction. I subsequently chart the reception history of one of Newman's most curiously popular works, *The Dream*, showing how Victorians themselves underwent a gradual conversion in their regard for Newman's writing and eschatology. Placing *The Dream* in the context of Newman's theological controversies allows for this new understanding of how eras and movements are themselves conversion stories writ large. Ultimately, if Tract 90 opened a rift in public discourse that resisted closure, artistic representations of purgatory as a maturational state helped purge resentments from previous generations. The popularity of Newman's vision of the afterlife consequently speaks not only to a Victorian fascination with theorizing development across discourses but also to an emerging sense of historical and artistic consciousness oriented around gradualism and mature deliberation rather than revolutionary fervor.

I. The Victorian Reinvention of Purgatory: Newman, Aristotle, and Eschatology

If Lucy Snowe in *Villette* comes to consider purgatory a source of consolation, it is largely because of the dramatic changes that this realm of the afterlife underwent in the wake of the Oxford Movement. Throughout the course of the nineteenth century, purgatory became the center of a national controversy over defining the ideological boundaries of the Church of England. Far from resembling Dante's vision of arduous ascent, in this new model spiritual *bildung* became the central process. In the *Purgatorio*, shades are depicted climbing Mount Purgatory, facing challenges on each terrace that are conveyed as physical torments, including starving, burning, and carrying heavy stones on one's back.[18] Newman espoused a dramatically different view in suggesting, as both an Anglican and a Catholic, that this punitive model of Judgment need not be the case. As he asserted in one of his Anglican sermons, "A great part of the Christian world, as is well known, believes that after this life the souls of Christians ordinarily go into a prison called Purgatory, where they are kept in fire or other torment, till, their sins being burned away, they are at length fitted for that glorious kingdom into which nothing defiled can enter. Now, if there were any good reason for this belief, we should certainly have a very sad and depressing prospect before us."[19] Instead, Newman presented purgatory as a kinder "Intermediate State,"[20] characterized as "a time of maturing that fruit of grace, but partly formed . . . in this life,—a school-time of contemplation" during which "the sins of youth are turned to account by the profitable penance of manhood."[21] Introspection and learning, not punitive duress, came to characterize his ideal of purgation in the afterlife. In reconceiving the afterlife to be gentler, Newman was at the forefront in redefining Judgment in two crucial ways: first, as a state of existence rather than a place with tiers, echelons, and geographical features as found in Dante's Mount Purgatory, and second, as a time centering on individual maturation, not the trial by fire, as a model of spiritually productive eventfulness.[22]

This story of the reinvention of purgatory in the Victorian era is one that unsettles familiar accounts of the trajectory of orthodox belief in the period. Despite the Victorian and modernist eras often being framed in terms of the decline of popular religion and a larger crisis of faith, the Victorians revived a long tradition of belief in purgatory. Historian Jacques Le Goff charts the entrance of the word *purgatorium* into the English lexicon in the twelfth century through the first stages of acceptance of this belief. Examining the history of Judgment four centuries later, Stephen Greenblatt gives an account of the "afterlife" of purgatory in post-Reformation England, finding literary evidence of the continued presence of Catholic eschatology in the figure of the ghost of Hamlet's father.[23] Yet in more recent times, purgatory could be found hovering long after the ghost of Hamlet's father first strode, or floated, offstage. Amid industrial expansion and the rise of liberalism, certain pre-Reformation beliefs once again found their way into mainstream British thought in the Victorian era. Beginning with the Oxford Movement, there was a resurgence of popular belief in the concept of purgatory.[24]

This controversy can be said to have begun in Oxford in 1833 when a group called the Tractarians began publishing pamphlets, several of which advocated that Anglicans return to primitive church doctrines. One such doctrine, the belief in a progressive realm of Judgment, became a central point of discussion with the publication of the movement's most provocative document in 1841, Tract 90, written by Newman. In the wake of the Catholic Emancipation and during a time of renewed anti-Catholic sentiment in England, Newman's suggestion that all Anglicans, and not just Catholics, might espouse belief in a progressive state of Judgment was taken as a profession of Romanism, a charge only confirmed for many critics retrospectively by his conversion in 1845.[25] What Newman was trying to achieve in Tract 90, however, was not proselytizing on behalf of Catholics. Instead, he used the tract to draw a distinction between the "Romish" purgatory, which he defines ominously as "the conflagration of the world," and a gentler alternative he presents as potentially appealing to his readers: "Another doctrine, purgatorian, but not Romish, is that said to be maintained by the Greeks at Florence, in which the cleansing, though a punishment was but a *poena damni*, not a *poena sensûs;* not a positive sensible infliction, much less the torment of fire, but the absence of God's presence. And another purgatory is that in which the cleansing is but a progressive sanctification, and has no pain at all."[26] The idea of the *poena damni*, which Newman characterizes as the pain of being deprived of God's presence as opposed to sensible pain such as Dante's penitents undergo in the *Purgatorio*, became integral to Newman's model of Judgment. At first, this milder vision of purgatory met great resistance, provoking outrage on a national level, but it also increasingly became an identifiable part of popular religion in the latter half of the nineteenth century and into the early twentieth century.

Despite the initial controversy surrounding Newman's eschatology, his concept of purgatory appealed to Victorians who, in their fervor for development, fused Newman's ideas about the afterlife with emerging scientific concepts of gradualism, such as evolution. As one Victorian theologian wrote in a sermon on the subject,

> "Evolution," it has been pointedly said, "is in the air. It is the category of the age; a *partus temporis*; a necessary consequence of our wider field of comparison." Evolution and Christianity have at last become partners, and although there is still some insecurity in this new alliance, yet every day, almost, seems to give to it a character and likelihood of greater permanence. Therefore it is only in agreement with the new method in the conception of things, and more especially of the essence of things, viz., life, that we pursue our inquiry about the Intermediate State in the direction of such development. For, apart from other considerations, if there be such a law of growth belonging to all life as we know it now, there is some antecedent probability in the hypothesis, that it may be the law which governs the life in other stages than those which we know at present.[27]

In other words, evolution could continue into the afterlife, an idea that accommodated both emerging scientific concepts of gradualism and eschatology. Theological models of development therefore provided both an important counterpoint and an often-overlooked complement to evolutionary models of change; evolutionary theory and eschatology both evoke a central "mystery" in insisting that change can be subtle enough *not to appear as change at all.* Nevertheless, evolution describes growth in fundamentally material terms. Changes witnessed on the time scale of eons can be observed in manifest evidence: bodies, features, mutations, markings. In Newman's conception of purgatory, all change was rendered intangible, bodiless, and abstract. A dramatic shift in temporal thinking is also similarly required by both models, each describing transformations that exceed the humble frame of an individual life span with *parousia* providing the limit of time and history in theological visions of the "last things."[28] Yet once again, theological models of growth, such as those innovated by Newman, adamantly resist invoking the sensory as a measure for individual change. Belief in afterlife maturation defied even the heightened insight provided by the microscope, that iconic instrument in Eliot's fiction, demanding a more abstract conception of "putting all the action inside," to quote D. H. Lawrence's praise of Eliot's ability to capture the inner life.[29]

This intermediate state of Judgment was notoriously difficult to represent in narrative form, eventually coming to be labeled "the problem child of theology" by theologians.[30] Victorians struggled to understand the basic storyline for purgatorial change. For example, in a piece titled *When a Man Dies Where Does He Go? or, Some Things about the Intermediate State*, one clergyman named John Thomas Pickering insisted, "Rest does not necessarily mean inaction. Rest of mind and soul does not imply cessation from energy and activity."[31] The idea that "rest" could equal "activity," while preferable in some circles to trial by fire, remained conceptually difficult to grasp and, furthermore, difficult to explain. It also raised ethical questions about the proper role of acts and trials in achieving spiritual betterment. In questioning what kind of "activity" takes place in Judgment during a state of "soul sleep," believers in the intermediate state came to be divided into two main factions: those who believed in a period of total unconsciousness while waiting for the Second Coming and those who believed in the soul's growth through lucid dreaming in the afterlife.[32]

On one side of the argument, the prospect of indeterminate, changeless waiting left little to the imagination. As Archbishop Richard Whately, Newman's former tutor at Oxford, observed, the main "objection" to this model "is that it seems as if there were a tedious and dreary interval of non-existence to be passed, by such as should be supposed to sleep, perhaps for some thousands of years, which might elapse between their death and the end of the world."[33] On the other side of the argument, theologians such as Pickering insisted that soul sleep was the highest form of action in the afterlife, a view similar to the one Newman expressed in Tract 90. In another tract on the subject, a Catholic woman named Sophia Scott sided with Newman in insisting that "souls are in a state of more activity and *clearer* consciousness"; she laments, "What shall we say to convince you that in that blessed separate state kept and guarded by the Good Shepherd Himself, there is a great work going on, and no *in*activity?"[34] Anglicans such as William Ince, Canon of Christchurch, coincided with many Catholics in further expressing the need for a conception of the afterlife that "allows room both for thought and [for] action,"[35] a position supported by one of the most high-profile Victorian writers on the subject, millenarianist E. H. Bickersteth, who described the intermediate state as "in the first place . . . a state of rest. . . . Secondly, it is a state of consciously living to God. . . . The rest of those who sleep in Christ is no condition of unconscious inactivity, but of intelligent fellowship with God and fruition of His love."[36]

This ideal of restful action and "consciously living" (despite being dead) raised a number of confounding paradoxes. Time in Judgment was conceived as being both terminal, or "intermediary" and hence leading to another state, and also immeasurable in quantifiable terms. Consequently, believers were faced with the prospect of dailiness without days, of endurance of the prosaic without a sense of the diurnal, and with an abstract idea that their souls would benefit from experiential learning without undergoing anything understood as an "experience" per se. Changes in the intermediate state could not readily be conveyed through trials and dramatic turning points, as in Dante's *Purgatorio*, but only through a more understated model of plotting. In Newman's conception, prolonged contemplation becomes tantamount to the highest form of action, an inward action not readily translated into narrative "events" but instead registering as a subtle accretion.

Newman on the Poetics

This kind of contemplative action, as Newman conceives it, runs counter to Aristotle's definition of "action" in the *Poetics*. Before

Newman wrote Tract 90 and *The Dream*, he approached the problems of describing eschatology in explicitly narrative terms in his essay "Poetry with Reference to Aristotle's *Poetics*."[37] In this essay, he insists, "Seldom does any great interest arise from the action" (2). Arguing against Aristotle for the precedence of character over action, Newman's essay is curiously replete with references to the afterlife. Modern critics have been nonplussed by Newman's repeated and incongruous invocations of the afterlife, most often dismissing this tangential focus on eschatology as Newman's imposition of Victorian morality on the *Poetics*. Yet rather than reading these passages as cultural artifacts or as strains of Newman's moral agenda, I read these intrusions of eschatology in another light. Indeed, underneath Newman's insistence that Greek tragedy be read in light of a Christian afterlife, there lies a provocative model of how we weigh actions—and inactions—in narratives. The afterlife occupies an important role in the essay, surfacing at critical points when Newman delves into what happens during plot lulls, or what he terms the "stationary" and "irregular" (2) parts of a composition, and why he finds these parts most satisfying. Connecting these lulls to a kind of development he associates with change in the afterlife, Newman begins to think through a model of inward action that receives its fullest treatment in his subsequent works, notably *The Dream of Gerontius*, a poem that both explicates and itself performs uneventful development.

As Newman insists in his essay on Aristotle's *Poetics*, the "charm of Greek Tragedy does not ordinarily arise from scientific correctness of plot":

> Seldom does any great interest arise from the action; which, instead of being progressive and sustained, is commonly either a mere necessary condition of the drama, or a convenience for the introduction of matter more important than itself. It is often stationary—often irregular—sometimes either wants or outlives the catastrophe. . . . The action then will be more justly viewed as the vehicle

for introducing the personages of the drama, than as the principal object of the poet's art; it is not in the plot, but in the characters, sentiments, and diction, that the actual merit and poetry of the composition are found. (2)

Newman provides an early incarnation of Markovits's present-day argument that character precedes action in nineteenth-century literature in focusing on those places where a plot is "often stationary—often irregular."[38] Grand turning points or "catastrophes" do not necessarily mark the most important parts of a composition for Newman. Instead, he asserts that the plot often continues onward and "outlives" them. In one place, he even posits the need for Christian belief in the "afterlife" to make sense of tragedy: "It is scarcely possible for a poet satisfactorily to connect innocence with ultimate unhappiness, when the notion of a future life is excluded. Honors paid to the memory of the dead are some alleviation of the harshness. In his use of the doctrine of a future life, Southey is admirable. Other writers are content to conduct their heroes to temporal happiness;—Southey refuses present comfort to his Ladurlad, Thalaba, and Roderick, but carries them on through suffering to another world" (17).[39] The injustice of tragic endings troubled Newman, who found the need for an afterlife (or a realm of "temporal happiness") to help right the imbalance of innocent characters dying in a state of misery. For Newman, sacrifices and grand gestures thus needed to be brought inside the orbit of Christian morality, and poetry—a term which he uses interchangeably with tragedy in this essay—is the medium through which the otherworldly can be imagined. As Newman states, poetry "provides a solace for the mind broken by the disappointments and sufferings of actual life; and becomes, moreover, the utterance of the inward emotions of a right moral feeling, seeking a purity and a truth which this world will not give."[40] The connection that he repeatedly draws in the essay between poetry and a form of understanding not available in earthly existence proves to be a twofold contradiction: Newman proposes that poetry captures the essence of the afterlife but also that it is still necessary to impose the afterlife on a tragic work to instill "right moral feeling." He thereby ushers all tragedies into a realm where earthly time is of no account, for in Newman's essay all tragedies properly end in the afterlife (whether they do so explicitly or by benefit of the reader's framing agency). Grand finales are dissolved into a continuing narrative that concludes in the indefinite hereafter, and individual acts of closure—especially those that are doomed, tragic, and without "solace"—are obliterated by being subsumed into an ending that *parousia* alone can provide. Newman's position can consequently be viewed as the inverse of Hannah Arendt's discussion of action and ethics in Greek tragedy. In Arendt's reading, actions have force because they occur in the absence of otherworldly retribution and reward, an essentially existentialist point of view.[41]

But if Newman diminishes the importance of death and closure in any given tragedy, it is not to privilege the "every-day" as the repository of meaning. Realism was never Newman's main interest either as a theologian or as a novelist. "Why interrupt so transcendent a display of poetical genius by inquiries degrading it to the level of every-day events, and implying incompleteness in the action till a catastrophe arrives?" he asks.[42] What, then, is Newman privileging in place of action if not the lulls of prosaic description? The simple answer would be lulls of a more transcendent nature—the lulls of an afterlife where action, in some form, "outlives" the catastrophe of death. It is no accident that in presenting his favored aspects of Greek tragedy, Newman speaks of "characters, sentiments, and diction," making the subtle choice of distinguishing "characters" from "sentiments." Newman's afterlife is one in which the world of "sentiments" continues past death and past, however contradictorily, the world of the senses. These disembodied sentiments, although passively framed, are the highest form of action for Newman. Death, consequently, is only the end of one kind of action—physical action—and in his essay the most affecting movements in a drama are not feats and the final "act" of dying but instead come from extending final moments into an indefinite lull, an intermediate state of existence.

If the essay on the *Poetics* accomplishes any central goal, it is to privilege poetry, and specifically, poetic suspension, as the means through which to understand slow changes that underlie dramatic turning points. The essay comes as a discursive rally against representing change through purely discursive means, for Newman urges that poetry can give readers access to understanding the afterlife in ways that are unavailable in sermons and tracts. It is no surprise, then, that later in his career Newman avails himself of poetry to explain his own model of the afterlife. In the case of Newman's *Dream*, his chosen poetic form allows him to accomplish something that proved out of reach in Tract 90; a quarter of a century after Tract 90, Newman turned to a new form that could allow him to explain and, moreover, to perform the eschatological conundrums he had previously discussed in tract form. Eschewing the purely explanatory (not to mention inflammatory) nature of the tract, Newman instead turned to devotional poetry. In taking a new, lyrical approach to the subject matter, he chose a poetic model that borrowed from both the circularity of liturgy and the suspended quality of dramatic monologues, thereby achieving a difficult balance between foregrounding Catholic concerns over death and the afterlife while still generating greater reader receptivity in his use of the soliloquy.

II. Victorians in Purgatory:
The Dream of Gerontius and Poetic Conciliation

Although *The Dream of Gerontius* is fabled for finding its way into the hands of men of action like General Gordon, the poem imagines change as the product of radical inaction, the result of bodiless contemplation occurring in a sensory deprivation chamber. As the poem in recent times is rarely considered outside of its theological and religious-historical interest, it has been bypassed by a contemporary tradition of literary scholarship focusing on the political work of Victorian poetry. Newman's prose is often included in considerations of the relation between poetry and politics, such as Isobel Armstrong's seminal *Victorian Poetry: Poetry, Poetics and Politics*, which discusses how Newman's sermons and tracts illuminate the political concerns of poets such as Arthur Hugh Clough and Matthew Arnold, but his poetry is overlooked in such studies.[43] Despite *The Dream*'s many potential critical points of interest—including the lingering mystery of its success, its controversial content, and the political turnaround it helped achieve—Newman's most popular poem has received little literary critical attention in our time. As a result, its popularity has yet to be addressed as a phenomenon firmly enmeshed in his poetics.

To understand Newman's success in *The Dream*, we must bring the poem into current conversations about the long Victorian poem that rely on narrative theory, from which it has been absent, including recent work on dramatic monologues, explorations of lyric versus narrative modes, and studies of Victorian experimentation with hybrid genres. This approach is embodied by scholars such as Monique Morgan, whose recent work provides a model for the kind of scholarship on the long Victorian poem that could yield new insights into Newman's approach in *The Dream*.[44] Indeed, *The Dream* is a worthy example for deeper study given the unusual narrative methods Newman employs to capture individual change over a substantial poetic duration. Considered alongside other long poems of the period, notably Tennyson's *In Memoriam*, the work with which it is most frequently compared, *The Dream* differs radically in its vision of a central speaker's development.[45] *In Memoriam* is oriented around a central figure whose anguished doubt gives the poem its vital trajectory and intimacy. For example, many passages are devoted to the urgent questioning of Hallam's existence after death and the possibility for future development.[46] In contrast, in Newman's vision of purgatory, Gerontius's salvation is ensured upon his entering the realm of Judgment. As a result, his journey is not one from doubt to increasing faith, for he instead undergoes a central process of dispossession of selfhood and the cleansing of self-interest. To put it slightly differently: the poem as a whole is not about personhood but about process, about conversion, not the convert. And just as the speaker's musings vary from those of Tennyson in *In Memoriam*, so too does the poetic form in which these musings take shape. The certainty of an afterlife that opens the poem marks an important distinction—a distinction that plays out on a formal level in *The Dream*. To capture his vision of conversion, Newman undermines a Tennysonian emphasis on the lyrical "I," found in both the epic melancholia of *In Memoriam* and Victorian dramatic monologues, borrowing instead from the suspension of liturgy.

This reading of *The Dream* as a poem that uniquely partakes of liturgy is necessarily situated in the context of poetics movements of the time, notably, the turn toward ritualism in the 1860s. As I contend, *The Dream* may be understood as part of a renewed interest in ritualism, but it is also something more. In brief, the poem is evidence of Newman's ability to navigate the shifting terrain of the 1860s and to make death-consolation literature the site of his own brand of subversive orthodoxy. It exemplifies Newman's ability to craft what I term a "poetics of conciliation," or a poetic form that accommodates Catholic liturgy and secular verse, as well as formal paradoxes including temporal suspension and narrative progression, sensory description and portrayals of disembodiment. In its interplay between quoted Catholic ritual and soliloquies, *The Dream* invokes ritual in ways more explicit, and potentially more off-putting, than were pursued by other popular devotional poets of his time, notably, Anglo-Catholic devotional poets such as Christina Rossetti, for Newman quotes directly and at length from rites performed in the Roman Catholic mass. At the same time, he also partakes of provocative dramatic monologues by Tennyson and Browning to upend their madhouse meditations. Newman thereby stages a conversion of the dramatic monologue itself from lyric to liturgy. He uses Gerontius's monologues to capture a suspended, lyrical quality and simultaneously to critique the "unconstrained lyrical 'I'" found in works such as "St. Simeon Stylites" and "Johannes Agricola in Meditation."[47] This blend of ritualist poetry and soliloquies allowed Newman to create a devotional drama with many speakers, a hybrid that against all odds effectively appealed to Victorians more disposed to reading Tennyson's *In Memoriam* than Catholic liturgy.[48] Newman's hybrid form also allowed him to use poetic methods to accomplish ideological ends: only in crafting a "poetics of conciliation" could he successfully perform, and not simply describe, the theological conundrums at the heart of his conception of purgatory as a place for gradual change.

Reading (Around) Ritual: The Organization of The Dream

On a surface level, *The Dream*'s clearly demarcated structure may have partly contributed to its success. The poem is divided into seven numbered sections and moves from quoting hymns and Catholic rites to including a greater number of subjective reflections on the state of the soul after death. In the first section, an old man named Gerontius lies on his deathbed. The priest and his assistants administer the final rites, and Gerontius passes into the afterlife. These rites and prayers for the dead, which dominate part 1, give way in part 2 to meditative soliloquies as Gerontius arrives in the afterlife. Gerontius's Soul then reflects on his disembodied state and his new understanding of time and the lack of senses in the afterlife. He subsequently encounters guiding angels and taunting demons, then glimpses God before finally being laid to rest in purgatorial waters at the poem's conclusion in section 7. These waters provide a final cleansing period of contemplation that readers glimpse before the poem ends.

As *The Dream* proceeds through its seven sections, visual divisions (including section breaks and line breaks between speakers) effectively separate the religious rites and liturgy quoted in the poem from the more seemingly secular soliloquies, making it easy to excerpt and favor certain passages—as readers like General Gordon evidently did. Soon after his death, Gordon's personal copy of *The Dream* was returned to England, where it found its way into Newman's hands.[49] The copy had Gordon's pencil notations throughout, and in 1889, reproductions of these selective markings were made available to the public.[50] Readers were known to copy these markings into their own editions of the poem, the most famous example being Newman himself.[51] Gordon's personal notations were thus one unofficially sanctioned way for non-Catholics to encounter the poem.

It is interesting that the poem's opening, which includes religious rites from the Catholic mass, is not marked in Gordon's personal edition. As Gerontius says in the opening,

> Jesu, Maria—I am near to death,
> And thou art calling me; I know it now.
> Not by the token of this faltering breath,
> This chill at heart, this dampness on my brow,
> (Jesu, have mercy! Mary, pray for me!)
> 'Tis this new feeling, never felt before,
> (Be with me, Lord, in my extremity!)
>
> (5)

Observations about his personal condition, "This chill at heart, this dampness on my brow," alternate with lines that echo hymns and biblical lamentation, "Mary, pray for me! . . . Be with me, Lord, in my extremity!" This division between personal reflection and ceremony becomes more pronounced later in the poem when the ritualism of part 1 meets the soliloquies of part 2. As part 1 proceeds, Gerontius's life ends and the poem increasingly yields to a full quotation of Catholic ritual, including a chorus of Assistants chanting the rite for commending a departing soul to God, "Kyrie eleïson, Christe eleïson, Kyrie eleïson," followed by "Holy Mary, pray for him," all taken from the Catholic mass (6). Newman here exceeds the ritualism ascribed to devotional writers of the period who were also influenced by Tractarianism, for example Christina Rossetti.[52] Although her poems include an array of ritualistic elements that invoke the Anglo-Catholic mass, including "Great mitred priests," "incense turned to fire / In golden censers," and "lamps ablaze and garlands round about," unlike Newman, she does not quote from religious services verbatim and at length.[53]

In contrast, Newman's direct, lengthy inclusions from the Roman Catholic mass in the first section could potentially be controversial content for Victorian readers and might give a staunch Evangelical Christian like Gordon pause. And indeed, pausing is most likely what happened for many readers of the poem—pausing, that is, and skipping. Tellingly, in his copy, Gordon marks the lines that precede the introduction of Roman Catholic rites and Gerontius's words "Pray for me, O my friends," but then skips over the rites themselves and the following parts where the Priest and Attendants speak. The next passage that he marks at length is the soliloquy following Gerontius's death that opens section 2, which gives the speaker's first impressions of the afterlife as a disembodied soul. This is the same passage cited by Doyle as being the best part of the poem: "The finest thing it contains is the early soliloquy of Gerontius when he finds himself, as he believes at first, alone with infinity" (115). Doyle further says that he prefers "the blank verse; the speeches rather. The lyrical portion are, in my judgment, less successful . . . [and] do not move me much more than those average hymns which people, who certainly are not angels yet, sing weekly in church" (117). By the "lyrical portion" Doyle means the more overtly religious parts that partake of Roman Catholic liturgy. Therefore, either implicitly or explicitly, Doyle and Gordon both recommend a strategy of reading around the most openly Catholic parts of the poem.

In thus reading along with Gordon and Doyle, as Victorian readers themselves did, contemporary readers can gain a new understanding of the poem's early reception history, and more specifically, of how Newman's demarcated structure allowed Victorian readers to skip, skim, and otherwise exclude the most overtly ritualistic elements of the poem. This insight into Victorian reading practices affords crucial new information about the poem's success, for it helps to explain how readers rationalized their own, seemingly perverse, delight in the poem; they did so through a strategy of selective reading based on the belief that they could excise the "Catholic parts" of the poem, in particular, the rites and rituals of part 1. But the question remains, is such an extraction really possible? By skipping or critically dismissing part 1, could Victorians truly quarantine themselves from the poem's Catholic content, as they so claimed? The answer, quite simply, is no.

Upon closer investigation, one finds that the most beloved parts of the poem, the soliloquies that readers gave themselves full license to enjoy, in fact contain the most controversial views in the poem. Indeed, in the soliloquies, Newman again sets forth the views on purgatory he had articulated in Tract 90. Yet for some reason, when presented in soliloquies in *The Dream*—and not in *Tracts for the Times*—these views passed muster. Newman had succeeded in fostering the illusion that readers could read around the Catholic parts of the poem, while in fact smuggling his most controversial eschatology in plain sight by embedding these views in the most accessible, comforting, and seemingly nondenominational parts of the poem: the soliloquies.

Progressive Suspension: The Soliloquies

The soliloquy that opens part 2 is especially pivotal in bringing Catholic ritualistic elements into a larger narrative of conversion between life and the afterlife. Lines assigned to "Gerontius" are now spoken by the "Soul of Gerontius" and soon after by a "Soul" after an Angel comes down to assure him that he is saved, a precondition for entering purgatory. By the end of the poem, Newman takes this process of deindividualization to its limit when Gerontius becomes one of a chorus of undifferentiated "Souls in Purgatory." Using the soliloquy, an introspective and self-revelatory form employed in dramatic monologues, Newman moves away from developing his protagonist's individual identity by way of first-person revelations. Instead, he has his protagonist reflect on becoming part of a general pool of unnamed souls. This diffusion of the protagonist's identity jars with the sense of character development as a process of increasing specification and self-exposure over time. In *The Dream*, the protagonist instead sheds character as the poem progresses, becoming less individualized as a character with a marked disposition. The soliloquies therefore help Newman to enact a central principle of his conception of purgatory, the cleansing of self-interest and the purging of individual persona, while working through a more seemingly secular form usually devoted to revealing character and presenting persona.

They also allow Newman to achieve a balance between suspension and progression that lies at the heart of his idea of purgatory as a state of productive waiting. After partaking of the suspended effect of apostrophe—exemplified by the lamentations, prayers, and spoken rites of the opening section—the poem further inducts readers into a purgatorial mode of progress with its soliloquies.[54] The apostrophic quality of Gerontius's cries—"Jesu, have mercy! Mary, pray for me!"—works much like his subsequent soliloquizing in providing lyric suspension while still contributing to the overall narrative of a man journeying to the afterlife. By definition, this *narrative* in verse must continue moving forward though Newman uses poetic devices to help suspend narrative elements and to create a sense of change that is internalized, reflective, and discursive in nature. As Jonathan Culler writes, "Apostrophe resists narrative because its *now* is not a moment in a temporal sequence but a *now* of discourse, of writing."[55] Newman, accordingly, employs apostrophe and soliloquy to resist narrative's pull, thereby capturing gradual development on the level of poetic plotting. But it is important to realize that he employs this model of poetic plotting with a larger goal in mind: that of making purgatorial gradualism understandable, despite its seeming contradiction between suspension and movement. Newman's use of devotional poetry thus allows him to *perform* purgatorial gradualism rather than simply explain it as he did in Tract 90.

Exploring the tension between narrative and lyric modes in the long Victorian poem, Morgan shows how verse meditations can yield this subtle form of narrative movement. She makes the case that the dramatic monologue especially exemplifies a "seamless blend of lyric and narrative temporalities" (160). Soliloquies can be said to function similarly in combining lyric with narrative elements to achieve equipoise between stasis and movement. This balance between lyric and narrative modes is the temporal essence of purgatory—a state caught between progress and suspension. Fittingly, this temporal paradox of progressive suspension is the subject of Gerontius's first soliloquy:

... How still it is!
I hear no more the busy beat of time,

> No, nor my fluttering breath, nor struggling pulse;
> Nor does one moment differ from the next.
> I had a dream; yes:—someone softly said
> "He's gone;" and then a sigh went round the room.
> And then I surely heard a priestly voice
> Cry "Subvenite;" and they knelt in prayer.
> I seem to hear him still; but thin and low,
> And fainter and more faint the accents come,
> As at an ever-widening interval.
>
> (14)

Time has not stopped; the "interval" between Gerontius's moment of death and his reflections is "ever-widening." The speaking of "Subvenite," the responsorial recitation in the Roman Catholic Requiem Mass, marks a countertime, reappearing at intervals to offset a subjective, lyrical, and discursive time of meditation from earthly time marked by ongoing spoken rites and the poem's meter.[56] He is reassured that change will continue unfolding even though it cannot be measured by even the smallest narrative unit, the moment, let alone more dramatic narrative markers such as events and turning points. As the Angel next explains, Gerontius's sense of time passing slowly is irregular and does not correspond to the actual speed of his journey between death and purgatory.

> Thou art not let; but with extremest speed
> Art hurrying to the just and Holy Judge:
> For scarcely art thou disembodied yet.
> Divide a moment, as men measure time,
> Into its million-million-millionth part,
> Yet even less than that the interval
> Since thou didst leave the body. . . .
> . . . .
> Precise and punctual, men divide the hours,
> Equal, continuous, for their common use.

> Not so with us in th' immaterial world;
> But intervals in their succession
> Are measured by the living thought alone,
> And grow or wane with its intensity.
> And time is not a common property;
> But what is long is short, and swift is slow,
> And near is distant, as received and grasped
> By this mind and by that, and every one
> Is standard of his own chronology.
>
> (22–23)

The "hurrying" that immediately follows Gerontius's death appears as stasis to him, and this sense of uneventful reflection is crucial to Newman's ideas about conversion as a gradual rather than revolutionary process. Depicting the ultimate conversion from life to the afterlife, Newman attempts to have the best of both worlds: the temporality of the earthly poet—"precise," "punctual," and metered—and the temporality of suspended time in which the "fruit of grace" can go through a process of "maturing" ("Intermediate State," 377) without being hurried and without conforming to measurable standards. This contradiction of a seemingly timeless duration is one of the central paradoxes Newman strives to represent. In his conception, purgatory occurs outside of earthly time, but it remains finite and telos-oriented. The goal of purgatory is to prepare souls for their exit from this state and their entrance into paradise. Yet despite unfolding in time, one's duration in purgatory is indefinite, immeasurable, and not for "common use." In trying to represent this temporal paradox, Newman uses soliloquies to explain his concept of the timeless duration while at the same time performing it, an effect uniquely achieved through poetic means. In other words, the soliloquies allow Newman to perform suspended contemplative action in the very act of describing it to readers, thereby uniting form and content in a way previously unavailable to him in his sermons and tracts.

Converting the Dramatic Monologue

Yet if Newman uses soliloquies to capture the "seamless blend of lyric and narrative temporalities" associated with the dramatic monologue, he also uses soliloquies to turn the dramatic monologue on its head. In featuring a lone central speaker, *The Dream* reframes the conflict between spiritual progress and egoism that Tennyson and Browning imagine in poems including "St. Simeon Stylites" and "Johannes Agricola in Meditation," respectively.[57] Johannes Agricola declares, "For I intend to get to God, / For 'tis to God I speed so fast" (lines 6–7) but circularly asserts that "God's Breast" (line 8) is "where I have always lain" (line 11). This form of spiritual claim jumping involves a problem of not knowing, or at least not acknowledging, the difference between "reach and grasp."[58] In trying to collapse this distinction, dramatic monologue speakers such as St. Simeon Stylites attempt to bypass the between state of being "unfit for earth, unfit for heaven" (line 3), a holding pattern that constitutes the central condition of growth in purgatory and also the suspended form of the dramatic monologue itself. But whereas Tennyson and Browning channel suspension and gradual revelation into doubt through dramatic irony, Newman tells us that Gerontius is saved from the beginning. This certainty of salvation marks an important difference between Newman's poem and Tennyson's and Browning's dramatic monologues, a contrast more starkly realized when considering a work such as "Tithonus,"[59] given Tennyson's emphasis on immortality without redemption and stasis without the promise of progress, however imperceptible. In its structure, *The Dream* consequently operates quite differently than dramatic monologues by Tennyson and Browning, for *The Dream* instead works as a reassurance against doubt, using the soliloquies first to entertain apprehension and doubts and then turning to the explicatory dialogue with the Angel to dispel them. In this way, doubt of a spiritual nature is shifted to doubt of an experiential kind: the uncertainty of an individual in unfamiliar circumstances, not the doubt of someone on the brink of damnation. Angels accordingly take a leading hand and demons are relegated to the sidelines, where they appear comical and impotent as Satan's cheerleaders, speaking in a doggerel reminiscent of Christina Rossetti's goblin men: "What's a saint? / One whose breath / Doth the air taint" (28).

The main threat in the poem instead comes from the isolation and fear of solipsism Gerontius experiences after first arriving in the afterlife, an anxiety that the poem itself performs by briefly collapsing into "the unconstrained lyrical 'I'" of the dramatic monologue.[60] Gerontius's experience as a lone speaker is one of "deep rest" but also of strenuous "pain" in having his "thoughts" driven back "upon their spring" (14). His initial meditations are portrayed not restfully but as an act of self-cannibalism: "I now begin to feed upon myself, / Because I have nought else to feed upon" (15). This negative isolation is remedied by the Angel's eventual appearance and the poem's expansion into dramatic forms; thus, conversation rescues Gerontius from the social vacuum imagined at the core of his soliloquies. In relief, his soul says,

> Now know I surely that I am at length
> Out of the body: had I part with earth,
> I never could have drunk those accents in,
> And not have worshipped as a god the voice
> That was so musical; but now I am
> So whole of heart, so calm, so self-possessed,
> With such a full content, and with a sense
> So apprehensive and discriminant
> As no temptation can intoxicate.
>
> (20)

Only by losing self-possession—the transition from "Gerontius" to nameless "Soul" in purgatory—can the central speaker become fully "self-possessed" and "full content." The pun on "content" as both an emotional state and one of repletion points up the paradox of feeling substantial only when removed from the world of earthly substance, but it also reconfigures the earlier cannibalism imagery as benign self-satisfaction: instead of eating away at oneself through depleting rumination, the Soul now feels "whole of heart," a strangeness of eating one's cake and having it too. This sense of paradoxical fullness counteracts the smug contentment of speakers such as Browning's Johannes Agricola, who asserts that he was made by God "because that love had need / Of something irreversibly / Pledged solely its content to be" (lines 28–30). Newman illustrates a contentment that comes only with the loss of one's physical body—a paradox at the heart of his ideas about purgatory as a place of disembodied substance.

Extremity: The Body in the Afterlife

To capture his speaker's newly disembodied contentment, Newman develops various techniques for representing the experience of complete sensory loss—a state that would seem to defy representation. In Gerontius's opening, the prayer "Be with me, Lord, in my extremity!" is echoed in his first concerns in the afterlife when he fears the loss of his body, this state of "extremity" involving a lack of his own physical extremities:

> 'Tis strange; I cannot stir a hand or foot,
> I cannot make my fingers or my lips
> By mutual pressure witness each to each,
> Nor by the eyelid's instantaneous stroke
> Assure myself I have a body still.
>
> (15)

At first Gerontius mistakenly thinks that he has maintained all of his senses except for sight, and this blindness functions as a synecdoche for complete sensory loss. As the Angel explains to him:

> Hast thou not heard of those, who after loss
> Of hand or foot, still cried that they had pains
> In hand or foot, as though they had it still?
> So is it now with thee, who has not lost
> Thy hand or foot, but all which made up a man.
>
> (33)

The Angel's metaphor of having a phantom limb is one that Newman extends to help readers understand the implications of having a phantom body. In Newman's clever poetic strategy, this phantom body is represented as an absence of sense perceptions that can be understood only through the uncanny continuance of perception. He therefore makes the task of representing this loss one that can in fact be understood in earthly terms. This retentive illusion allows his character to recount experiences that readers can comprehend while they can still interpret them as otherworldly. Absent senses are thus invoked through synesthesia, or as a ghostly presence recalled only through other senses, notably, hearing and touch, which act as surrogates for a full range of sensation: "I hear a singing; yet in sooth, / I cannot of that music rightly say / Whether I hear or touch or taste the tones" (16).

In addition to describing the sensation of having a "phantom body," Newman also presents this disembodiment as a feeling of being physically enfolded in God's giant palm.

> Another marvel: someone has me fast
> Within his ample palm; 'tis not a grasp
> Such as they use on earth, but all around
> Over the surface of my subtle being,
> As though I were a sphere . . .

(16)

Gerontius finds himself safely in the womb-like palm of God, a divine and surprisingly literal realization of God being with him in "extremity," Gerontius's lack of physical extremities being soothed by God's celestial hand. Worries of exhaustion and depletion are now replaced with images of gestation, later echoed in the final scene of immersion in the prenatal waters of purgatory. Gestation, with its creative rather than destructive potential, functions as an analogous temporal model for Newman's idea of purgatorial progress and proves central to the poem's appeal as a work focused on regeneration as consolation.

From Consolation to Conciliation

The ability to give consolation, a quality prized by Victorian readers of *The Dream*, has been framed as the legacy of Tractarian poetry but a modest and ephemeral one at best. G. B. Tennyson asks, "What, for example did the Tractarians accomplish in their poetry as poetry? Certainly it could not be argued that they left any single work of great poetry or even a single great short poem."[61] In the long term, he finds that consolation was simply not enough: "Most readers of poetry want more than a soothing tendency. . . . Readers who cannot bring to the reading of poetry a sympathy with the ideas the Tractarians were at pains to advance will probably not be won over by the power of the poetry alone" (190). Although twentieth-century interest in Newman's poetry waned, many Victorians with little sympathy for Tractarianism were in fact professedly won over by Newman's "poetry alone"—the "alone" part being a crucial component in their approval, at least as they understood it.[62] This early perception of the poem as a work made up of discrete, isolatable parts proved crucial to its acceptance—though it was by no means true that readers could perform a neat excision of the poem's theological content and achieve sanitized readings, as they believed. The frequently excerpted soliloquies were in fact the center of Newman's eschatological musings. Newman's success resides precisely in fostering this illusion. The poetic form he chose allowed readers to come to a consoling, albeit false, conclusion: namely, that a distinction could be made between his poem's Catholic content and its "poetry."

This distinction was made by Kingsley, Doyle, Gordon, and many others in their praise of *The Dream*. As Doyle says of the poem, "Of the doctrines involved in this striking production it is unnecessary to say more than that there is nothing, except the bare idea of purgatory (a theological and not a poetical blemish), which need prevent any Christian, or, indeed, any one who believes in the providence of God, from valuing it according to its deserts. It is built mainly upon those noble foundations which were laid eighteen hundred years ago, and which are still the common inheritance of Christendom, the common centre of our European civilisation."[63] After suggesting that the poem's subject and form can be considered separately—lyricism outweighing and even redeeming or canceling out the religious content—Doyle immediately claims the same religious heritage for all Catholics and Anglicans and urges an Oxford ceasefire. He ends by lamenting the "antagonism," "hostile zeal," and "unsympathetic demeanor" of those at Oxford with grudges against Newman, and he appeals to his audience's "genuine respect" and "undiminished affection" for an individual of such worth (123). Doyle's final comments are evidence of a widespread phenomenon in the poem's reception history: its ability *as a poem* to foster a slippage between consolation and conciliation, even when there is nothing especially compromising about the poem ideologically speaking. After all, it is almost exactly the same model of purgatory that Newman presented in Tract 90.

Thus, despite its controversial content, *The Dream* became renowned for offering relief to its readers, but it ultimately succeeded because it offered readers something more: a cleansing of animosities from the Oxford Movement. As Newman writes in his essay on Keble, "Poetry is the refuge of those who have not the Catholic Church to flee to and repose upon, for the Church herself is the most sacred and august of poets. . . . Now what is the Catholic Church, viewed in her human aspect, but a discipline of the affections and passions? What are her ordinances and practices but the regulated expression of keen, or deep, or turbid feeling, and thus a 'cleansing,' as Aristotle would word it, of the sick soul?"[64] Newman distinguishes the "cleansing" of Catholics from the lesser consolation prize of nonbelievers reading poetry to find "refuge." In taking *The Dream* to heart, many of Newman's non-Catholic readers may not have followed the kind of cleansing regime its author imagined as a strictly Catholic (and indeed purgatorial) experience, instead finding consolation in his work. But this consolation was nevertheless not without wider implications than merely soothing a few "sick souls." Newman's consoling poem did not merely provide refuge for those facing death and seeking a literary balm. It also helped many of its readers perform a different kind of purgation—a cleansing of bitterness following Tract 90.

Accordingly, religious historians have marveled at the poem's conciliatory powers. Geoffrey Rowell observes not only that *The Dream* "reached a far larger audience" and "enjoyed great popularity" but also that, ultimately, through *The Dream*, Newman "presented an understanding of purgatory which was acceptable to many outside his own communion."[65] Novels such as *Villette* reveal this process of consideration midcentury, and subsequent chapters discuss the resonance of Newman's theological writing and midcentury eschatology in works of fiction more broadly, showing how a new consoling model of the afterlife eventually surfaced in an array of novels as a metaphor for gradual change and maturation of the most subtle, beneficial kind. Consequently, regardless of whether or not Anglicans fully came around, the poem certainly helped Victorians (including Kingsley) to purge their bitter feelings about Tract 90 and its fallout. The model of the afterlife that had once been a source of vexed conflict instead became a site of soothing consolation. Therefore, more than just offering refuge and relief, purgatory finally came to occupy a central position as both a point of controversy and grounds for larger compromise. In the end, *The Dream* can be said to have helped Newman accomplish one of his previous, and most ambitious, goals: that of making purgatory into a via media after all.

The Afterlife of The Dream

Newman's intermediate model of purgatory would continue to permeate Victorian literature and culture long after the appearance of Tract 90. Most explicitly, Newman's eschatology surfaced in literary visions of the afterlife and theological tracts published later in the nineteenth and early twentieth century. Such literary visions of judgment include Margaret Oliphant's "The Land of Darkness" and "A Beleaguered City" as well as C. S. Lewis's *The Great Divorce*, all works that present a non-Catholic vision of purgatory in which the soul's main "activity" is to interpret its own state, as Gerontius does for most of *The Dream*.[66] In Oliphant's "The Land of Darkness," readers at first cannot be sure whether they are encountering a vision of purgatory as they follow the newly dead protagonist through regions in the afterlife dedicated to everything from hedonism to totalitarian tidiness. The tale concludes with a hellish circling back that casts doubt on the protagonist's potential for progress. Yet this humbling regression simultaneously gives value to the difficulty of achieving progress in a place of unforeseeable duration. If limbo is desire without hope, purgatory is desire *with* hope, and in Oliphant's open-ended conclusion the protagonist's potential for hope gives the narrative the chance of being one of progressive linearity, instead of merely a story of circular resignation.[67] Similarly, in Lewis's *The Great Divorce* a penitent soul enters an intermediate place of Judgment that slips either into hell or into heaven, depending on the choices he or she makes there. Those who continue in error are already in a state of hell without knowing it. Those who persist in improvement, often without it being recognizable to them, are living in a purgatory that can only retrospectively be understood as such.

In theology of the twentieth century, Newman's influence is even clearer. During World War I, Newman's gentler ideal of purgatory as a place for maturation experienced a tremendous resurgence, offering grieving families the consolatory prospect of continued growth for the many young men who had died in battle. General studies of modernism and twentieth-century religion rarely mention this facet of postwar fervor, but taking this brief interval in Britain's religious history into account may contribute to a new understanding of twentieth-century responses to Victorian theology, ranging from tracts and war documents to literary works. As one professor of theology wrote in 1918, "Men are seeking assurance of life to come for those who have given their lives.... We hope as never before for an assured and abundant life after death."[68] Letters home from the trenches reveal that soldiers deeply feared going to hell, especially when their last act might be that of killing another person. As one British soldier wrote home to his parents, "So you think that if a man is fighting on the side of righteousness and mercy no matter what kind of life he has led in the past he will not go to the purgatory as pictured by Dante. I agree."[69] The belief in heaven offered the strongest comfort possible for many, but not everyone could embrace the idea of the soul's immediate translation to paradise without a period of purgation, especially when acts of war had been committed in life. In response to an urgent desire for answers to philosophical quandaries, preachers, theologians, and popular writers began proposing that soldiers would go to a place for purging, but not "purgatory as pictured by Dante."[70] Instead they would go to a purgatory as pictured by Newman. To soothe congregants, preachers increasingly recurred to the gentler Anglican models of purgatory that came to prominence in the Victorian era. Reflecting on the Oxford Movement's influence during the war, one clergyman wrote in 1916,

> The Oxford Movement helped to restore the old faith and practice.... The great European War has forced the sense of the loss of prayer for the dead not merely on numbers of Church people, but on very many who belong to Nonconformist bodies. The Reformers denied any intermediate state or place between Heaven and Hell; their descendants find little difficulty in the thought of a state of progress hereafter, and great difficulty in the belief that all but the pious "elect" are abandoned to an endless Hell.
>
> It is surely, the duty of all, who have the opportunity, to help in bringing England back to the faith and practice of the Primitive Church.[71]

What had once been regarded as highly controversial Oxford Movement theology became an acceptable alternative for those seeking a model that eschewed continued violence in favor of gradual learning and growth.[72]

As discussed in chapter 4, this conception of purgatory as a gentler state provided modernist writers, notably Woolf, with a metaphor for the nonviolent change that her characters contemplate and seek to achieve in *The Years*, a postwar novel that imagines the possibility for "another life" by way of a dramatic rereading of Dante's *Purgatorio*. This reading of the *Purgatorio*, however, is crucially inflected with progressive ideas about the afterlife popularized in the previous century, for she presents purgatory as a maturational state and model of peaceful historical change. Purgatory, which appears by way of Dantean allusion and also as an extended metaphor, recurs to reveal both Eleanor Pargiter's individual development from the Victorian period onward and, also, larger historical changes that Woolf's characters hope to observe as the postwar future dawns.

Such examples make clear that the most profound influence of Newman's writing was not to be found in overtly religious documents or in religious literary works that imaginatively sought to portray the afterlife per se. The Victorian fascination with purgatory as he conceived it received its most interesting treatment in secular fictions that used purgatory as a metaphor for gradual adult maturation. In the chapters that follow, I explore how methods for representing slow change in the afterlife came to appear, often as extended metaphors, in a range of novels from *Little Dorrit* to *The Years*. These works of fiction not only borrow from Victorian visions of the afterlife in using purgatory as a metaphor for the protagonist's journey, they also borrow from the representational techniques that theologians such as Newman developed to put, as has been written of George Eliot, "the action inside."

CHAPTER TWO

George Eliot's Winter Tales

*I*f Henry James famously criticized *Daniel Deronda* for being more like a lake than like a river in terms of its narrative flow, Gwendolen Harleth's widowhood can be considered the deepest and stillest part of Lake Deronda.[1] She begins the novel as a willful young woman, a "spoiled child," as the novel labels her, but concludes as a widow quietly returning to live with her mother and sisters at Offendene. Early readers found this ending frustrating enough that one American fan anonymously penned a sequel called *Gwendolen*, published in 1878, two years after the original, which culminates in the heroine's marriage to Daniel (Mirah having been conveniently dispatched).[2] Evidently, though Gwendolen in Eliot's novel at first worried that marriage would be painfully "humdrum,"[3] readers have had a bigger problem with the "humdrum" once it is divorced from the marriage plot and made a conclusion on its own, a divorce that Eliot insists upon for her heroine at the end of *Daniel Deronda.*

Although Eliot grants the marriage plot to her hero and Mirah instead, she does not leave her heroine bereft, as many have claimed.[4] Instead, she refocuses Gwendolen's storyline on a gradualist vision of change that many have been tempted to overwrite as punitive stasis. Echoing early reader malaise, critics have called Gwendolen's widowed end "tragic," seeing her as "fixed in her tableau of tragic dread."[5] On the contrary, the narrator insists that Gwendolen is not "fixed" in her concluding state but may be "supposed to move, like the limpet, by an apparent sticking, which after a good while is discerned to be a slight progression" (*DD*, 701). We learn that Gwendolen's current and future transformation will be enacted on the scale of the "quiet recurrence of the familiar" instead of "the revolutionary rush of change which makes a new inner and outer life" (*DD*, 701). The tendency to reject this gradualism as stasis can be identified as part of a larger scholarly trend that flirts with branding Eliot a "conservative," thereby refusing to accept Eliot's vision of gradual progress as true progress at all.[6] As a counter-reading to such scholarship, this chapter explores Eliot's insistent fascination with extreme gradualism and how it is linked to her most unconventional approaches to plotting stories for her mature protagonists. In these works, which include *Scenes of Clerical Life*, *Silas Marner*, *Middlemarch*, *Romola*, and *Daniel Deronda*, Eliot resists the pull of the marriage plot to give failed first endeavors less attention in a larger story of second chances.[7] This period of adulthood attained becomes the subject of Eliot's most radical writing, for in depicting maturity at length and, in some cases, as a "humdrum" conclusion protested by readers, Eliot launches an embedded critique of the marriage plot and the bildungsroman as the main plots available in Victorian fiction.

I. Adventures for "Grown-Up People"

This approach to plotting the "humdrum" would seem to be completely at odds with the vim of the adventure story. Adventures are for young people, at least if one believes Georg Simmel, whose definition has shaped numerous studies of the bildungsroman and its tumultuous plots. As Simmel writes,

> The adventure does not belong to the life-style of old age. The decisive point about this fact is that the adventure, in its specific nature and charm, is a *form of experiencing*.... The old person usually lives either in a wholly *centralized* fashion, peripheral interests having fallen off and being unconnected with his essential life and its inner necessity; or his center atrophies, and existence runs its course only in isolated petty details, accenting mere externals and accidentals. Neither case makes possible the relation between the outer fate and the inner springs of life in which the adventure consists; clearly, neither permits the perception of contrast characteristic of adventure, viz., that an action is completely torn out of the inclusive context of life and that simultaneously the whole strength and intensity of life stream into it."[8]

Despite this common affiliation between adventure stories and plots of youth, Simmel's concept resonates no less evocatively with novels about adult renewal. Indeed, one reason the adventure offers such a supple model of the plot "event" is that, in Simmel's conception, the adventure is not wholly destructive or dismissive of the prosaic; it is at once removed from the daily ("torn out of the inclusive context of life") and continuous with and encompassing it ("the whole strength and intensity of life stream into it"). In this way, Simmel defines the adventure as both a turning point with a definite "beginning and end" and, contradictorily, as amorphous in its borders, an advent that cannot be understood solely in terms of outward occurrences but which depends more particularly on the way these factors are internalized over time into personal experience. Youth, he says, is the condition most favorable to this inward processing and openness. Yet in considering the novels of George Eliot, we see a curious reversal of his dictum: adventures arise more commonly for her adult and middle-aged protagonists, those characters who seem least likely to have them, according to Simmel.

Many, if not most, of her works feature figures well past the first throes of youth. In contrast, in Eliot's novel starring a child heroine, *The Mill on the Floss*, Maggie Tulliver has her adventure cut short, the sense of a grand new beginning never coming to fruition before her story ends. Eliot instead cedes "the adventure" as a life experience to her mature characters, those protagonists who find the excitement of renewal in developments such as unexpected parenthood, as in *Silas Marner*, or the prospect of an adult homecoming that both Gwendolen and Daniel find in varying ways at the end of *Daniel Deronda*. These delayed stirrings may be understated and misunderstood, at times emerging from periods of resignation, quiescence, or even despair, but they prove to be "adventures" in the truest sense of the word: they are George Eliot's late-blooming visions of advent. Presenting readers with these alternatives to the dramatic turning points we associate with the bildungsroman, Eliot gives us a new kind of adventure: "English novels for grown-up people," as Woolf characterized *Middlemarch*.[9] Untraditional adventures like these necessarily demand a different approach to plot than the bildungsroman affords.

To capture these plots of midlife, Eliot turns to an array of metaphors for slow growth that she opposes to stasis: economic models of hoarding, art historical discussions of pictorial stasis versus narrative movement, and theological models of development in the afterlife. Purgatory, in particular, appears as a central trope in her fictions of maturity that draws on and overlaps with these other gradualist discourses. Tracing references to purgatory as a recurrent metaphor, I focus on two central figures of mature advent in her novels: the miser and the widow. Silas Marner's hoarding, a period that Eliot presents metaphorically as the germination of a buried seed, sets a precedent for the kind of narrative accretion that she expands on in her fictions about young widows, anticipating her methods for depicting Gwendolen's widowhood in *Daniel Deronda* as a "purgatory ... on the green earth" (669). Purgatory, in turn, becomes a trope Eliot uses at great length to capture the quandaries and struggles of adulthood. Casting Gwendolen as a modern La Pia of Siena, Eliot performs a dramatic reinterpretation of Dante's famous penitent from the *Purgatorio* and also of Pre-Raphaelite depictions of this well-known victim, responding to artists such as Dante Gabriel Rossetti, John Everett Millais, and Gustave Doré. In plotting Gwendolen's course through purgatory on earth, invocations of the visual arts prove essential to Eliot's gradualist approach, for she frames her heroine's development as partaking of the stillness of pictorial images and statuary, an immobility that masks underlying movement and development.

My larger contention in this exploration of Eliot's ekphrasis is that she resists concluding *Daniel Deronda* with a "fixed" tragedy, as many have claimed, instead giving readers one of purgatory's plots: the story of Gwendolen's adult maturation. Existing studies discuss how Dante provides Eliot with a trove of purgatorial references, but few have noted that in her novels the summit of Dante's Mount Purgatory accommodates itself to the flatter topography of a distinctively Victorian conception of the afterlife. Whereas Newman evolved a narrative model of extreme gradualism to explain his theological concept of purgatory, Eliot can be said to approach purgatorial plotting from the opposite direction: she uses contemporary eschatology as a metaphor by which to capture the gradual momentum of her characters' secular conversions.

Plotting Mature Adventures: Theology and Form

Eschatology occupies an important position in Eliot's secular vision of mature conversion. As Mary Ann Evans remarked early in her career as a writer, "Religious novels are more hateful to me than merely worldly ones. They are a sort of Centaur or Mermaid and like other monsters that we do not know how to class should be destroyed for the public good as soon as born."[10] Despite this critique of religious novels, rendered at age nineteen and while still a practicing Evangelical Christian, George Eliot's missing prose debut was almost certain to have been a religious book. Its title, *The Idea of a Future Life*, appears in several letters from 1853, along with publication negotiations and its estimated prospects ("I am to have 'half profits' = o/o!"). No notes or portions of the book have been found.[11]

Although this mysterious text has intrigued many, it has rarely earned attention as a potentially theological work. Perhaps taking a cue from the author's move toward secularism, most critics invoke this ghostly beginning to treat it as "The Idea of a Future *Novel*" instead, thereby allowing the religious implications of its alluring title to go largely unexamined.[12] Given Eliot's youthful call to exterminate religious novels, it would seem impertinent to suggest that her lost first book resembled any such chimerical breed of religious fiction. Neil Hertz has gone as far as to speculate that this first work "would have consisted of reflections on belief in an afterlife, probably more wide-ranging both historically and cross-culturally than Feuerbach's,"[13] but his and other critical works illustrate how Eliot's sense of futurity was transposed into secular models of development, such as economics and evolutionary theory. Gillian Beer further refers to the text in exploring evolutionary theory and *Daniel Deronda* in *Darwin's Plots:* "Indeed 'the future Life' is the absolute form of fiction," she notes, and particularly "that sense of futurity intensified by evolutionary theory which is preoccupied with the future of life on this earth" (171).

In directly seeking the "future life" of her lost work in Eliot's subsequent allusions to scientific developmental discourses, scholars have tended to overlook how nineteenth-century theological debates themselves influenced Eliot's methods.[14] The question that remains is whether a nonmonstrous form of religious fiction can be imagined, and whether Eliot achieved this fusion in novels starring mature protagonists, such as *Silas Marner* and *Daniel Deronda*. Such analysis requires a broader conception of the ways that religion can inflect fiction. Currently, the critical tendency to cite Eliot's *The Idea of a Future Life* only to sidestep its potential theological content demonstrates a biographical fallacy of eliding belief with other forms of religious knowledge that Eliot certainly possessed. Her title, *The Idea of a Future Life*, not only speaks to her knowledge of debates about the afterlife that characterized midcentury public intellectual life but also speaks to her desire to participate in these debates via her writing.

As discussed in chapter 1, many of the discussions taking center stage during Eliot's early career focused on the possibility of an intermediate state of Judgment, a topic encompassing an array of concerns about whether change and growth occur in the afterlife, whether the dead can hear the prayers of the living, and whether Anglican eschatology should ultimately include a form of purgatory. Nevertheless, despite Eliot's seeming interest in writing a book on the subject of the afterlife, studies of the presence of intermediate state theology in her work seem to have fallen in the gap between two major groups of criticism. The first focuses on developmental theories in Eliot's works, mostly turning toward evolution, economics, geology, and anthropology. The second strain devotes itself to Eliot and religious studies and usually concentrates on the author's spiritual and intellectual (dis)affiliations: Feuerbach's "Religion of Humanity," Comte's Positivism, pantheism, and—in the few works that combine religious studies with narratology—the Apocalypse and Eliot's conception of history, eventfulness, and closure.[15] A renewed Victorian fascination with purgatory is rarely invoked in either of these more specialized fields, despite the topic's history of crossing cabalistic boundaries and exerting a diffusive influence in both ivory tower Oxford debates and the personal lives of many Victorians. Indeed, George Eliot was one such Victorian.

The afterlife was a recurrent topic of interest for Eliot, both as a young parishioner and as an author and translator. Not only did her first realized publication, a poem in *The Christian Observer*, describe a soul's preparation for the afterlife, her well-documented struggle with Evangelical Christianity also involved a final objection to "personal immortality," a belief that part of the self continues after death.[16] In addition to Feuerbach's writing on the subject of personal immortality, translated by Eliot in 1854, several of Eliot's accounts of her reading give further evidence of her interest in the afterlife.[17] These books include Joseph Butler's inquiry into afterlife "probation" in *The Analogy of Religion* and Isaac Taylor's *Physical Theory of Another Life*.[18] Oxford Movement discussions of the future state may have played a prominent role in Eliot's theological reading and education too. During the early years of her career, the publication of Tract 90 in 1841 only intensified preexisting public argument about the nature of the hereafter in advocating that purgatory not be dismissed as a time of spiritual preparation in the Anglican faith. Eliot's letters written during this period reveal her conflicted considerations of the Oxford Movement's ideologies and main figures, typified later by her sympathetic response to Newman's *Apologia Pro Vita Sua*.[19]

In considering this nexus of theological concerns, we find that it is not coincidental that many intermediate state tracts share markedly similar titles to Eliot's proposed debut. Among a wealth of collected sermons, essays, and other published material on the subject are William Ince's *The Future Life—The Intermediate State—Heaven*, R. E. Hutton's *The Life Beyond*, and a more widely recognized work, *A View of the Scripture Revelations Concerning a Future State* by prominent Anglican churchman and Newman's former Oxford tutor, Archbishop Richard Whately. Eliot's intellectual attraction to these theological texts and debates is also abundantly apparent in her fictions, for regardless of her increasing personal disbelief in the hereafter, intermediate state models of purgatory appear in her novels starring mature protagonists on several levels: on the level of allusions to Dante's *Purgatorio*, on the level of purgatorial figures of self-improvement (notably Silas Marner and Gwendolen Harleth), and most significantly on the level of what might be termed a theological narrative form.

To propose that a "theological form" exists in Eliot's stories of midlife is to observe that nineteenth-century eschatology infuses her novels on a pervasive formal level, not merely arising in isolated references to doctrinal texts and controversies. Eliot was one of many Victorian novelists who, separate of personal religious beliefs, converged with theologians in trying to represent a development that transcended the physical. If George Henry Lewes described evolutionary theory as making "the implicit explicit,"[20] intermediate state theology imagined an opposing model of involution, whereby all change would be rendered implicit and invisible. Although Lewes's description of evolution better fits traditional ideas of narrative explication, or making explicit, novelists and theologians such as Eliot and Newman, respectively, shared an interest in trying to explain a kind of growth that would not readily speak its name or show its stripes but proved to be of substance nonetheless.

It is notable that these discussions of development in the afterlife far preceded Darwin's publication of his *Origin of Species* (1859), thereby corresponding with Eliot's early career and her development as a writer. When she began reading the *Origin of Species*, Eliot famously expressed a sense of the inadequacy of evolution to capture a full understanding of growth: "To me the Development theory and other explanations of processes by which things came to be, produce a feeble impression compared with the mystery that lies under the processes."[21] Addressing this statement, critics have suggested that if evolution fell short of encompassing this "mystery" for Eliot, then theology went further toward addressing a perceived deficiency.[22] But rather than serving as substitutes for one another, theological and evolutionary models of development held many features in common, sharing a similar intellectual root in seeking to understand growth as "an invisible process, registered only in retrospect," to use Beer's definition of growth.[23]

Eliot's method of "putting all the action inside" overtly partakes of contemporary theological discourses, in particular in her works that represent the "intermediate state" between youth and old age. Purgatory and the journey through Judgment become recurrent metaphors for the slow progress of her figures of adult arrested development, two of which shall be discussed at greater length: the miser and the widow.

II. *Silas Marner*: Misers and Narrative Hoarding

On a formal level, Eliot's slimmest novel, *Silas Marner*, demonstrates an array of techniques that appear in her longer fictions featuring mature protagonists. Eliot opens her story with a dispossessed weaver of about forty who lives in exile from his past. After giving a brief flashback to his youth, and the cataclysmic disappointments that shaped him into a hermit, she lingers over his midlife stagnation for the first half of the novel. This strategy caused her publisher deep concern. Upon receiving the first half-volume installment of *Silas Marner*, John Blackwood commented that the "first 100 pages are very sad, almost oppressive," and he questioned Eliot's pacing: "Are you sure you will be able to wind up in the space you allot to yourself? I should almost doubt it."[24]

Despite these early concerns, Eliot maintained the approach of leaving her hero with little dramatic action to call his own, presenting Marner at the outset as prematurely dead.[25] Raveloe's eligible females deem him as alluring "as a dead man come to life again"; Jem Rodney echoes these morbid sentiments in discovering the weaver leaning up against a stile, with his eyes "set like a dead man's"; and finally this witnessed moment of catalepsy gives rise to considerable tavern speculation that "there might be such a thing as a man's soul being loose from his body, and going out and in . . . and that was how folks got over-wise, for they went to school in this shell-less state to those who could teach them more than their neighbours."[26] Like Dante entering the *Divine Comedy*, Silas enters the story as a living man initiated into the afterlife, but in this case, a uniquely nineteenth-century view of the hereafter. His cataleptic fits appear to the townspeople as a "shell-less" intermediate state, a suspended period characterized by two main, if conflicting, features: sensory deprivation and experiential learning (though in this case, as the townspeople presume, his instruction comes from the devil).

His move to Raveloe is thus portrayed as a move to the afterlife itself. In describing his departure from Lantern Yard, the narrator remarks upon the "Lethean influence of exile, in which the past becomes dreamy because its symbols have all vanished, and the present too is dreamy because it is linked with no memories" (19). Like Dante in *Purgatorio*, Canto XXXI, Silas has drunk from the river of the dead, his weaving and hoarding providing him with a fresh daily balm of Lethean amnesia. Hoarding, as Susan Stewart notes, typically serves this amnesiac function of forestalling painful recollections: "The point of the souvenir may be remembering . . . [but] the point of the collection is forgetting."[27] Jean Baudrillard similarly observes that hoarding, like mourning, is not without its internal logic, its consolatory rationale: "Objects allow us to apply the work of mourning to ourselves right now, in everyday life, and this in turn allows us to live—to live regressively, no doubt, but at least to live."[28] While Silas forgets his past losses through collecting, he finds himself spinning to "live regressively . . . but at least to live," an ethos of bare survival that connotes a proximity to death and the afterlife's encroachments into life itself. His hoarding therefore comes to represent a life lived on the borderlands of life and death, an activity that is at once stigmatized and yet, in its warped way, sustaining.

Indeed, amassing coins offers certain recuperative benefits that distinguish the miser hero from the dying and the dead that litter Eliot's tale in large numbers. His period of accumulation emerges as a period of self-preservation symbolized by the "attempt, marked by desperation, to 'keep body and soul together,'"[29] Stewart's diagnosis of the collector's woe recalling the central image of shadow folklore that is the focus of the next chapter: the separation of body and spirit. Coin fondling, his cherished method of record keeping, gives him a way to unite body and spirit, providing him with an emotional pivot for his daily rotations, the sensory enjoyment of touching each coin allowing him to forget "everything else but his immediate sensations" (24), everything but the body experiencing a transient, if repetitious, pleasure. This pleasure, no matter how onanistic, opens a productive course for Silas, and his miserhood is figured as a time for him to collect, among many other things, himself.[30] To collect, as Baudrillard notes, is always to collect oneself, for "any collection comprises a succession of items, but the last in the set is the person of the collector."[31] Silas provides a surprisingly direct illustration of this concept, coming to resemble several of his possessions, most notably a broken-off "handle" (25), like the one belonging to his destroyed earthenware pot, and his coins with their graven faces: his "face and figure shrank and bent themselves" (25) and his gold "gathered his power of loving together into a hard isolation like its own" (50). Burying his treasure in a dark hole, Silas relegates himself to the same existence, becoming an integral part of his collection. His sixteen years of miserhood may appear dehumanizing, cramping his body into "mechanical relation to the objects of his life" (25), but despite their bleakness, they allow for him to begin a new course of development: recuperation, configured as the literal work of pulling himself together.

This attempt to pull himself together is realized symbolically midway through the novel when his hoard is stolen and he bursts into the Rainbow to protest its loss. In this scene, his integration into the community comes by way of that great social conduit, the tavern, registering as a physical reintegration of "wandering" spirit and the laboring body:

> [T]he next moment there seemed to be some evidence that ghosts had a more condescending disposition than Mr. Macey attributed to them; for the pale thin figure of Silas Marner was suddenly seen standing in the warm light, uttering no word, but looking round at the company with his strange unearthly eyes. The long pipes gave a simultaneous movement, like the antennae of startled insects, and every man present, not excepting even the skeptical farrier, had an impression that he saw, not Silas in the flesh, but an apparition; for the door by which Silas had entered was hidden by the high-screened seats, and no one had noticed his approach. Mr. Macey, sitting a long way off the ghost, might be supposed to have felt an argumentative triumph, which would tend to neutralize his share of the general alarm. Had he not always said that when Silas Marner was in that strange trance of his, his soul went loose from his body? Here was the demonstration: nevertheless, on the whole, he would have been as well contented without it. (65)

> The slight suspicion with which his hearers at first listened to him, gradually melted away before the convincing simplicity of his distress: it was impossible for the neighbors to doubt that Marner was telling the truth... because, as Mr. Macey observed, "Folks as had the devil to back 'em were not likely to be so mushed" as poor Silas was. (67)

It is notable that Silas begins this climactic scene by interrupting a tavern conversation about ghostly "phenomena," his timing causing all present to wonder whether he has arrived "in the flesh" or whether it is his "soul" once again gone "loose from his body" (64–65). By the end of the scene, he has transformed in the eyes of his fellow townspeople; while neither cool, nor calm, he does seem miraculously collected, a shade restored to human form. He appears, as Mr. Macey proclaims, suddenly "mushed," or freed from the collector's desperation to "keep body and soul together" (Stewart, 154). His visible anguish proves to all those present that, far from being a ghost, his body and soul must be conjoined and working in tandem to register his "passionate preoccupation with his loss" (67).

Yet while the townspeople's immediate sympathy for Silas's "mushed" state may not be misplaced, the narrator makes it clear that they comprehend Silas's suffering, and by extension his humanity, only through blatant symptoms of woe—the implicit made explicit, to use Lewes's phrase. The narrator suggests that in noticing transformations through visible affect—or even only *as* visible affect—something important may be elided, a "mystery that lies beneath" the surface of physically recognizable symptoms. Silas's great moment of release from being a miser unfolds between hearth and tavern, but on another level, this "old-fashioned" folkloric transformation overlies a less easily perceived narrative development that occurs during Silas's previous uneventful years as a miser, or rather, during the first hundred pages that Blackwood called into question. In insisting on depicting this period at length in a short work, Eliot makes clear that the miser's years of hoarding are not simply a preface to the main story but are central to a larger goal: that of depicting imperceptible, gradual change occurring over time, and revealing how this change often goes unrecognized.

As the narrator explains, Silas's sixteen years of isolation appear to his fellow townspeople as a period of complete arrested development, but we are cautioned that the townspeople have a tendency to understand only the visible and therefore to overlook changes that occur on another level. They are described as trusting only those whom the community deems "honest folk, born and bred in a visible manner" (8). As a foreigner and as a recluse, Silas represents an opposing model of having been born and bred in seemingly invisible conditions. As if to counterbalance the townspeople's introductory perspectives on Silas, the narrator includes a running commentary about the dangers of mistaking wonders for signs. We receive warnings about the incommensurability of "form" to "feeling" and how the "visible" may obscure rather than reveal inner states: "But while opinion concerning him had remained nearly stationary, and his daily habits had presented scarcely any visible change, Marner's inward life had been a history and a metamorphosis, as that of every fervid nature must be when it has fled, or been condemned to solitude" (12). As we shall see, Eliot's apparent distrust of the visual garners even more attention in *Daniel Deronda*.

For Silas Marner, the scarcity of "visible change" in his person also coincides with a scarcity of plot events. A beloved earthenware pot breaks. Silas offers Sally Oates an herbal remedy, only to be further misunderstood and rebuffed by his neighbors. These minor events provide landmarks in the flatlands of his lonely years, but the narrator insists that they are not the main "action" generated by the protagonist during this time. Instead, the narrator states that another form of action has taken place on a different plane, a "history and a metamorphosis" having occurred in a sphere beyond Raveloe's apprehension, if not beyond the reader's—the sphere of "Marner's inward life" (12).

The Phantasm of Desire: Beginnings as Invisible Events

If Eliot provides Silas Marner with any "action" during his years as a miser, it is a type of eventfulness not readily represented through the workings of plot. As a figure of passivity, Silas does not "act out" even when faced with injustice. Instead, Eliot renders "Marner's inward life" as an "acting-in," in which personal changes do not correspond proportionately with external narrative events. As she writes of the development that occurs in Silas's climactic scene in the Rainbow, "This strangely novel situation of opening his trouble to his Raveloe neighbors, of sitting in the warmth of a hearth not his own, and feeling the presence of faces and voices which were his nearest promise of help, had doubtless its influence on Marner, in spite of his passionate preoccupation with his loss. Our consciousness rarely registers the beginning of a growth within us any more than without us: there have been many circulations of the sap before we detect the smallest sign of the bud" (67). The difference between the bud and its preceding circulations of sap gives a sense of the distinction between signs and wonders, or rather, between plot events that mark milestones and less easily observed occurrences; the whole process of development is a wonder and mystery, but only one part comes to stand for the process as a whole—or even to efface the process in presenting readers with an emblem of the results. The phrase "circulations of the sap" provides an appropriately ambiguous unit for understanding this effaced process of growth, connoting both a bounded cycle with beginning and end, and also a continuity that resists the artificiality of division. Parsing the process into individuated rounds only creates an imaginary starting point, or as Eliot writes in the epigraph to *Daniel Deronda*, a "make-believe of a beginning": "Men can do nothing without the make-believe of a beginning. Even Science, the strict measurer, is obliged to start with a make-believe unit, and must fix on a point in the stars' unceasing journey when his sidereal clock shall pretend that time is at Nought.... No retrospect will take us to the true beginning; and whether our prologue be in heaven or on earth, it is but a fraction of that all-presupposing fact with which our story sets out" (*DD*, 1). In *Silas Marner*, we are told that there "have been many circulations of the sap" before we "detect the smallest sign" of change, detection and representation being decidedly belated affairs. In this inward model of action, the ever-receding "make-believe" of a beginning shifts retrospectively from bloom to seedling to the preceding "loam": the "habit of looking towards the money and grasping it with a sense of fulfilled effort made a loam that was deep enough for the seeds of desire" (22). A definitive beginning cannot be grasped, but Eliot nevertheless tries to position the first growth that can be recognized and represented further inward, closer to the mythical source where it is "born and bred" *invisibly*.

And for Eliot, these make-believe beginnings, though illusory, provide real sustenance. Evidence for this can be seen in a fleeting first-person recollection in *Silas Marner* in which we are presented with a small mystery. In the narrator's personal recollection, an old laborer dies because he has no recourse to this "make-believe," perhaps explaining the verbal subtlety that he perishes not for lack of "appetite" but because he cannot "raise the phantasm of appetite": "'Is there anything you can fancy that you would like to eat?' I once said to an old labouring man, who was in his last illness, and who had refused all the food his wife had offered him. 'No,' he answered, 'I've never been used to nothing but common victual, and I can't eat that.' Experience had bred no fancies in him that could raise the phantasm of appetite" (9). This humble death scene, the first in a novel replete with dramatic demises, emerges in a curious aside. It is the only death discrete from the main storyline, and one perhaps forgotten in the onslaught of subsequent fatalities that forward the plot: Mollie's opiated death crawl, Dunstan's corpse rising from the stone pits (a surprise hoard Eliot keeps for the grand finale), and less brutally if no less dramatically, the demise of the senior deacon of Lantern Yard, whose death touches off a spasm of plot disasters for Silas. In keeping several of these deaths as surprises to be sprung on characters at the conclusion, Eliot shows how narratives themselves hoard, both in being gradually accretive and also in keeping secrets. The old laborer's dying pales in comparison to the pyrotechnics of these later fatalities, though its casual insertion belies its centrality, for Eliot establishes an unspoken parallel between Silas and this first briefly mentioned laborer. While hoarding may deaden Silas to the outside world, the reawakening to "fancy" it provides distinguishes him from the dying man. As the narrator explains, the old laborer exemplifies "the minds of men who have always been pressed close by primitive wants" but who differ from the weaver in that their "imagination is almost barren of the images that feed desire and hope" (9).

In contrast, Silas's imaginative, if pathological, relationship with each coin allows him to raise the "phantasm" of desire that the old laborer lacks, Silas's hoard being described, in an unmistakable echo, as his "phantasm of delight" (90). The repetition calls attention to a critical distinction: the difference between the "phantasm of appetite" and "appetite" itself, or rather, the phantasm of a sensation and the sensation itself. The distinction is not at once apparent, for one would suppose that an old laborer could perish for lacking appetite as easily as for lacking "the phantasm" of it. To distinguish the "phantasm" of a feeling from the feeling itself seems like a task tantamount to separating one circulation of the sap from another. Nevertheless, we find this curious construction repeated throughout Eliot's work, not only in Silas's "phantasm of delight" but also in "Janet's Repentance": "She tried to have hope and trust, though it was hard to believe that the future would be anything else than the harvest of the seed that was being sown before her eyes. But always there is seed being sown silently and unseen, and everywhere there come sweet flowers without our foresight or labour. We reap what we sow, but Nature has love over and above that justice, and gives us shadow and blossom and fruit that spring from no planting of ours."[32] The idea of sowing without conscious knowledge proves central to Eliot's depictions of the gradual fulfillment of "shadow and blossom and fruit," "shadow" being an unusual choice for harvest, unless one understands this phrasing to invoke another example of the "make-believe of a beginning." The phantasmic nature of an urge before it is recognized gives the sense that renewal begins before the sign of renewal, desiring before full-blown desire, and the preparation for growth well before anything recognized as growth itself. Eliot makes clear that for every marked beginning we have a moment right before that eludes classification, existing as a ghostly fore-life—and not simply as a shadowy afterlife. This anticipatory "phantasm" gives a sense of the "make-believe beginning," which is no less vital for seeming unreal before any visible signs of confirmation. If narrative studies give few models for this unseen "action" in theoretical conceptions of plot, botany for Eliot provides important models for how to tell the story of invisible development.

The botanical imagery Eliot uses to give a sense of the "make-believe of a beginning" or the "phantasm" of growth is typical of many nineteenth-century tracts explaining purgatorial development. In intermediate state tracts, the soul in the afterlife is often envisioned as a latent seed, a favorite trope of those advocating "soul sleep" as the dominant model of existence after the dead body has been "planted" in the earth. In outlining the positions of the two main factions of intermediate state believers in 1856, Archbishop Whately suggested a surprisingly literal understanding of how the human body becomes a seed in preparation for the Second Coming. He envisioned long-deceased bodies rising up from a preserved "essential part" for reunification with their waiting souls:

> If, however, a man's body at his death, remained, though inanimate, yet sound, entire and uncorrupt, and so continued, in a torpid state, ready for the soul to reanimate it,—even as some seeds may be kept in a dry state for many years, and will be ready to vegetate as soon as exposed to moisture and warmth,—then, indeed, by a very bold figure of speech, the body might be said to be asleep; even as we might, figuratively, speak of the seed as asleep. But we know that all this is very far from the fact; that the body decays, and is dissolved into its elements. . . . It is conceivable,

however, that the whole of the body may not be dissolved; that some portion of it, perhaps many times less than the smallest grain of dust, may be exempted from the general decay,—may be, however minute, very curiously organized—(for *great* and *small* are only comparative) may be the really essential part of the body, so as to be properly called by itself, the body—and may remain in a torpid state, like a seed, ready to be again connected with the soul. All this, however, is merely a string of suppositions.[33]

In *The Shadowed Home*, Bickersteth made his own suppositions, using seedling analogies from Scripture as evidence of each individual's potential for resurrection after the millennial Second Coming.

First, how can that mouldering frame be raised again? . . . St. Paul answers both perplexities by one analogy. The seed-corn is not quickened to life, except it die; it is sown as naked grain; it is raised, clothed in new and beautiful apparel. What is this but a prophecy and proof from the natural creation that the resurrection is possible, and that the resurrection body is in one respect diverse from, in another respect identical with, that which is buried in the tomb? The objection is this: the body dies, it decays, it turns to dust; surely it utterly perishes. The answer is, so does the seed-corn die, and yet it does not utterly perish. Yea, more, it dies that it may live. As naked grain, it is hard and dry and fruitless; it must needs die before it can obtain its higher and nobler life as a graceful, fruitful, reproductive plant.[34]

The idea of literal afterlife regeneration held little sway with Eliot, who wrote in her review of Robert William Mackay's *The Progress of the Intellect* that "for succeeding ages to dream of retaining the spirit along with the forms of the past, is as futile as the embalming of the dead body in the hope that it may one day be resumed by the living soul."[35] Eliot did envision the possibility of a Second Coming, a rising up from a regenerating seed, but she imagined this renewal happening on earth.

In *Silas Marner*, the miser's time of self-collection reduces him, or consolidates his energies, into a buried seed state from which the second half of his story springs. We learn that his body "shrank," his "life had reduced itself more and more into a mere pulsation" (25), the dual meaning of pulse as heartbeat and as seed grain having been noted in Hertz's seminal *George Eliot's Pulse*.[36] In his "hardening," Silas becomes akin not simply to the "dead disrupted" coin, rendering him a member of his own collection, but to something generative, if similarly inert. The seed models this inert promise, its action occurring underground and in unrecognized circumstances. Eliot's desire to follow a likewise invisible course of development is crucial to her portrayal of Silas's uneventful miserhood as a seed state, or as an "intermediate state" of growth in which the events of the story, much like the main character, have simply gone underground.

Making Progress: Coincidental versus Sequential Plots

For every epoch of hiding underground in Eliot's tale, there comes a season of revelation. Godfrey's development as a man who fears accepting responsibility for his actions unfolds alongside Silas Marner's storyline. Yet for Godfrey, his life of secrets is the natural outgrowth of his early decision to worship "blessed Chance": "The evil principle deprecated in that religion, is the orderly sequence by which the seed brings forth a crop after its kind" (87). This excoriation of Chance—the only explicable agent of Silas's early misfortunes—shifts the focus away from one model of plot demonstrated early in the novel: that of *coincidence* being the main source of *incident*. Shunning Chance as the sole "mighty creator of success" (or failure, for that matter), Eliot presents a second model of plotting that coexists with this first one, even if it does not displace it completely. In warning about an overmastering belief in Chance, Eliot suggests a model of plot in which events are based on consequences rather than coincidences. Godfrey and Silas are both great believers in Chance, Godfrey optimistically and Silas pessimistically. This lack of faith in consequences, be they negative or positive, yields two different stories of descent and escapism: Godfrey's, motivated by a fear of looming consequences, and Silas's, motivated as a response to coincidences beyond his control. In both cases, the decision to hide passively away, in Jonah fashion, is driven by the belief that Chance is the sole agent of change. This subservience to forces beyond one's control manifests itself in severe near-sightedness, myopia being one of Silas's most remarked-upon attributes, though both men share an inability to foresee that "a seed brings forth a crop after its kind" (87).

Silas's hoarding is his first move away from being a victim of Chance, or one trapped in a "coincidental" model of plot, for his hoarding initiates a linear plot based on sequence and consequence. The daily act of contributing to his stash can be viewed as his incipient belief in sequential accomplishments—his previous sequential accomplishments at Lantern Yard having been interrupted by the cruel interventions of Chance. Sixteen years later, the disappearance of Silas's hoard would seem to return his plot to a storyline governed by coincidence, but not for long or even to negative effect. Dunstan's theft does not dismantle everything that Silas's hoarding has accomplished: it takes away his money but not his ability to watch something grow—this ability being the seed planted during these miserly years that comes to fruition in his fathering of Eppie.[37]

> The heap of gold seemed to glow and get larger beneath his agitated gaze. . . . [I]t was a sleeping child—a round fair thing, with soft yellow rings all over its head. Could this be his little sister come back to him in a dream—his little sister whom he had carried about in his arms for a year before she died, when he was a small boy without shoes or stockings?. . . . [T]here was a vision of the old home and the old streets leading to Lantern Yard—and within that vision another, of the thoughts which had been present

> with him in those far-off scenes. The thoughts were strange to him now, like old friendships impossible to revive; and yet he had a dreamy feeling that this child was somehow a message come to him from that far-off life: it stirred fibres that had never been moved in Raveloe. . . . He had plenty to do through the next hour. The porridge, sweetened with some dry brown sugar from an old store which he had refrained from using for himself, stopped the cries of the little one. (127–28)

Upon finding Eppie on his hearth, Silas mistakes her for his most immediate object of loss, his gold, but the impulse toward association with all things lost does not end there. His mind spans outward to losses of the most irretrievable nature: his little sister, whom he will never see again, and his life at Lantern Yard, the memory of which is almost "impossible to revive." The far-off life will not be resurrected, and Eppie's cries, her demands for porridge and dry shoes, move the story forward, even as her presence opens for Silas a retrospection that is also part of his reconstruction of a sequential story for his life. Retrospection is as important to Silas's recovery of a sequential story as the sense of futurity that comes with raising Eppie. Nevertheless, Eliot insists that retrospection can never be mistaken for restoration. Unlike Shakespeare's *The Winter's Tale*, with its similar interlude of sixteen years passed in insanity and isolation, in *Silas Marner* those lost do not magically—or by tremendous coincidence—return. Silas's gold is restored to him but devoid of the meaning it once held for him. The coins that once had individual faces in his imagination are now, like thoughts of Lantern Yard, "friendships impossible to revive." Equivalencies will be denied; not even currency can ever equal itself once imbued with desperate personal significance. Eppie is not Perdita come back to her father after his season of error, nor is she Silas's younger sister, Hepzibah, returned under the same name. Sixteen years pass in Silas's time as a miser, and again, sixteen years pass as Eppie's youth flies by. If a happy ending is possible in *Silas Marner*, it is largely because of the development these interludes provide. In the case of Silas's time as a miser, this time is one of gradual growth that offers recuperation, if not an "old-fashioned" fairy tale of restoration.

III. *Daniel Deronda:* Widows and the Afterlife of the Marriage Plot

A sixteen-year interlude, as in *Silas Marner*, surfaces again in *Daniel Deronda* when Eliot invokes *The Winter's Tale* in Gwendolen's tableau vivant of Hermione's resurrection. In Shakespeare's play, as opposed to Eliot's novels, the major temporal gap at its center passes offstage and between the acts. Eliot works to fill in these lacunae, gravitating toward periods in which development unfolds slowly between recognized turning points. Gwendolen Harleth's widowhood is one such interlude.

Widows appear in Eliot's novels repeatedly and under a wide range of guises: we meet resigned mothers such as Mrs. Raynor and Mrs. Davilow; self-sacrificing heroines, including Dorothea and Romola; vibrant scene-stealers turned penitent, such as Gwendolen and her prototype, Janet Dempster. Despite differences in age, personal circumstance, and disposition, each one faces the same recurring dilemma: a problem of negotiating the void that follows the end of the coming-of-age story. As Eliot's comic widow, Mona Brigida, complains in *Romola*, "Holy Madonna! it seems as if widows had nothing to do now but to buy their coffins, and think it a thousand years till they get into them, instead of enjoying themselves a little when they've got their hands free for the first time."[38] Later, in *Daniel Deronda*, the Alcharisi, Eliot's most imperious widow, similarly describes her life in terms of premature death: "Another life! Men talk of 'another life,' as if it only began on the other side of the grave. I have long entered on another life" (666).

In foregrounding these complaints and rebellions, Eliot comments on the roles assigned to widows in British culture. She addresses two different stereotypes: the aged widow who sits, propped up, an unchanging fixture in the corners of Victorian fiction—the "lone lorn creeturs" of Victorian fiction represented by *David Copperfield*'s Mrs. Gummidge—and also youthful widows and their plots of remarriage. These young widows are frequently sentimentalized, their mourning rendered tragic in the face of such patent nubility. "Poor Eleanor Bold!" declares the narrator of *Barchester Towers*. "How well does that widow's cap become her, and the solemn gravity with which she devotes herself to her new duties."[39] In scuttling Eleanor out of her cap and back into orange blossoms, the narrator questions the benefits of a widow's dutifulness: "As the parasite plant will follow even the defects of the trunk which it embraces, so did Eleanor cling to and love the very faults of her husband" (14). Eleanor Bold finds a sister in Amelia Sedley in *Vanity Fair*, whose worship of an unworthy late husband, George Osborne, suspends and elongates her midlife doldrums. Both Trollope and Thackeray make the widow a central figure in their fictions of maturity, caricaturing and critiquing the sentimentalism associated with this state, but unlike Eliot they do not offer a more complex, nuanced depiction of widowhood as a state of midlife female *bildung*. *Little Dorrit*'s Flora Finching lies between these two poles of youthful widowhood and old age, though she is, like other Dickensian widows, treated parodically and unsparingly. Dickens presents her midlife attempts at attracting Clennam as an unseemly masquerade of her younger self, a masquerade made all the more ridiculous for the tumorous accessory of Mr. F's Aunt—a constant reminder of the perils of female aging in Dickens's fictive world. Elizabeth Gaskell's *Cranford* uniquely provides a more active view of widowhood as a state of companionship and social standing for "ladies of good family."[40] Yet the concern remains that their closed society of "elderly spinsters, or widows without children" needs to "become less exclusive," at the risk of atrophying into "no society at all" (*Cranford*, 64). This anxiety plays out on a formal level in Gaskell's approach to plot. As in the bildungsroman as a form, in many novels of maturity female marriageability and reproduction provide a reliable story arc, and in Gaskell's episodic and meandering sketches she cannily skirts the limits of *Cranford* dissolving into what might be termed "no *story* at all."

Amid this abundance of fictions featuring widows of all ages, Eliot's portrayals are unusually complex and problematic. She protests the stifling plot assigned to widows, often via outspoken minor characters, yet nevertheless seems to perpetuate the same uneventful storylines herself. In *Middlemarch*, Dorothea finds herself at loose ends months after Casaubon's death: "The widow's cap of those times made an oval frame for the face, and had a crown standing up; the dress was an experiment in the utmost laying on of crape; but this heavy solemnity of clothing made her face look all the younger, with its recovered bloom, and the sweet, inquiring candor of her eyes" (335). His demise might be expected to return her to a story of youthful possibility, her mourning garb framing this eligibility all the more clearly—as it does in the case of Eleanor Bold—but Eliot resists indulging this convention. Instead, Dorothea's storyline appears inert for the expansive middle of the novel, with hundreds of pages separating her husband's death and the major events that crowd the finish, including her epiphany about loving Ladislaw and her "ardent action" on behalf of Lydgate. Whereas Anthony Trollope immediately reengages the marriage plot for his young widows in *Barchester Towers*, Eliot lets Dorothea squirm.

Middlemarch in this way sets a precedent for Eliot's refusal to renew the heroine's marriage plot at all in *Daniel Deronda*. In Gwendolen's marriage to Grandcourt, his "presence and surveillance seemed to flatten every effort to the level of the boredom which his manner expressed: his negative mind was as diffusive as fog, clinging to all objects and spoiling all contact" (*DD*, 587). The flattening effect of his surveillance affects the narrative itself, and scene after scene of unchanging discord fill the chapters devoted to their union. When his drowning finally comes, readers are not released from the previous stalemate, for Gwendolen's recourse to aid and absolution involves replaying scenes from her marriage, a penitential storyline that decrescendos into her final return to Offendene.

Rather than reengage a courtship plot for Gwendolen, Eliot achieves her vision of "another life" outside of the marriage plot and the bildungsroman by contrasting her heroine to two examples of exilic female martyrdom: Hermione in *The Winter's Tale* and La Pia of Siena, the murdered wife, in Dante's *Purgatorio*. Eliot uses these works as touchstones for capturing a gradual change that appears outwardly like stasis, invoking Shakespeare's wintry interlude and Dante's journey through purgatory as metaphors for this process. She further alludes to these iconic female figures from Shakespeare and Dante to write against contemporary visual representations of female abjection in Pre-Raphaelite art. La Pia and her sisters—Mariana, the Lady of Shalott, and the Blessed Damozel—are presented as "fixed" in their abandoned state by Victorian artists including Dante Gabriel Rossetti, John Everett Millais, and Gustave Doré. In contrast, Eliot uses ekphrasis at once to conjure up and simultaneously undermine contemporary visual images of aestheticized female abjection, evoking Pre-Raphaelite paintings to illustrate her heroine's struggle against stasis. It is not uncommon to see continuity between Eliot's literary realism and the detailed aesthetic vision of female subjects created by Pre-Raphaelite painters and contemporary visual artists, and scholars contend that paintings such as Millais's *Mariana* were internalized in her writing after she saw an exhibit of their works at the Royal Academy in 1852.[41] Nevertheless, in considering Eliot's expressed discomfort with static and beautiful images of abandoned women—a discomfort raised with special insistence in *Daniel Deronda*—we can clearly see that Eliot invokes images of famous stricken women to revisit and, in many ways, revise our understanding of the abandoned woman in literature and art.

Ekphrasis thus proves central to Eliot's method of plotting adult maturation, for references to visual art become a locus in her novels for counterposing still visual surfaces to inner turmoil, a method similar to the one she uses earlier in contrasting "Marner's inner life" to his unchanging external appearance. Presenting Gwendolen not only as La Pia but also as a living statue in the tradition of Shakespeare's Hermione, Eliot uses La Pia and the figure of the living statue to engage art historical debates about the distinction between still and moving art forms, a method that allows her to develop a new form of extreme narrative gradualism. In scenes featuring the trope of the living statue, in particular, she alludes to G. E. Lessing's model of *ut pictura poesis*, playing with his categories of visual stasis versus narrative movement to muddle his distinctions; Gwendolen is presented as a hybrid, a figure of *moving stasis* whose gradual maturation is captured through metaphors borrowed from the visual arts and Victorian eschatology alike.[42] Eliot's use of painting and statuary in her fiction in this way allows her to rehabilitate the tragic female figure in Victorian painting and poetry by putting this figure in motion—albeit slow motion—thereby staging the clash of *pictura* and *poesis* as the drama of her heroine's "slight progression."

The Hermione Syndrome: Ekphrasis, Stasis, and Aestheticizing Female Abjection

"Let him scream, and see."[43] This challenge, issued by Lessing in his essay on *Laocoön and His Sons*, comes as a warning to visual artists who would depict raw fear at the risk of alienating viewers. It is a challenge that George Eliot, who invoked Lessing's "masterful" essay in her reviews, takes up directly in *Daniel Deronda:* she lets her heroine scream and be seen, most notably in the tableau vivant. In this scene, Eliot stages a clash between static visual art and the novelistic heroine's penchant for mobility—a central tension between visual stasis and narrative movement present in Lessing's seminal essay on ekphrasis.

Scholars of Eliot's ekphrasis tend to focus on Gwendolen as a medusa figure in this scene, a common reading that has overshadowed another source for Eliot's take on the screaming statue: Lessing's essay.[44] Eliot was more than familiar with the *Laocoön*, having discussed it in an 1856 Belles Lettres column for the *Westminster Review* in which she cites Lessing's "masterly distinction between the methods of presentation in poetry and the plastic arts," or his insistence that the visual arts are static and poetry unfolds over time.[45] She then repeats Lessing's warning that painters and sculptors must refrain from depicting pain at full blast, though writers, as he says, have greater leeway.[46] As Lessing wrote of the statue of Laocoön: "Pain, in its disfiguring extreme, was not compatible with beauty, and must therefore be softened. Screams must be reduced to sighs not because screams would betray weakness, but because they would deform the countenance to a repulsive degree. Imagine Laocoön's mouth open, and judge. Let him scream, and see."[47] In *Daniel Deronda*, Eliot responds to Lessing. Depicting Gwendolen's moment of recoil, she does something no visual artist, under Lessing's decree, should do: she lingers over her heroine's shrieking face, describing her "expression terrifying in its terror" and how she "looked like a statue into which a soul of Fear had entered: her pallid lips were parted; her eyes, usually narrowed under their long lashes, were dilated and fixed" (55). If Gwendolen "looked like a statue," it is obviously not one that Lessing would have praised. Mouth agape and composure lost, she produces a far more original production than the one she had intended, for instead of capturing Hermione's stoic gravitas at this moment, she emerges as a feminized parody of the statue of Laocoön. This comparison, which has yet to be fully identified by critics, is further reinforced by subsequent descriptions of Gwendolen's "fits of spiritual dread" (63), which also recall Laocoön's serpentine predicament; in her "shrieking fear," she too experiences the sensation of "evil spirits . . . hissing around her with serpent tongues" (762).

Recognizing the tableau as a parodic staging of Lessing's essay proves essential to understanding Eliot's complex response to his theory of ekphrasis throughout *Daniel Deronda*. As I contend, Lessing's writing scaffolds crucial scenes in the novel in which Eliot invokes the visual arts to achieve her own brand of what I term "narrative gradualism," a reading that argues for a new understanding of Eliot's relation to Lessing's writing. Scholars often view Eliot as coinciding uncritically with Lessing, and the argument has been made that she both paraphrases his views and aligns herself with them.[48] Yet in *Daniel Deronda* she plays with his distinctions, going so far as to offer readers a send-up of his model of sculpted decorum while simultaneously putting his central binary—the difference between narrative movement and visual stillness—on stage to startling effect.

This new perception of how Lessing's essay is parodically dramatized in the novel has wider implications: Lessing shaped Eliot's depiction of the visual arts as well as her response to contemporary visual artists. Ultimately, her presentation of Gwendolen as a screaming statue proves crucial to her unconventional approach to plotting a finale for her flawed, complex heroine. Critics have expressed disappointment at Gwendolen's displacement in the concluding nuptials, framing her widowed return to Offendene as punitive, as the fate of "a monster, a witch, a Medusa figure," "the novel's tragic figure" who is "fixed"[49] in a stasis akin to her frozen horror in the tableau vivant. In contrast, perceiving the nature of Eliot's response to Lessing and the Pre-Raphaelites gives new context for recovering a recuperative, rather than abject, understanding of the heroine's ending. Instead of sacrificing Gwendolen, as some have claimed, Eliot envisions a future of continued growth for her heroine, giving Gwendolen room to grow while at the same time, as an author, evading being "held captive by the ordinary wirework of social forms" (*DD*, 53) that constitutes the marriage plot. In the novel's conclusion, ekphrasis allows Eliot to capture the kind of change she envisions, for instead of recurring to the portrait of the dead face as an icon in Gwendolen's finale, Eliot moves beyond its suspended Gothic terror toward a model of gradual change embodied in the moving statue, the figure to which Eliot once again compares Gwendolen in describing her "humdrum" homecoming to Offendene and the second chances this return offers.

Staging Lessing: Beauty, Stasis, and the Trope of the Living Statue

Lessing's central role in the tableau vivant becomes apparent from the outset in the unorthodox form it takes. Even when considered within the context of other fanciful home theatrical productions in nineteenth-century literature, including the charades of *Vanity Fair* and *Jane Eyre*, this tableau is unusual in the seeming excess of artistic media on display in short succession: a tableau from a play is interrupted when a picture of a dead face springs forward, triggered by forceful piano playing. The effect is to turn the heroine, even more effectively, into a statue. That this intermixing of the arts takes place *on stage* is itself noteworthy. It becomes clear that Eliot is presenting readers not simply with an abortive performance of *The Winter's Tale* but instead with a dramatic staging of the conflict between different art forms at the heart of Lessing's essay. Drama in this scene offers a compromise between the stillness of the image and the movement of narrative, arising as an important third term in the adulterated form of the tableau; as Gwendolen urges, "instead of the mere tableau there should be just enough acting of the scene to introduce the striking up of the music" (59). For Gwendolen, "just enough acting" means "enough" to satisfy her penchant for movement but not so much that it incurs her uncle's censure against acting of any kind. And it is precisely this attempt to smuggle acting into the still form of the tableau vivant that sets off a chain of performative disasters. In stepping off the pedestal to display her attractive "foot and instep" (60), Gwendolen sets in motion a different kind of production, a staging not simply of Hermione's awakening but, more to the point, of Lessing's theory about the conflict between still and moving art.

This conflict between movement and stasis is embodied in the figure Gwendolen chooses to play: the living statue. The trope of the living statue recurs at critical junctures in the novel, opening a space of contemplation that drives the plot inward to where action unfolds slowly below the surface of a character's observable façade. As Kenneth Gross observes in *The Dream of the Moving Statue*, "Despite this sense of their exteriority . . . statues can simultaneously attract to themselves a strong, if elusive feeling of *interiority;* statues can become the foci, the troubled bearers of an interior life that is at once their own and not their own."[50] The living statue, as a trope, provides Eliot with a means through which to conceive her approach to narrative gradualism. In both *Daniel Deronda* and *Middlemarch*, references to living statues touch off omniscient third-person observations about what lies beneath the still, or in Gwendolen's case frozen, surface of outer appearance, allowing Eliot to counterpose visual surfaces to inner turmoil. But it is in *Daniel Deronda*, in particular, that these references to living statuary are further imbued with an underlying parodic engagement with Lessing. The appearance of Gwendolen midscream makes Eliot's departure from her previous works of fiction clear. Eliot is not simply casting her heroine as a living statue, as she does to aesthetically pleasing effect in *Middlemarch,* but instead she presents readers with a variant of this trope, the *screaming* statue, a figure that immediately recalls Lessing's sculptural dicta and reveals George Eliot's direct engagement with his writing.

This unflattering treatment of her leading lady is a central part of Eliot's response to Lessing, a response to his theory of *ut pictura poesis* that is evident from the first page of the novel onward. As in the tableau vivant, the opening description of Gwendolen is discreetly underwritten by Lessing, for it introduces a line of inquiry familiar to Lessing's argument about the relation between visual beauty and viewer sympathy, but at the same time it departs from Lessing in a crucial way: it pushes toward further separating physical beauty and literary, as opposed to visual, methods of creating sympathy. The opening reads, "Was she beautiful or not beautiful? and what was the secret of form or expression which gave the dynamic quality to her glance? Was the good or the evil genius dominant in those beams? Probably the evil; else why was the effect that of unrest rather than of undisturbed charm? Why was the wish to look again felt as coercion and not as a longing in which the whole being consents?" (7). In Lessing's conception, still and stoic beauty is a primary source of sympathy in visual depictions of suffering, and his ideal of beauty in suffering guides Pre-Raphaelite artists and Victorian poets alike who fixate on representing female abjection as stoic, even erotic. These artists and poets poise figures such as Mariana, the Blessed Damozel, the Lady of Shalott, and La Pia of Siena in moments of contemplated and composed affliction. But while these famed figures may suffer beautifully, Gwendolen, we are pointedly told, does not. Eliot instead presents her from the very first page onward as a curious composite: both beautiful and "evil," both snake and quivering prey, she is the enchantress in a green gown who "has got herself up as a sort of serpent" (12), but she is also the victim of an even more "dangerous serpent" (668), a husband skilled in being both constricting and venomous. Gwendolen's "iridescence" of "character," her ability to attract people and inspire both "fear" and "fondness" in equal measure, thus results from "the play of various, nay, contrary tendencies" (42). She may fashion herself to be a "daring" (63) young "princess in exile" (41), but she nevertheless experiences "fits of timidity or terror" (64) at "suddenly feeling herself alone, when, for example, she was walking without companionship and there came some rapid change in the light. Solitude in any wide scene impressed her with an undefined feeling of immeasurable existence aloof from her, in the midst of which she was helplessly incapable of asserting herself" (63). These suspended moments of sublime "spiritual dread" contrast with her desire for motion and self-assertion—for escape, however heedless, from the "narrow theatre which life offers to a girl of twenty" (63). As she is torn between frozen fear and undirected dynamism, Gwendolen's course of action is unclear in any given moment, let alone moments of crisis. Her "iridescence" or fluctuation between opposing impulses has a repellant dimension, an ambiguity that Eliot portrays as dually moral and aesthetic in nature. The problem of "being many opposite things in the same moment" (42) translates into a problem of knowing how to act—"we cannot kill and not kill in the same moment" (42)—an ethical concern that Eliot establishes early in the novel as being intimately bound up with questions of beauty, and in Gwendolen's case, with *questionable* beauty.

Even in the moment of Gwendolen's greatest stillness, her fright in the tableau vivant, Eliot disallows any simple appreciation of Gwendolen as a beautiful art object. Our sympathy for her, which Eliot later demands outright in chapter 54 of the novel in comparing her to La Pia, cannot be based on any simple sense of her visual surface appeal. The opening series of questions heads off any such impulse. Lessing may align beauty with the static visual image, but Eliot plays with this affiliation, going so far as to suggest that Gwendolen's potential lack of beauty, her tinge of "evil genius," generates our interest in her, and with it, narrative momentum. Gwendolen, accordingly, does not arrest viewers with her striking appearance but causes "*un*rest," an important difference.[51] This unrest provides the combustive spark that jolts the novel forward, propelling Daniel's and the reader's interest in her as a "dynamic" character. Beauty might yield the "effect . . . of undisturbed charm," but we are led to believe that our heroine's more questionable forms of attraction drive narrative more effectively.

Gwendolen's subsequent appearance as a screaming statue further makes an ethical problem in the text manifest: the problem of aestheticizing female suffering, or rather, of representing distressing emotional states through eye-pleasing visual means. It is an aesthetic conundrum that Eliot often broaches through statuary, as she does in *Middlemarch* in depicting Dorothea in the galleries of Rome. In this scene, Eliot's most famed example of ekphrasis, Will Ladislaw and his artist friend Naumann stumble upon Dorothea in a moment of stillness in which she appears to them as a statue of Ariadne. "They were just in time to see another figure standing against a pedestal near the reclining marble: a breathing blooming girl, whose form, not shamed by the Ariadne, was clad in Quakerish grey drapery" (121). In comparing Dorothea with the sculpture, the painter Naumann focuses immediately on her beauty: "There lies antique beauty, not corpse-like even in death, but arrested in the complete contentment of its sensuous perfection: and here stands beauty in its breathing life" (121). Irritated by Naumann's rival fixation, Ladislaw voices his displeasure via Lessing, parroting Lessing's stance that the narrative arts transcend static visual representation: "Your painting and Plastik are poor stuff after all. They perturb and dull conceptions instead of raising them. Language is a finer medium. . . . Language gives a fuller image. . . . After all, the true seeing is within; and painting stares at you with an insistent imperfection. I feel that especially about representations of women. As if a woman were a mere coloured superficies! You must wait for movement and tone" (122). Whether or not George Eliot aligns herself with Ladislaw has been the subject of much of the critical debate on this passage.[52] It is tempting to read Ladislaw's opinion as Eliot's own, and critics have warned against assigning Eliot a one-sided view in the debate between narrative and visual art. Rather than assert the superiority of narrative over visual means, Eliot "affirms the dynamic and expressive power of art by using the statue as a catalyst for the birth of desire," according to Abigail Rischin.[53] Missing from Rischin's and others' arguments, however, is an investigation of the unstable place of beauty in Eliot's discussions of ekphrasis.

Eliot implicates beauty as a source of volatility at the fraught crossroads between the visual and the verbal. This discussion of the problematic nature of beauty arises both in the Belles Lettres piece in which she cites Lessing and also in her essay "The Natural History of German Life." In these reviews, the perils of visual beauty are presented as twofold: the beautiful image, invoked in narrative, is often a shortcut used to engender "sympathy ready-made";[54] conversely, beauty's absence, plainness or ugliness, becomes a common source of mishandling by writers and not just by visual artists, this point of Eliot's marking an important departure from Lessing's essay.[55] When discussing the vexed role beauty plays in engendering sympathy, Eliot does not target the visual arts as an inferior medium but rather reserves her criticism for writers who flatten their subjects when invoking the beautiful image in literature. As she insists, writers who fail to translate *pictura* into *poesis* with due deftness settle for the "symbolism" of visual art,[56] neglecting to do what poets and writers can uniquely do: capture the invisible movements of the mind.

The problem, then, that arises in *Middlemarch* is that Ladislaw and Naumann may adopt different stances on Lessing, but their differing stances mask a problematic similarity: they both fail to perceive what lies beneath the surface of a beautiful face. As the defender of *poesis*, Ladislaw joins his artist friend in finding Dorothea an object of supreme aesthetic interest; he, too, is captivated by the "superficies" of her loveliness, failing to intuit her struggle "within." This surface appreciation is one that Eliot works to undermine in succeeding pages of narration. Picking up where Ladislaw falls short, the next chapter is devoted to delving into Dorothea's "inward amazement," revealing the process of disillusionment that has characterized her marriage: "[T]hat new real future which was replacing the imaginary drew its material from the endless minutiae by which her view of Mr. Casaubon and her wifely relation, now that she was married to him, was gradually changing" (224). Opening such invisible processes to her readers, Eliot uses ekphrasis at this critical juncture in Dorothea's story to create a specific effect: she invokes the visual arts, in particular the trope of the moving statue, to achieve her own narrative gradualism, revealing the slow change that belies her heroine's outward stasis or melancholy poise. Ekphrasis in this way proves central to Eliot's purgatorial approach to plotting stories of midlife, and it is no coincidence that a quotation from Dante's *Purgatorio* serves as the epigraph for the chapter that introduces Dorothea's dismal Roman holiday, a reference that prefigures Eliot's continued investment in purgatory as a metaphor for marital and midlife struggle in *Daniel Deronda*.[57]

In *Daniel Deronda*, Eliot more aggressively bars attempts to consider her heroine as a still and lovely aesthetic object. Moments of statuary stasis that would most allow for this kind of appreciation are immediately tainted by her heroine's uncontrolled horror, a discomposure that is neither stoical nor beautiful. Our heroine, as Eliot insists, is not an icon of patient suffering but instead a fundamentally novelistic character, a mobile creation who gladly attracts attention even as she resists being regarded as a purely aesthetic object. This dynamism, however, is under constant threat. Eliot invokes visual artworks to give the threat of stasis symbolic weight at the same time that she uses ekphrasis to reveal her characters' inner torment. Young women in the novel are repeatedly represented as statues, a comparison that often emerges in scenes of fear and distress. Gwendolen's first extended conversation with Grandcourt marks one such scene of distress. In keeping with Eliot's pattern of ekphrasis, Gwendolen is described as a statue: "She was perfectly silent, holding up the folds of her robe like a statue, and giving a harder grasp to the handle of her whip, which she had snatched up automatically with her hat when they had first set off" (130). Again, the statue metaphor comes at a crucial juncture, a turning point in the novel when the moment, as Daniel reflects in the opening casino scene, becomes "dramatic" (9). Statuary is again used in this scene to enact a gradualist temporality, ekphrasis being employed to show how fear and excitement "stretched the moment with conflict" (10). This "stretched" and suspended quality is one that Eliot creates by invoking the visual arts.

Eliot echoes her description of Gwendolen as a "statue into which the soul of Fear had entered" in Mirah's subsequent introduction as a statue during her failed suicide attempt: "her eyes were fixed on the river with a look of immovable, statue-like despair" (183). In this scene, it is notable that Daniel, unlike Ladislaw, feels "an outleap of interest and compassion toward her" (183), a desire to understand her inner motivations that he, in turn, checks, questioning it as an outgrowth of his attraction to her beauty. He "smile[s] at his own share in the prejudice that interesting faces must have interesting adventures" but concludes inwardly, "I should not have forgotten the look of misery if she had been ugly and vulgar. . . . But there was no denying that the attractiveness of the image made it likelier to last" (183). Following Mirah's introduction as a statue, several female characters are likewise depicted in terms of the stasis of visual artworks, and characters including Lydia Glasher and the Alcharisi serve as cautionary examples of the oubliette that waits just outside the marriage plot. Their condition of waiting, abandonment, and illegitimacy is conveyed in an array of images of frozen dread that flash upon readers like afterimages of the "picture of a dead face" that first horrifies Gwendolen. Lydia Glasher can be said to spring from the woodwork as if launched by the same mechanism as the painting in the tableau vivant, and she angrily haunts the novel from her outpost in the moated grange of Gadsmere. Later, the Alcharisi stands as another cautionary example of dynamism quelled and made weary. These women, like Gwendolen, have a penchant for drama and action but find themselves stilled and marginalized within the world of *Daniel Deronda*. The trials of stasis are on full display in the novel, and as Eliot forces readers to conclude, they are not always pretty.

This refusal to make female abjection beautiful puts Eliot at odds with many of her contemporaries. In works by Victorian artists and poets, abandoned female characters become a recurring source of sympathy partly through their condition of immobility. These female subjects are often presented as weary, still, and beautifully ossified in conditions of abjection. In *Daniel Deronda*, Eliot challenges these contemporary portrayals of abandoned women who find themselves ejected from the marriage plot and forced to reside in a form of limbo. Pre-Raphaelite artists and Victorian poets aestheticize this limbo, but Eliot works against their examples, most clearly in her own remaking of La Pia of Siena, a popular source of inspiration for Victorian artists. In comparing her heroine to La Pia, Eliot both counters other Victorian representations of female abjection and uses this figure from the *Purgatorio* to imagine Gwendolen's ensuing maturation as a form of gradual movement, as a "purgatory . . . on the green earth" replete with references to Dante's *Divine Comedy*.

La Pia: Siena Made Her, Eliot Remade Her

To imagine the afterlife of the marriage plot, Eliot invokes Dante's *Purgatorio* as an extended metaphor by which to capture Gwendolen's uneventful progress.[58] The *Purgatorio* was a work that had various marital associations for Eliot, as evidenced by the anecdote that she and John Cross took a copy with them on their honeymoon to read out loud as a romantic activity.[59] Nevertheless, by any standards, this volume is an unusual choice for honeymoon literature, for it is replete with images of marital disappointment. This emphasis on discord in marriage perhaps explains why the last two books of *Daniel Deronda*, the portion devoted to Gwendolen's unhappy marriage and widowhood, include the highest number of allusions to Dante's *Purgatorio* of any stretch of Eliot's writing.

Given the central role of widows in purgatorial doctrine, the connection between widows and *Purgatorio* references in *Daniel Deronda* is not surprising. In Dante's vision of the afterlife, widows are often described as the living keepers of purgatory, fulfilling a crucial role of speeding the upward climb of souls through prayer and intercession. The process of purgatory thus always begins "on earth" for widows, but usually on someone else's behalf. Like that other figure of toilsome waiting, the miser, widows are envisioned in the *Divine Comedy* as collectors—and specifically, as re-collectors—for it is through their acts of repeated remembrance and recollection that loved ones can achieve their own spiritual composure more efficiently in the afterlife. Dante is accordingly beseeched throughout his imagined journey to contact the living relations of the deceased, especially widows who remain on earth, and to encourage their prayers.

In one such scene in Canto VIII, which Eliot translated and copied into several of her notebooks, a husband laments that his wife has remarried and is slow with her forthcoming prayers. He pleads with Dante to contact his daughter when he returns to earth to ask that she pray for him instead:

> "[W]hen you are far from these wide waters,
> ask my Giovanna to direct her prayers for me
> to where the innocent are heard.
>
> "I think her mother has not loved me
> since she stopped wearing her white wimple,
> which, in her coming misery, she may long for.
>
> "There is an easy lesson in her conduct:
> how short a time the fire of love endures in woman
> if frequent sight and touch do not rekindle it.
>
> "The viper that leads the Milanese afield
> will hardly ornament her tomb as handsomely
> as the cock of Gallura would have done."
>
> He spoke these words, his face stamped
> with a look of righteous indignation
> that burns with proper measure in the heart.[60]

The plight of the man whose widow remarries earned Thomas Carlyle's homage in *On Heroes, Hero-Worship, and the Heroic in History*. Citing the above passage by way of example, Carlyle describes the *Purgatorio* as potentially the most "excellent" volume of the *Commedia*:

> I do not agree with much modern criticism, in greatly preferring the *Inferno* to the two other parts of the *Divine Commedia*. Such preference belongs, I imagine, to our general Byronism of taste, and is like to be a transient feeling. The *Purgatorio* and *Paradiso*, especially the former, one would almost say, is even more excellent than it. It is a noble thing that *Purgatorio*, 'Mountain of Purification;' an emblem of the noblest conception of that age. . . . Repentance is the grand Christian act. It is beautiful how Dante works it out. . . . "Pray for me," the denizens of that Mount of Pain all say to him. "Tell my Giovanna to pray for me," my daughter Giovanna; "I think her mother loves me no more!"[61]

Carlyle makes an example of the dead husband's "righteous indignation," and the dilemma presented in *Purgatorio*'s Canto VIII appears in Eliot's novels as well.[62] Through figures such as Bardo in *Romola* and Casaubon in *Middlemarch*, she depicts the dying man's desire to be remembered and properly memorialized after death. Eliot treats these patriarchs sympathetically but pointedly does not focus on their "righteous indignation," choosing to retell the story of Canto VIII from another perspective—that of living widows and daughters whose struggles with bequeathed burdens provide a center for her fictions. Rather than delve into the dead husband's indignation, Eliot focuses on another character in the *Purgatorio*: the first woman that Dante encounters in purgatory, La Pia of Siena, the murdered wife. Eliot introduces La Pia into Gwendolen's story by imagining the marital strife that precipitated the lady's death:

> Madonna Pia, whose husband, feeling himself injured by her, took her to his castle amid the swampy flats of the

> Maremma and got rid of her there, makes a pathetic figure in Dante's Purgatory, among the sinners who repented at the last and desire to be remembered compassionately by their fellow-countrymen. We know little about the grounds of mutual discontent between the Siennese couple, but we may infer with some confidence that the husband had never been a very delightful companion . . . [and] in relieving himself of her he could not avoid making the relief mutual. And thus, without any hardness to the poor Tuscan lady who had her deliverance long ago, one may feel warranted in thinking of her with a less sympathetic interest than of the better known Gwendolen who, instead of being delivered from her errors on earth and cleansed from their effect in purgatory, is at the very height of her entanglement in those fatal meshes which are woven within more closely than without, and often make the inward torture disproportionate to what is discernible as outward cause. . . . She had a root of conscience in her, and the process of purgatory had begun for her on the green earth: she knew that she had been wrong. (668–69)[63]

The juxtaposition of Gwendolen with a murder victim becomes increasingly jarring given the subsequent revelation of her homicidal impulses and Grandcourt's death. It would seem that Eliot calls attention to similarities between the two women's marital states only to contrast more sharply La Pia's "deliverance long ago" with Gwendolen's current purgatory. As Eliot asserts, her own creation must be of greater "sympathetic interest" than La Pia of Siena. This is a bold statement, for La Pia was a subject of tremendous sympathy in Victorian art, her plight having captured the imagination of several of Eliot's contemporaries, including Gustave Doré and Dante Gabriel Rossetti.[64] In his 1868 illustrations of Dante's *Divine Comedy*, Doré devoted an individual etching to La Pia of Siena.

In Doré's conception (see figure 2.1), La Pia looks uncommonly good for a woman who has just been murdered, but moreover, she

FIGURE 2.1 "La Pia of Siena," Canto V, *Le Purgatoire*, Gustave Doré, 1868. From Dante Alighieri's *Purgatory and Paradise*, translated by the Rev. Henry Francis Cary, M.A., and illustrated with the designs of M. Gustave Doré (New York: Cassell and Company, 1883). *Image courtesy of Princeton University Library.*

also looks very good for someone in the beginning stages of Dante's purgatory, where she resides in a waiting area Dante scholars term "ante-purgatory," a region at Mount Purgatory's base that functions as a form of eschatological lobby for saved penitents.[65] Far from being merely a placid prelude to the trials of Judgment, ante-purgatory is a place where waiting is a grueling trial in itself. In Doré's vision of La Pia, this waiting area differs strikingly from Dante's descriptions, for it appears peaceful, verging on edenic. La Pia's sylvan setting resembles Doré's later depictions of the earthly garden of bliss, a place that marks the end of purgatory and provides souls with respite after they have finished expiating their sins (see figure 2.2). Doré's images of both La Pia and the Garden of Eden have a similar composition in centering on a trio in conversation amid almost identical landscapes. But despite the ambiance of rarified air in both etchings, La Pia is not at the top of the mountain in Dante's vision, the region where the garden of earthly bliss lies, but at the bottom among a group called the "late-repenters" who wait to enter purgatory (see figure 2.3).

Picturing the late-repenters in a state of misery, Doré dramatizes the trials of ante-purgatory as a dehumanizing endurance test. Naked and hunched under a rocky overhang, his masculine group of late-repenters contrasts with La Pia's poised and contemplative stance in a woodland setting. Nevertheless, as self-collected as La Pia appears, she occupies the same space as the other sufferers, the main difference being that her state of waiting and "lonely lamentation" is aestheticized, even eroticized, by Doré.[66] La Pia receives similar treatment at the hands of Dante Gabriel Rossetti (see figure 2.4). In his *La Pia de' Tolomei* (1868–80), she gazes out from the frame wistful and elegantly garbed, an image not of violent marital violence but of contemplative victimization. Fondling her wedding ring with her rosary nearby, the Pious One waits, and Rossetti draws attention both to time's passage and to its apparent stasis in including a sundial in the foreground, a timekeeper that appears frozen in the still iconography of La Pia's grief.

p. 142.	Already had my steps,
Though slow, so far into that ancient wood
Transported me, I could not ken the place
Where I had enter'd.

Canto XXVIII. lines 22-25

FIGURE 2.2 "The Earthly Garden of Bliss," Canto XXVIII, *Le Purgatoire*, Gustave Doré, 1868. From Dante Alighieri's *Purgatory and Paradise*, translated by the Rev. Henry Francis Cary, M.A., and illustrated with the designs of M. Gustave Doré (New York: Cassell and Company, 1883). *Image courtesy of Princeton University Library.*

And there were some, who in the shady place
Behind the rock were standing, as a man
Through idleness might stand.

Canto IV., lines 100–102.

FIGURE 2.3 "The Late-Repenters," Canto IV, *Le Purgatoire*, Gustave Doré, 1868. From Dante Alighieri's *Purgatory and Paradise*, translated by the Rev. Henry Francis Cary, M.A., and illustrated with the designs of M. Gustave Doré (New York: Cassell and Company, 1883). *Image courtesy of Princeton University Library.*

FIGURE 2.4 *La Pia de' Tolomei*, Dante Gabriel Rossetti, 1868–80, oil on canvas, 104.8 × 120.6 cm. *Spencer Museum of Art, University of Kansas, Lawrence, Museum purchase, 1956.0031.*

In contrast to Doré and Rossetti, Eliot firmly situates La Pia among the late-repenters, introducing her as residing "among the sinners who repented at the last." She thereby foregrounds La Pia's placement in ante-purgatory, a detail that Doré and Rossetti elide. In painting La Pia as separate from the regular throng of sinners, both artists idealize La Pia to focus on only one aspect of her story: the tragedy of her stasis. By making the dilemma of La Pia's waiting the central focus of our sympathy, their portraits of La Pia correspond with a concurrent trend in Victorian art and poetry of imagining the tragic fate of the woman who has been abandoned by her love and whose greatest trial is one of stasis. This model is typified by Mariana in Tennyson's eponymous poem, who spends "[a]ll day within the dreamy house," uttering the refrain:

> "My life is dreary,
> He cometh not," she said;
> She said, "I am aweary, aweary,
> I would that I were dead!"[67]

Another poem in this genre is Rossetti's *The Blessed Damozel*, a work often paired with his painting *La Pia de' Tolomei*, which includes a deceased female speaker who waits for her beloved on earth, lamenting,

> "I wish that he were come to me,
> For he will come," she said.
> "Have I not pray'd in Heaven?—on earth,
> Lord, Lord, has he not pray'd?
> Are not two prayers a perfect strength?
> And shall I feel afraid?"[68]

The poem ends with her weeping, her tears being witnessed by another speaker who emerges as an invisible and voyeuristic "I," making his presence known in parenthetical statements at the end of the poem:

> Her eyes pray'd, and she smil'd.
>
> (I saw her smile.) But soon their path
> Was vague in distant spheres:
> And then she cast her arms along
> The golden barriers,
> And laid her face between her hands,
> And wept. (I heard her tears.)

This voyeuristic "I" of the lover in the poem corresponds with the position of the implied viewer in portraits of La Pia of Siena, her sadness and stasis being presented to a gazing subject just outside of her bounding frame.

With these depictions of depressed and frozen femininity in mind, I ask that we return to Eliot's assertion that we should have more sympathy for Gwendolen than for La Pia to think about Eliot's description of Madonna Pia in the context of these other contemporary images of the murdered wife. Eliot states that we are "warranted" in thinking of La Pia "with a less sympathetic interest than the better known Gwendolen who... is at the very height of her entanglement in those fatal meshes which are woven within more closely than without." In contrasting Gwendolen with a dead and static image of Dante's murdered wife, who had her "deliverance long ago," Eliot flies in the face of Victorian sympathy for the murdered Italian lady by suggesting that she might be better off dead, death having ended her marriage and made the "relief mutual." Eliot's emphasis on Gwendolen's living, earthly entanglement, by contrast, reads as a rejection of idealized and eroticized images of La Pia as calm, peaceful, and resigned—Eliot's wording even going so far as to critique the visual medium itself as a misleading surface depiction. She insists that Gwendolen's dilemma cannot be properly understood from the outside, her "inward torture" being "disproportionate to . . . outward cause." Rather than aestheticize a calm exterior of waiting suffering, Eliot reveals a desire to distance her Gwendolen from other artistic takes on the plight of the abandoned woman, making a claim that fiction can achieve a perspective on inner turmoil that is unavailable to audiences on a purely visual level—and that writers, rather than try to imitate the still grief of visual iconography, are under an obligation to perform acts of emotional excavation—a point she made earlier in her Belles Lettres review when invoking Lessing.

Through the flawed, if mobile, character of Gwendolen, Eliot transmutes La Pia's dilemma into a more hopeful—but also more inward—vision of the afterlife of failed unions. In taking this approach, she is more successful than her contemporaries in visual art, such as Doré and Rossetti, at effectively transmuting images from

Dante's *Purgatorio* into a distinctly Victorian conception of purgatory as a place for active, if uneventful, maturation—not one of mournful stasis. These artists all give prominence to the aspects of purgatory that have to do with waiting, but Eliot's fictions alone convey the internal struggles that accompany the act of waiting, showing how these struggles are part of a larger process. In Dante's theological framework, La Pia's deliverance would have included a series of spiritual trials conceived in physical terms. The starving, crawling, and burning shades we meet in *Purgatorio* illustrate how painful activities may function metaphorically to represent metaphysical exertions. In the case of "the better known Gwendolen," regardless of her purgatory being a bodily experience "on earth," her torment emerges as a more internalized conception of the trial by fire than Dante's suffering penitents undergo, for Eliot insists that Gwendolen's struggles are "woven within" and that the "inward torture" must be fundamentally "disproportionate to what is discernible as outward cause." In thus juxtaposing Gwendolen with Madonna Pia, Eliot reanimates the role of the tragic waiting woman as a figure of inward action, rather than of inaction—inward action being the dominant feature of Victorian concepts of purgatory. Gwendolen can properly be said to undergo a "school-time of contemplation" and a "time for maturing," to borrow Newman's description of his Victorian notion of the intermediate state.

Although allusions to Dante's *Purgatorio* align Gwendolen's marital drama with the time of Judgment, it is important to note that Eliot is not necessarily envisioning Dante's medieval conception of the afterlife—a place of enumerated trials and marked events. Eliot presents readers with a different purgatory than Dante's, depicting Gwendolen's progress along the lines of nineteenth-century visions of "the spirit-world" (*DD*, 763) where thoughts are drawn inward and progress may look like stasis. Several critics have studied Eliot's fascination with Dante and his influence upon her writing, but with the exception of Alison Milbank, few note that nineteenth-century theologies of purgatory often inflect Victorian references to the *Divine Comedy*.[69] The divergence of Gwendolen's story from Dante's precedent has troubled critics, especially those who do not acknowledge the availability to Eliot of other purgatorial models. In analyzing Gwendolen's marriage plot alongside the *Purgatorio* and the *Inferno*, David Moldstad concludes that for "most of Gwendolen's marriage, the purgatorial metaphor follows the Dantean pattern. But at the end . . . her final forsaken state is virtually opposite that of Dante."[70] He also claims that with Grandcourt's death, "suddenly, the worst of Gwendolen's purgatory is over."[71] On the contrary, far from being over, Gwendolen's purgatory has barely begun. Her continued penitential repetition aligns her all the more firmly with purgatorial expiation, just not perhaps Dante's model of purgation. Rather than being freed from this purgatory as a conclusion, she is seemingly left in this state at the novel's close. Moldstad is nevertheless correct in observing that Gwendolen's story does not follow Dante's ascent when Eliot quotes from *Purgatorio* in an epigraph to chapter 64, a deceptively upbeat epigraph when taken out of context. This epigraph in fact comes from early in Dante's journey, from Canto IV of the *Purgatorio*:

> "Questa montagna è tale,
> Che sempre al cominciar di sotto è grave,
> E quant' om più va sù, e men fa male."
> [This mountain is so formed that it is always wearisome when one begins the ascent but becomes easier the higher one climbs.][72]

Specifying where this passage appears in Dante's text is important. Taken out of the context of the *Purgatorio*, Virgil's quoted assurance gestures at an impending end, a time when the course will shortly become easier. In fact, these words come before Dante has begun his ascent up the mountain—before he has even entered the portal to purgatory proper, when he must dwell in ante-purgatory. Ante-purgatory is a place where the preparation for growth is deemed important but is also difficult to recognize. For example, Dante does not recognize Belacqua's state of waiting as one of progress, chiding him for being "as indolent as sloth's sister" until Belacqua explains that he has not yet reached the place of recognizable spiritual growth:

> The angel of God who sits in the gateway
> would not let me pass into the torments.
> I must wait outside as long as in my lifetime
> the heavens wheeled around me
> while I put off my sighs of penance to the end,
> unless I'm helped by prayers that rise
> from a heart that lives in grace.[73]

Eliot calls attention to Gwendolen's similarly stalled pace in finding redemption but with an insistence, as in Dante's text, that the preparation for a time of growth constitutes a form of progress itself, however difficult to observe. Eliot's choice of the epigraph for chapter 64 aligns Gwendolen's "purgatory . . . on the green earth" with the very beginning stages of Dante's journey, a strategy in keeping with Eliot's demonstrated interest in capturing elusive beginnings and her conception of them as a time of "shadow" before "blossom and fruit."[74]

It is not coincidental that all of Eliot's *Purgatorio* citations in *Daniel Deronda* are taken from these first eight cantos of the work, the portion of the text devoted to the poet's time in ante-purgatory. This is the realm in Dante's vision of the afterlife that most resembles nineteenth-century intermediate state models, and the dominance of ante-purgatory references in the novel may speak to the familiarity of this purgatorial mold to Eliot and her readers. After all, it is in ante-purgatory that we find the *Divine Comedy* figure whom Eliot most explicitly compares to Gwendolen: "Madonna Pia." It becomes clear that Madonna Pia represents a model of religious "deliverance" fundamentally unlike Gwendolen's current struggle, while also serving as a figure through whom Dantean models of purgatory can be conceived in uniquely nineteenth-century terms.

Like Gwendolen, La Pia appears in *The Divine Comedy* in an anticipatory state of purgation, a time devoted to the uneventful growth that

Eliot also seeks to capture in showing how a spoiled child can grow into a "crushed penitent," a late-repenter in her own right:

> If the swiftest thinking has about the pace of a greyhound, the slowest must be supposed to move, like the limpet, by an apparent sticking, which after a good while is discerned to be a slight progression. Such differences are manifest in the variable intensity which we call human experience, from the revolutionary rush of change which makes a new inner and outer life, to that quiet recurrence of the familiar, which has not other epochs than those of hunger and the heavens.
>
> Something of this contrast was seen in the year's experience which had turned the brilliant, self-confident Gwendolen Harleth of the Archery Meeting into the crushed penitent impelled to confess her unworthiness where it would have been her happiness to be held worthy. (705)

In Gwendolen's continued remorse as a widow, Eliot shows how individuals change not solely in explosive bursts, or rapidly at "the pace of a greyhound," but how we also move "like the limpet, by an apparent sticking, which after a good while is discerned to be a slight progression." The lesser "intensity" does not necessarily effect a lesser change—on the contrary, it often enacts the most pervasive changes, including the depiction over three volumes of "the year's experience which had turned the brilliant, self-confident Gwendolen Harleth of the Archery Meeting into the crushed penitent impelled to confess her unworthiness." For Gwendolen this is just the beginning of gradual self-improvement. We as readers are left to speculate that patience and acceptance of slow growth are to be Gwendolen's lot after the close of the novel, given her desire, as she writes to Daniel on his wedding day, that she "may live to be one of the best of women, who make others glad that they were born," though she confesses, "I do not yet see how that can be" (810). The inability to "see" how such changes will occur seems to be par for the course, for Gwendolen looks forward to a type of growth that is not readily observable by any quantitative means of making "the implicit explicit." As Eliot implies, Gwendolen is to have the glorious course of the limpet, an adult maturation to be accomplished on the humble level of prosaic continuity. In using fiction to make these implicit changes explicit, Eliot charts a course in which Gwendolen's growth is not driven by vivid narrative turning points, or "revolutionary" personal events. Her growth is instead transmuted through the slower movements of "a history and a metamorphosis," as Eliot first described Silas's sixteen years of miserhood that presented "scarcely any visible change." This gradual, internal movement requires a model of storytelling that not only accommodates a dearth of dramatic events but also seemingly emerges from this very quietude.

Nostos and the Novel: "Humdrum" Endings

By following Gwendolen's story through the end of her marriage and into her widowhood, Eliot pursues an unusual course. Marriage may mark the end of many a bildungsroman, but Eliot pushes past this terminal point to explore what might be termed, in a literal sense, the "afterlife" of the genre itself, or the life that follows after a coming-of-age story: the married state, widowhood, and even those second attachments lamented in *Purgatorio*'s Canto VIII. Capturing this time of adult maturation appears to call for a different storyline and closural method than the marriage plot readily provides. Indeed, the widow's plot in Eliot's novels appears remarkably smoothed out in terms of events, though despite this lulling approach, Gwendolen's course has changed. The transition from wife to widow, from one type of regretful penitence to another just a few shades apart, becomes a major turning point (or turning *stretch*) in Gwendolen's journey, one that Eliot brings inside into the realm of the "inner life."

In the introspective ending, Gwendolen is at last released from the fits of terror that punctuate her story. Her vacillation during Grandcourt's drowning marks a final turn in which her problematic "trembling" (61) between "opposites"—the "iridescence" of being beautiful and not beautiful, the impossibility of killing and not killing—reaches a head. The shocking image of the dead face, at last embodied in Grandcourt's drowning figure, becomes the final catalyst for pushing Gwendolen out of her pattern of horrified, sublime immobility and undirected desire into a new course of action offered by the path of gradual self-improvement, however "humdrum":

> She saw the gray shoulders of the downs ... the neatly-clipped hedges on the road from the parsonage to Offendene, the avenue where she was gradually discerned from the window, the hall-door opening, and her mother or one of the troublesome sisters coming out to meet her. All that brief experience of a quiet home which had once seemed a dulness to be fled from, now came back to her as a restful escape, a station where she found the breath of morning and the unreproaching voice of birds, after following a lure through a long Satanic masquerade. (761–62)

Yet this newfound quest for maturity is not rewarded, as many readers have hoped, with a corresponding reengagement of the heroine's marriage plot and the eventual union of Gwendolen with Daniel. Instead, Eliot divorces the conjoined storylines of female *bildung* and marriage, defying closural conventions and creating a narrative asymmetry in which the heroine and hero go their separate ways, as do, simultaneously, the story of female development and the marriage plot. Although some critics have labeled this conclusion a "tragedy" for Gwendolen, regarding *Daniel Deronda* as one of Eliot's curiously "retrogressive plots" because of its ending,[75] my reading recuperates an understanding of Gwendolen's ending as salutary and, further, of Eliot's open-ended approach to closure as progressive.

The visual arts play a crucial role in allowing Eliot to illustrate the introspective gradualism with which she controversially ends Gwendolen's story. In the conclusion, Eliot recurs to the trope of the living statue one last time to once again achieve a gradualist vision of Gwendolen's growth. After hearing that Daniel will be leaving England to marry and pursue a religious vocation, Gwendolen is once more surprised into statuary stillness, her immobility being mirrored in Daniel's stance: "There had been a long silence. Deronda had stood still, even thankful for an interval before he needed to say more, and Gwendolen had sat like a statue with her wrists lying over each other and her eyes fixed—the intensity of her mental action arresting all other excitation" (804). As Eliot insists, Gwendolen's appearance as a statue is not evidence of inactivity, but quite the opposite; it makes manifest the "intensity of her mental action." Critics, in protesting that Gwendolen is "fixed in a tableau of tragic dread" befitting a "tragic scapegoat,"[76] liken this ending to her appearance in the tableau vivant, but this visual echo does not necessarily hold the tragic implications many attribute to it. Instead, the living statue once again appears as a figure of insight, allowing Eliot to reveal a temporality associated both with contemplation and with the unfolding of character. These changes, which defy visual witness in being fundamentally "disproportionate to outward cause" (668), are often overlooked by critics, who dismiss or pass over the insistent appreciation and gentle humor Eliot conveys in depicting Gwendolen's new mature outlook and limpet's course after returning to Offendene.

Ekphrasis again allows Eliot to achieve a gradualism that partakes metaphorically of the stillness of the tableau, of statuary, and of painting but pushes past stasis and translates immobility into subtle advancement. As Carolyn Williams shows us in addressing the melodramatic tableau in Eliot's fiction, the "very structure of Gwendolen's character . . . posits or institutes the melodramatic oscillation between durational, quotidian reality and graphically foregrounded, static moments of uncertain meaningfulness."[77] As I have shown, this tension between what Williams terms "static moments" and the "durational" span of narrative itself takes center stage alongside Gwendolen in the tableau vivant, resurfacing in other crucial scenes in which the heroine appears as a figure of moving stasis, a gradualist vision expressed through Eliot's critical engagement with Lessing. Gwendolen's final appearance as a living statue thus fulfills a different role than one of simply revealing the heroine's tragic stasis, as many have argued. Instead, it is through this iconic figure of the living statue that Eliot simultaneously stages a response to contemporary artists while also enacting a central temporality in her fiction: the purgatorial pace of progress.

For Gwendolen, this purgatorial entrance into widowhood marks an advent without the fanfare of adventure that Daniel's conclusion receives. Simmel presents this quality of adventure as one restricted to youth and not common to tales of maturity and, in drawing this distinction, he asserts that although a person may feel that he has "ventured into spheres of life from which one returns home as if from a strange world," this feeling does not in itself constitute an adventure. Experiences become adventure "only by virtue of a certain experiential tension whereby their substance is realized."[78] In Offendene, we find a domesticized vision of the "spirit world," a calming purgatory for reflection that provides a new beginning for our heroine: an advent, though one not clearly recognized as an adventure from its outward appearance.

> The plan of removal to Offendene had been carried out; and Gwendolen, in settling there, maintained a calm beyond her mother's hopes. She was experiencing some of that peaceful melancholy which comes from the renunciation of demands for self, and from taking the ordinary good of existence.... There is a way of looking at our life daily as an escape, and taking the quiet return of morn and evening—still more the starlike out-glowing of some pure fellow-feeling, some generous impulse breaking our inward darkness—as a salvation that reconciles us to hardship. (795)

Beer has noted that in a novel with a complex temporal organization, we are given a beginning as an ending, and Eliot prefaces her final chapter of *Daniel Deronda* with an image of the cyclical merging of conclusions and commencements—an image that further recalls intermediate state tropes of seed cycles.[79] "Nay, in each of our lives harvest and spring-time are continually one, until Death himself gathers us and sows us anew in his invisible fields" (808). While this epigraph anticipates Mordecai's death that ends the novel, the purgatorial image of the soul transformed into a seed applies to the living Gwendolen and Daniel as much as to the dying visionary. They too are shown entering a time of renewal in the "invisible field" that lies in the afterlife of the novel itself. Daniel sets off with the promise of an epic voyage, and readers are left to imagine his rise to leadership as an adventure that more closely exemplifies Simmel's definition. On a less global scale, Gwendolen embarks on a course of personal regeneration as well, but without any external signs of it being an adventure. Earlier, Gwendolen complains, "We women can't go in search of adventures—to find out the North-West Passage or the source of the Nile, or to hunt tigers in the East. We must stay where we grow, or where the gardeners like to transplant us. We are brought up like the flowers, to look as pretty as we can, and be dull without complaining. That is my notion about the plants; they are often bored, and that is the reason why some of them have got poisonous. What do you think?" (131). Gwendolen seemingly comes to prove her own offhand truism: "We must stay where we grow." No grand voyage awaits her. She is likewise denied the more feminized return to the conquests of the marriage plot.

Scholars including Beer and Gates have noted the imbalance in Daniel's and Gwendolen's ending positions, claiming, as Gates does, that Daniel coopts both the adventure plot and the marriage plot, leaving Gwendolen bereft of closural events. Nevertheless, the narrator assures us that her ending, however anticlimactic, is salutary: "The plan of removal to Offendene had been carried out; and Gwendolen, in settling there, maintained a calm beyond her mother's hopes" (*DD*, 791). The critical tendency has been to consider Gwendolen's final state one of exile, and not a happy homecoming. Unearthing the source of this frustration, I would suggest that this readerly disappointment stems from unfulfilled expectations about *nostos*, the returning drive of all adventures to the familiar and the domestic. From *The Odyssey* to *David Copperfield*, final homecomings offer a happy coincidence of marriage and domestic stability. This novelistic vision of *nostos* is complicated in a work that presents Scylla and Charybdis in marriage itself and not in an exotic world of adventure. Although Eliot gives us a story of remarriage and a concluding return to the marriage plot in *Middlemarch,* she refuses to align second chances with second marriages in *Romola* and *Daniel Deronda*. In these novels, she chooses to divorce the novel for "grown-up people" from the marriage plot as the dominant storyline for the female bildungsroman. In doing so, she instead charts a new course by concluding with widows as figures of unorthodox homecoming: Romola finds domestic contentment as the surrogate head of Tito's illegitimate family, and Gwendolen finds peace and room for future growth in resuming the role of daughter and sister she had previously spurned.

Thus, rather than label Gwendolen a "scapegoat" and a figure of exile, we could say the reverse: perhaps it is the marriage plot, embodied in Daniel and Mirah as a couple, that gets sent packing. Daniel and Mirah exit the novel, moving into the narrative hinterlands of an eastern homeland. It is Gwendolen who remains staunchly grounded in the familiar, domestic center of the novel. Critics, in protesting the scapegoat's tragedy of Gwendolen's finale, have often overlooked the sincere appreciation Eliot conveys for Gwendolen's new mature outlook as an Offendene transplant; Gwendolen finds "a way of looking at our life daily as an escape," despite the presence of both "calm" and "hardship"—or perhaps, in a familiarly purgatorial model, calm *as* hardship. As with Silas's miserly going to seed, when Gwendolen replants herself at Offendene it marks not so much a traditional story of beginnings, as Daniel's does, but instead the potent make-believe of one. If Eliot leaves her heroine in purgatory, she leaves her with a "generous impulse breaking" through the "inward darkness," or rather, in a gentler "intermediate state" where the preparation for growth can be recognized as an important form of growth itself.

CHAPTER THREE

The Bachelor's Purgatory

Arrested Development and the Progress of Shades

When George Gissing asked in 1898, "Who, in childhood, ever cared much for *Little Dorrit?*" he did so at a time when he might just as easily have wondered who in adulthood cared for the novel either.[1] Dickens's friend and biographer John Forster had already deemed the heroine "tiresome by want of reality," and G. K. Chesterton would soon after pronounce *Little Dorrit* the "fugitive grey cloud" of the Dickens canon, locating this meteorological low front not in the heroine—as Forster first did—but rather in Arthur Clennam's mature model of heroism. "For the first time in a book by Dickens perhaps we really do feel that the hero is forty-five."[2] Despite his active defense of *Little Dorrit*, Gissing similarly attributed the book's reputation for being "tedious" and having a "prevalent air of gloom" to its concern with the trials of middle age, in particular, Dickens's middle age grafted onto the figure of Clennam: "There were reasons why the book should be lacking in the old vivacity—never indeed to be recovered, in so far as it had belonged to the golden years of youth.... Here and there the hand of the master is plainly weary."[3] These early studies of Dickens, founding works in a critical tradition that remains fascinated by *Little Dorrit*'s unwieldiness, came to the shared conclusion that the novel's long, ruminative stretches are symptomatic of its mature content. Far from arguing that nothing happens in a book that allegedly "bores Dickensians,"[4] they established that the development in *Little Dorrit* is at once more "subtle," to use Chesterton's favored adjective, and more protracted than the collapse of a house or the repossession of a fortune. The question they posed serves as a vital source for critical discussion today: what exactly happens in *Little Dorrit* when nothing seems to be happening?

Modern critics have continued to take up this question in addressing Dickens's apparent lack of plot in the novel. In 1953, Lionel Trilling insisted that in *Little Dorrit* "we do not have the amazing thickness of fact and incident that marks, say, *Bleak House* or *Our Mutual Friend*—not that we do not have sufficient thickness, but we do not have what Dickens usually gives us."[5] He expressed the view that Dickens's leaner handling of "incident" in a long form allows the author to reveal, as never before, the inward struggles of the will. Critics following Trilling also have questioned Dickens's move away from "incident" in *Little Dorrit*, the most extreme strain of this scholarship labeling *Little Dorrit* "in essence, a plotless novel," one that possesses a paradoxically "plotless plot."[6] Ruth Bernard Yeazell goes so far as to link Clennam's failure to "do it" with a midlife resignation verging on premature death: "In Arthur Clennam [Dickens] imagines a middle-aged man who nobly resigns himself to the inevitability of death rather than aggressively do it in any way."[7] This critical trajectory reveals that contemporary scholars increasingly found Clennam's "inaction" troublesome in the novel form, linking the novel's mature protagonist with a perceived structural shapelessness, a lack of plot altogether.

Centering on the aging bachelor as one of literature's ultimate late-bloomers, this chapter discusses how the middle-aged single man presents a special challenge as a protagonist, requiring novelists to develop methods for keeping the plot moving, often in the absence of dramatic turning points. Avuncular bachelors abound in Victorian fiction, although they are often minor characters, not protagonists, who fulfill helper roles in facilitating the marriage plots of others—in certain cases, to the detriment of their own.[8] The Reverend Farebrother in *Middlemarch* and John Jarndyce in *Bleak House* fall into this category, being described initially in terms that simultaneously foreground their virility and their precariousness on the outer bounds of the novel's reproductive plotlines. Mr. Farebrother is "a handsome, broad-chested but otherwise small man, about forty" with "brilliancy . . . in his quick gray eyes" (103) who adapts himself to his family's "small needs" (113) rather than the pursuit of his own larger desires, for example, for Mary Garth: "Very few men could have been as filial and chivalrous as he was to the mother, aunt, and sister, whose dependence on him had in many ways shaped his life rather uneasily for himself" (113). John Jarndyce, as observed first by Esther Summerson, is similarly described as having a "handsome, lively, quick face, full of change and motion; and his hair was a silvered iron-grey. I took him to be nearer sixty than fifty, but he was upright, hearty, and robust."[9] That both men are described as being "handsome," followed by the caveat of their being of a certain age, is telling. In the limited roles they play as minor characters rather than protagonists, their peripheral heroism culminates in a single grand gesture—the gesture of giving up a position within the marriageable world of the novel that they never fully occupied. If anything, their final acts do not dispel, but only more fully expose, an underlying source of discomfort: their odd mix of inertia and "robust" longing, gentlemanly altruism and regenerative self-interest.

This combination of inaction and desire proves even more challenging to plot as a central storyline, as opposed to being merely a minor character's subplot. Nevertheless, the self-consciously middle-aged bachelor appears as a hero in many works of the period, including *Silas Marner, Little Dorrit,* and *The Ambassadors.* The "make-believe beginnings" that characterize the widow's renewal in *Daniel Deronda* in these fictions of maturity meet with a related representational conundrum: the aging bachelor's delayed beginnings and arrested development. This sense of arrest most commonly registers as the protagonist's frustrated inability to jumpstart his own life story, let alone a multivolume novel, after it has come to rest in a narrative trough. In gravitating toward these extended troughs, *Little Dorrit*—far from being a plotless novel—is the work in which Dickens introduces some of his most complex and interesting plot techniques for keeping the story moving while, paradoxically, withholding major events. It also represents the culmination of Dickens's interest in a figure James would later call "the poor, sensitive gentleman." Although Dickens is famed for his representations of youthful development, he also reveals himself to be the exemplary Victorian writer of male middle-aged stasis and renewal.

Clennam is not alone in Dickens's canon, as early critics protested, but finds himself in good company. His condition of chronic suspension appears in no less potent form in Pip's waiting for his expectations to materialize, a delayed gratification that leads to his final midlife limbo. As Pip tells Biddy in the novel's conclusion, he is "already quite an old bachelor."[10] *David Copperfield*, another classic Dickensian bildungsroman, descends into midlife midway through the story's arc, the novel's vast middle period corresponding with David's adult travails. Another late novel, *Our Mutual Friend*, is no exception; John Harmon faces long periods of biding, incognito and otherwise. In his self-imposed death and adopted identity, we find a recurrence of Clennam's self-absenting alter ego "Nobody," Harmon's stint among the officially dead being another clear example of the hero's bifurcation into a living and a dead soul, the state of being haunted by his own past self. When these examples are considered, it becomes clear that *Little Dorrit* is far from an anomaly among Dickens's novels. It can more accurately be said to extend and fulfill a pattern of mature plotting that is well established throughout the author's body of work. Where it differs from these other novels is in beginning with a self-consciously middle-aged protagonist, rather than simply ending with a young man who has graduated to this state. In *Little Dorrit*, in particular, Dickens is forced to depart from bildungsroman protocols, illustrating the midlife odyssey at greater length and using new methods for creating a sense of progressive suspension.

One of the main ways in which Dickens achieves his gradualist approach to plotting midlife growth is by reinventing the doppelganger tradition in the realist novel. My reading in this chapter hinges on identifying Amy Dorrit's "Fairy Story," a pivotal tale within a tale that occurs early in the novel, as a rewriting of the folktale of Peter Schlemihl, the man who sold his shadow, and of Hans Christian Andersen's later adaptation of this folktale in "The Shadow." These sources for the novel have not previously been recognized for their pervasive influence on Dickens's approach to plot, and I show how shadow folklore provided Dickens with a model for how a longer form, like the Victorian novel, can absorb a protagonist's lengthy inactivity into a story that demands progress. In shadow folktales, the action is displaced into a counterfactual realm embodied by a shadow or "No-body" figure—in *Little Dorrit*, Clennam's aptly named alter ego "Nobody." Dickens gives Clennam a more exciting double but upends the traditional doppelganger formula in which the story focuses on the badly behaved, and more plot-worthy, half of the pair. In contrast, Dickens maintains the central perspective of the sedentary bachelor, relegating the exciting alter ego to the periphery. Dickens, in this manner, uses Clennam's doppelganger to evacuate action to the narrative's margins, preserving an uneventful central storyline while still giving the novel a fresh infusion of desire—albeit unrealized desire. Alter egos, when handled thus, become a useful plot device for embodying desire and keeping it quarantined away from the central plotline. They therefore do more than simply give shape to fantasized alternative histories, a narrative technique that Andrew Miller insightfully discusses in his work on counterfactuals.[11] Instead, Dickens's unorthodox use of doppelgangers allows him to achieve a new level of extreme gradualism in plotting.

Gerald Prince notes that eruptions of counterfactual thinking can "become a rhythmic instrument by regularly slowing down narrative speed," for as he writes of "disnarrated" elements in fiction, "reference to nonevents or hypothetical events plays a role similar or equivalent to that of descriptive or commentarial information."[12] But these "hypothetical" events—those roads not taken in Victorian fiction, as Andrew Miller describes them—do more than merely mimic the temporality of description. If counterfactual stories like Nobody's in *Little Dorrit* help achieve a gradualist tempo it is in service of another goal: that of representing an understated change in midlife that unfolds at a "descriptive" pacing and yet distinguishes itself as narrative proper—though perhaps not the most exciting *kind* of narrative.

Indeed, to depict midlife is often to choose, with seeming perverseness, a less eventful course, which raises the question, as Moretti does, "Why build a story with materials that are *reluctant* to narration?"[13] Or, as Thomas Hardy says in *Tess of the D'Urbervilles*, "let the elder be passed over here for those under whose bodices the life throbbed quick and warm."[14] The actualized narrative in many midlife tales is posed as the story that should never have been told, the story that should have been "passed over" in favor of the "quick and warm" accounts of youthful firsts. By drawing our attention to more exciting possibilities, counterfactual moments in *Little Dorrit* often foreground the frustrations that attend centering on middle-aged subjectivity. Prince discusses how hypothetical events "show why the narrative is tellable, why the situations, happenings, and actions it recounts are sufficiently poignant, funny, terrifying, uncommon, or problematic to be worthy of recounting" and how "tellability is related to virtual embedded narratives."[15] Yet, curiously, Dickens's invocation and dismissal of Nobody raises the conundrum: What happens when virtual embedded narratives point up the opposite—the untellability, the commonness, the drabness of the road actually taken in a novel? What happens when the more "poignant, funny, terrifying, uncommon" story gets away, or is purposefully ejected? And how might a new understanding of midlife plotting, in all its seeming untellability, open possibilities for perceiving the nineteenth century's fascination with the everyday, its ability to exalt a quality of dailiness as transformative and not merely as descriptive dross?

Nobody's ejection proves to be a pivotal moment for understanding Dickensian midlife plotting and the significance of this subgenre of novel for studies of realism more broadly. Dickens's interest in representing extreme gradualism, or rather, his insistence on creating his own form of purgatorial plot, becomes fully apparent only when Nobody is dismissed from the novel altogether and Dickens turns to another form of shadow story as a dominant metaphor: the story of shades in Judgment, conveyed as Clennam's penitential odyssey through the Marshalsea Prison. Subtle developments such as the ones Clennam undergoes during this period are truly "arrested developments," for they come to fruition when a character and his plotline most seem to stop moving. Dickens thus blends two shadowy sources, Peter Schlemihl folklore and Victorian conceptions of purgatory, to envision a redemption born not of trial by fire but of a much less pronounced trial by monotony. As I argue, the transition between these two modes of storytelling—the hellish stasis of the folkloric model and the productive purgatorial model offered by theology—illustrates a variance in the two kinds of arrested development that I explore. The term *arrested development* holds dual possibilities in my argument in connoting both stalled development and a more promising kind of development that occurs in a seemingly arrested state but proves progressive nonetheless.

In exploring the aging bachelor's arrested development, I conclude with a discussion of Dickens's afterlife in the works of Henry James. James employs doppelganger stories and counterfactual narratives in a way very similar to that of Dickens in his fictions starring his favorite protagonist, the "poor, sensitive gentleman." In his supernatural stories and in *The Ambassadors*, James, like Dickens before him, uses counterfactual narratives and references to purgatory to drive the story further inward, making highly internalized action the only action fueling the central plotline for long stretches at a time. The purgatorial model of plotting he evolves is, much like Dickens's and Eliot's, one that borrows from contemporary theology to serve uniquely secular and narrative ends, providing a bridge, as we will see, to later modernist works and writers across the chasm of the First World War.

I. *Little Dorrit:* Arthur Clennam's Shadow Story

At the heart of *Little Dorrit* lies a curious story within a story. When Maggy asks for a bedtime tale, Amy Dorrit embarks on story about a tiny seamstress who lives by herself, spinning all day with only one source of consolation: a shadow that she keeps locked away, left behind by a man who will never return. Much like *Silas Marner*, this tale revolves around the dual activities of spinning and hoarding, yet where Eliot's novel offers redemption, Amy's story does not. In the conclusion, the tiny woman dies alone and the shadow sinks into the ground with her. Although Maggy does not seem to mind this offering, it breaks with the form of the bedtime tale in being, simply put, dismal.

If Little Dorrit's effort at storytelling aggressively fails to please, being a "Fairy Story" that does not have much in the way of "faerie" whimsy or "story," it succeeds at accomplishing more insidious narrative goals. Whereas the inset tale reveals what Elaine Ostry describes as Little Dorrit's "belief that not much will change,"[16] it does more than merely allegorize Amy's unhappiness. In its insistent portrayal of confinement and repetition without release, the story succinctly describes and enacts a quality of stasis that pervades the much larger space of the novel. In this sense, Little Dorrit's tale functions as a microcosm for the larger narrative in its portrayal of imprisonment and dispossession, its doppelgangers, and its curiously static form. But the tale also presents a more interesting possibility in its adaptation of an earlier, overlooked folkloric source.[17] In recasting the folktale about Peter "Fool" (that is, "Schlemihl"), the man who exchanges his shadow for a limitless sack of gold,[18] Dickens uses Amy's tale to present a new model of counterfactual narration that he adopts in the rest of the novel to achieve his own brand of gradualism.

Peter Schlemihl and the Uses of Disenchantment

We begin with the long shadow cast by Peter Schlemihl. In choosing a folktale to serve as a touchstone in the novel, Dickens could not have picked a more saturnine one. Dickens's retelling of this tale, also found in his stories "The Haunted Man" and "A Christmas Carol," partakes of eighteenth- and early nineteenth-century versions of the myth of Peter Schlemihl, including Adelbert von Chamisso's *Peter Schlemiel* (1814) and Ludwig Tieck's tales, but it most markedly evokes Hans Christian Andersen's "The Shadow," a story that Andersen presented in a volume dedicated to Dickens a decade before *Little Dorrit*'s publication.[19] To enable us to better understand the analogous features shared between Little Dorrit's Fairy Story and the novel as a whole, those aspects of her story that derive from original folkloric versions must be distinguished from embellishments that reveal a distinctly Dickensian agenda. In terms of similarities, first, the melancholic fixity that predominates in Little Dorrit's tale also prevails in *Peter Schlemiel* and Andersen's "The Shadow." Second, like Amy's story, both of these earlier folktales showcase troublingly irresolute endings in refusing to conclude by reunifying the man and his shadow, seeking alternative forms of narrative closure instead.

In the original published source by Chamisso, the short novel *Peter Schlemiel*, we encounter a character who, much like Arthur Clennam, is returning from a "less than pleasant voyage" with "modest plans at self-improvement."[20] Recently returned home and at a loss for direction, Peter soon encounters a strange gray man at a party who offers to buy his shadow in exchange for a magic purse that infinitely refills with gold coins. Just as Clennam's modest plans for self-improvement crumble after investing with Mr. Merdle, another "strange" party-goer with a mysterious cash source, so do Peter's business transactions result in misery and isolation. The deal done, Peter finds himself shunned everywhere because of his disquieting lack of a shadow, a stigma that makes wooing the woman of his choice very difficult, not to mention displeasing to her parents. He begins a period of depressed inertia, analogous to Clennam's mood at various points of the novel, and relates, "I lay like Faffner beside his hoard, far removed from the balm of any human consolation, fondling my gold, not lovingly but cursing it all the while.... Day and night I pined away alone in my rooms, and grief gnawed at my heart" (19).

This melancholy pining also appears for large stretches in *Little Dorrit*; because Dickens focalizes the novel mostly through Clennam's perspective, his pining and heart-gnawing grief dominate the surface level of the text. But if, as the narrator professes, the novel "must sometimes see with Little Dorrit's eyes,"[21] within the small world of her tale, the tiny woman and not the male "Someone" appears as the quietly and exclusively suffering star. When Maggy asks for a story about "a Princess . . . and let her be a reg'lar one. Beyond all belief you know!" (286), the story that emerges features a wealthy and ambiguously psychic princess but concerns itself increasingly with the fate of a less exciting character, the unhappy little cottager:

> The Princess passed the cottage nearly every day, and whenever she went by in her beautiful carriage, she saw the poor tiny woman spinning at her wheel, and she looked at the tiny woman and the tiny woman looked at her. . . . [The Princess] had the power of knowing secrets, and she said to the tiny woman, Why do you keep it there? This showed her directly that the Princess knew why she lived all alone by herself, spinning at her wheel, and she kneeled down at the Princess's feet, and asked her never to betray her. So, the Princess said, I never will betray you. Let me see it. So, the tiny woman closed the shutter of the cottage window and fastened the door, and, trembling from head to foot for fear that any one should suspect her, opened a very secret place, and showed the Princess a shadow. . . .
>
> It was the shadow of Some one who had gone by long before: of Some one who had gone on far away quite out of reach, never, never to come back. . . . [N]o one so good and kind had ever passed that way, and that was why [she kept it] in the beginning. She said, too, that nobody missed it, that nobody was the worse for it, that Some one had gone on to those who were expecting him . . . and that this remembrance was stolen or kept back from nobody. The

Princess made answer, Ah! But when the cottager died it would be discovered there. The tiny woman told her No; when that time came, it would sink quietly into her own grave, and would never be found. (287–88)

In Chamisso's *Peter Schlemiel*, the plot revolves almost entirely around the fate suffered by a man who unwisely sells his shadow, but in Little Dorrit's Fairy Story, the misadventures of a shadowless male could not prove less consequential. "Some one" has proceeded without much ado "far away quite out of reach, never, never to come back." The usual consequences of shadow severance, shame, and self-imposed solitary confinement—key constants in many versions of the folktale—do not attend this absent male "Some one," or the Clennam figure in Little Dorrit's telling. They fall instead rather uncharacteristically upon the shadow's female keeper. In this uniquely female-centered version, the tiny woman adopts both the antagonist roles presented in *Peter Schlemiel* (that of Peter, the tormented hermit with a dread secret, and that of the strange grey man, the shadow's sinister possessor), thereby casting the abstemious tiny woman as both a glutton for punishment and a glutton for all the major roles in the original folktale.

Although Little Dorrit dramatically changes the folktale to usurp both the main parts for a single female lead—played by none other than a veiled version of herself—she makes a point of preserving the story's Faustian strain in an understated form, signaling to readers her tale's affinity with the earlier *Peter Schlemiel*. In *Peter Schlemiel*, a man's shadow may be exchanged for money. In Little Dorrit's tale, she likewise connects the shadow with "treasure" but removes any direct reference to the commodified relationship between shadow and gold, displacing this relationship from the explicitly economic realm to the metaphorical realm of the linguistic exchange of signifiers. As the tiny woman makes no reference to buying the shadow, the shadow and golden coins are interchangeable only on the metaphorical level, where the shadow is the treasure: "It was bright to look at" and "she was proud of it with all her heart, as a great, great, treasure" (288).

This presentation of the shadow as "bright" contradicts the common conception of shadows as the absence of light, until the adjective adheres to "treasure." Just as Peter in *Peter Schlemiel* sits caressing "his hoard, far removed from the balm of any human consolation, fondling [his] gold" so too does the little woman bestow similarly unreturned touches upon her hoarded treasure.

The shadow, though ostensibly pleasing as something "bright" to have around the cottage, never transcends its status as an object by converting from being an "it" into the more satisfying company that would be provided by a "him," a grammatical transition from "it" to "him" that Andersen's Shadow makes with ease, eventually rising from "it" to "him" to "master." The shadow in Little Dorrit's tale instead remains cupboarded in a state of objectified alienation from its original body, existing in a secondary state as a representation of a body long gone, rather than any sentient representative of the body itself. As Victor Stoichita relates in *A Short History of the Shadow* when speaking of "Man and his Doubles," according to the Plinian fable, art was born of an act of love when a shepherdess traced the shadow of her beloved as a keepsake.[22] As in Stoichita's description of the lovers, the shadow in *Little Dorrit* cannot be mistaken for a representation of the "kind" man who "passed that way" but is instead a representation of this kind man's very absence. The use of the word *remembrance* also figures the shadow as a form of memorial, or a representation of a person's absence. The tiny woman explains that she keeps the shadow because the man had "gone on to those who were expecting him, and . . . this remembrance was stolen or kept back from nobody"—"remembrance" strangely replacing the expected word "shadow" to give the line the slippery feel of a legal disclaimer exculpating the tiny woman of having stolen or unlawfully detained another's property. In this passage, the word *remembrance* may be read not only as suspiciously vague but also as the verbal equivalent of *shadow*, binding remembrance and shadows together in their shared definition of being "representations of absence." In this reading, the "shadow" *is* the "remembrance," a memorial of a person gone out of reach.

If a shadow can be seen as a memorial for a person, or as a representation of an absence, then Little Dorrit's tale is in itself a "representation of absence" on many levels, at once describing qualities absent in the tiny woman's ascetic life—a special "Some one," daily variety, basic human contact—and simultaneously performing absence on the level of the story's form: the story evacuates itself of features that normally constitute a tale, such as plot, emerging as a story without "story," in the Shklovskian sense.[23] Amy Dorrit's tale achieves an uncanny quality of being haunted by the unverifiable possibilities of its own plot, reading not only as the story of a shadow but also as the elusive *shadow of a story*. In contrast, *Peter Schlemiel* and Andersen's later work "The Shadow" abound in recognizable plot events despite their similar tendency toward melancholic fixity. At the end of *Peter Schlemiel*, Peter goes through a rapid series of actions: he confronts the strange gray man, casts the bottomless purse into a bottomless abyss, and refuses to sell his soul for the return of his shadow. His actions have clear consequences. He never regains either his shadow or his lost love, who as a widow devotes herself to working in a hospital dedicated to Peter, complete with a "Schlemilium" (84) for tending the sick—a detail that Maggy would perhaps have appreciated in Little Dorrit's version, given her predilection for hospitals. Peter ends the story having reconciled himself to his life as an outcast, and like many retired persons, he decides to travel the world, this time in seven-league boots and comfortable with the knowledge that he can "console [him]self with the fact" that he has "not used them idly but [has] employed them consistently for the pursuit of knowledge and progress" (87). As in Little Dorrit's Fairy Story, the main male figure is never reunited with his shadow, but if Chamisso's earlier version also features unchanging isolation for its main character, it includes a greater sense of resolution, of initial transgression, and of positive development at the end of the tale. In Little Dorrit's tale, readers are left with a story that spins itself out, like the little woman perpetually spinning at her wheel, with no tangible skein of storyline to grasp as a final result.

Dickens accomplishes this shadowy approach to storytelling by clouding the tale with linguistic indeterminacy, using passive constructions and employing "nobody" as the subject in many sentences, a strategy that reappears in altered form in Henry James's later shadow stories, such as "The Beast in the Jungle." Little Dorrit's story serves the larger formal function of telling a cautionary tale about arrested development and does so by enacting an absence of development on the level of both form and content. Accordingly, in the end readers are left with only traces of what may have happened:

> At last one day the wheel was still, and the tiny woman was not to be seen. [The Princess] was informed that the wheel had stopped because there was nobody to turn it, the tiny woman being dead. . . . [The Princess] went in at once to search for the treasured shadow. But there was no sign of it to be found anywhere; and then she knew that the tiny woman had told her the truth, and that it would never give any body any trouble, and that it had sunk quietly into her own grave, and that she and it were at rest together. (289)

This conclusion, if it can be called such, is conveyed through the absence of events: "the wheel had stopped because there was nobody to turn it," and as for the shadow, "there was no sign of it to be found anywhere." All of the major occurrences are further cloaked in passive grammatical constructions; instead of saying that the Princess finds the little woman dead, for example, the story reads "the tiny woman was not to be seen."

Like a miser on holiday, Dickens uses the active voice sparingly, reserving it for habitual activities or actions performed by "nobody," and therefore potentially not performed at all. Looking, spinning, driving—these activities garner Dickens's use of the active voice but do not register as "eventful." They are the habitual activities that occur when nothing else is happening, and by sheer force of their repetition, they become activities emblematic of the lack of activity.

Taking, stealing, dying—these are the more exciting acts that never occur outright but which Dickens hints at as possibilities, obscuring their potential force by using the passive voice, by attributing anything resembling action to "nobody," and by placing them outside of the frame of the story in an inaccessible past. A first act of acquisition provides the usual starting point for most versions of the folktale, but the tiny woman's acquisition of the shadow has been curiously elided, relegated to a space outside of the tale, a space where "Some one" has also disappeared, taking much of the original folktale plot with him.

"Nobody's Rival": Andersen and the Counterfactual

Thus, we come to another critical exchange: in a tale about disappointing transactions, the little woman gets the shadow but the plot adheres to the absent man. The arrangement seems fitting, for if the tiny woman has taken a shadow from "nobody," then perhaps nobody has reciprocated by stealing the action from her story. This reading restores some of the "story" to Little Dorrit's tale, or at least to its margins, for if one reads "nobody" as a proper name, the name of the lost action figure in Little Dorrit's fantasy, we find active verbs reinfused back into the tale. After the shadow was "stolen" and "kept back from nobody," in turn "nobody missed it" and "nobody was the worse for it." As Janice Carlisle observes in *The Sense of an Audience: Dickens, Thackeray, and George Eliot at Mid-Century*, "This interpolated narrative is the counterpart of Clennam's conception of himself as Nobody. . . . Clennam is 'Some one.' In a curious way, both their tales reduce him to an indefinite pronoun."[24] If by linguistic trickery Odysseus escapes from Polyphemus by telling him that "No Man" has blinded him, so does "Nobody" escape from the confines of Little Dorrit's tale, disappearing with the bounty of the traditional storyline. He would then seem to reappear in the outer sphere of the novel in Clennam's self-fashioned yarn starring a livelier alter ego, also known as Nobody.

It is well known that Dickens originally intended to name the novel *Nobody's Fault* in his early plans for a social commentary about a man who shrugs off responsibility, to calamitous result. The novel named for "Nobody" soon dissolved into the novel named for somebody, a young prison-born heroine, yet the kernel of this original title remains in the chapters where Clennam imagines pursuing a romantic course with Pet Meagles. "'Suppose that a man,' so his thoughts ran, 'who had been of age some twenty years or so . . . were to persuade himself that he could hope to win her; what a weakness it would be! . . . Why should he be vexed or sore at heart? It was not his weakness that he had imagined. It was nobody's, nobody's within his knowledge" (200). Although this interpretation has not been considered in the critical literature, the four chapters starring Clennam's more exciting alter ego—titled "Nobody's Weakness," "Nobody's Rival," "Nobody's State of Mind," and "Nobody's Disappearance"—may spring from a source other than the dismissed novel *Nobody's Fault*. Indeed, at the nexus between Clennam's story of "Nobody" and Little Dorrit's Fairy Story about "Some one," we find a similar rupture between active desires and passive resignation, an important division in most doppelganger folktales and one that testifies to the influence of Andersen's "The Shadow" in *Little Dorrit*.

Andersen's "The Shadow" presents an interesting possibility that Dickens adopts, for this short story features a version of Nobody that we find in Clennam's alter ego: the figure of "the Shadow," or as one might term him, "No Body." Demonstrating more independence than the shadow in Amy's story, the shadow in Andersen's tale secedes from his kindly but sedentary master, disappearing to the margins of the tale to live a life of action and romance. The story begins by introducing readers to this master, a "learned man" (Andersen 264) from the "cold countries" (264) who has traveled to a place that could be a prototype for the opening scene in *Little Dorrit*'s first chapter, "Sun and Shadow." Dickens writes that "[t]hirty years ago, Marseilles lay burning in the sun, one day" and goes on to observe that "[a] blazing sun upon a fierce August day was no greater rarity in southern France then, than at any other time, before or since. . . . Blinds, shutter, curtains, awnings were all closed to keep out the stare" (15–16). Similarly, Andersen's tale opens in a place where "the sun can really scorch you!"

The learned man finds that "[a]long with all other sensible souls, he had to stay indoors. All day long, the shutters were drawn and the doors were kept closed. It looked just as if everyone was still sleeping or not at home. The narrow street on which the man lived was lined with tall buildings and was laid out so that it was flooded with sunshine from morning until evening. It was really unbearable!" (264). In yearning for change, the sequestered scholar entertains a voyeuristic impulse to see inside his neighbor's house, but unfortunately, only his projected shadow can extend unnoticed across the balconies and into the abode. He jokingly asks his shadow, "Kindly step inside" (267), upon which request his shadow enters the other house and leaves him. In a pointed reference to Chamisso's *Peter Schlemiel* that highlights the self-conscious genealogy of folkloric influence (a genealogy that Dickens in turn extends), Andersen slyly tells how "[w]hat annoyed him most was not so much the loss of his shadow as the fact that there was already a story about a man without a shadow. Everyone back home in the cold countries knew that story. If he returned home and told them his own story, they would just say that he was copying the other one and shouldn't bother going on" (267).

In recognizing past influences, Andersen distinguishes his tale from Chamisso's *Peter Schlemiel* by giving his shadow agency and a body. In Andersen's story, the man and the shadow seem to change places, with the protagonist growing more shadowy in his isolation and the shadow becoming more corporeal with the passing of time. After many years, the runaway shadow returns to his master transformed into a "distinguished fellow" (268), complete with flesh and finery, "a wealthy man in every way," (268) who has made his fortune as a blackmailer. The scholar relates how he has, in contrast, been living alone writing about "the good, the true, and the beautiful" (273). The two subsequently travel together and the shadow finds a princess to marry him, though as with the bride in *Peter Schlemiel*, his lack of a shadow at first impedes their union. With the return of the shadow, the learned man—already more suited to the passive role—finds himself coerced into addressing the shadow as "Sir" and attending the shadow wherever he goes, Finally, the shadow insists that they change places once and for all. When the learned man protests, he is imprisoned until the fateful day of the shadow's wedding to the princess, upon which occasion the crowds cheered and the "learned man didn't hear any of that, for by then they had taken his life" (279).

In his version of the folktale, Andersen presents an interesting possibility that Dickens adopts in imagining Clennam's alter ego, Nobody. Andersen uses this shadow figure to funnel the action out of the main storyline and into a shadow narrative that lies just beyond the immediate arena of attention, a space that serves to absorb the action from the main tale. His folktale envisions a realm of counterfactual possibilities where the scholar's double performs illicit actions while he stays at home working, a strategy common in doppelganger stories and one found in Robert Louis Stevenson's *The Strange Case of Dr. Jekyll and Mr. Hyde* and Oscar Wilde's *The Picture of Dorian Gray*. This method of rendering the counterfactual provides a narrative model for how a longer work such as *Little Dorrit* can encompass large amounts of stasis while moving forward as a story.

As a novelist, Dickens extends this technique of displacing action into a counterfactual storyline by playfully manipulating the boundaries between Nobody's world and Clennam's own. Charitable work properly accomplished by Clennam—as opposed to romantic feats only wishfully accomplished—also gets attributed to "Nobody." In one illustration of this phenomenon, Little Dorrit tries to thank Clennam for funding Tip's release from prison, but he refuses to accept her gratitude directly, deflecting her thanks to a third-person version of himself: "[H]e would probably need no thanks, Clennam said" (169). Insisting on tactfully recognizing his good deed, she follows his lead and turns her intended "thank you" into a "thank him": "And what I was going to say sir, is, that if I knew him, and I might—but I don't know him and must not . . . I would go down on my knees to him, and take his hand and kiss it, and ask him not to draw it away, but to leave it—O to leave it for a moment—and let my thankful tears fall on it, for I have no other thanks to give him!" (170). Although both Little Dorrit and Clennam perform this small fiction with a firm understanding of who has performed the charitable act and who should be thanked for it, Amy's wording corroborates Clennam's own private fiction that "Nobody" accomplishes all the action while he, himself, sits contemplatively by the riverside. The sensual thanking she imagines, kneeling and kissing his hand and asking "him not to draw it away," accordingly occurs in the same displaced, conditional state. If kisses have been bestowed, they have been bestowed, as usual, upon Nobody.

Affery calls further attention to Dickens's trick of presenting the actual as the counterfactual, for she comes to believe that events in her life can be transposed into a fictional dream realm. When she observes Jeremiah Flintwinch and Mrs. Clennam plotting by noticing "the shadows of the two clever ones in conversation" (181), her husband sets about convincing her that the scheming she overheard did not occur, claiming it to be merely her sleepwalking reverie. The force of Flintwinch's suggestion—that actions performed by shadowy "nobodies" were not performed at all—leaves Affery to wonder whether, in all her dreaming, "life was not for some people a rather dull invention" (181). This statement can be read as Dickens's self-referential observation that the realist plot of his novel may seem "a dull invention" when opposed to the more exciting shadow stories he offers his readers.

Indeed, it makes sense that many doppelganger stories, such as *The Picture of Dorian Gray*, make the shadow plot dominant. These doppelganger narratives also tend to differentiate the doubles not solely by a naughtiness quotient but by an age division too. Dorian Gray's active but dissipated self remains preternaturally youthful, whereas his secluded self, the Dorian immured in the painting, rapidly and ungracefully ages. Dickens preserves this same traditional age division between Clennam and Nobody, as is apparent in the contradictory beliefs that "[a] man was certainly not old at forty" versus Clennam's later insistence to Amy, "[always think of me as quite an old man" (371).[25] In contrast to these other doppelganger models, both Andersen's tale and

Little Dorrit take an interesting detour: they choose not to follow the shadow's more plot-conducive path of misadventure, instead prioritizing the middle-aged protagonist's perspective and his less stimulating course of events. Dickens's decision to present a doppelganger story in a full-length novel, and then to follow a protagonist evacuated of his desires, can be seen as a boldly understated approach. If he already gives center stage to the sedentary half of a doppelganger duo, dismissing the more exciting double from the novel altogether only increases the risk of narrative languor. The difficulty of this approach has been made clear by a host of narratologists who posit desire as the basic fuel for narrative. Under such models, *Little Dorrit*'s readers may wonder what exactly happens when desire is embodied in a figure that subsequently leaves the storyline. How does one "read for the plot" after "Nobody's Disappearance"?

This last chapter in the installments featuring "Nobody" marks the beginning of an increased lassitude in Clennam's story that persists almost until the end of the novel. After Pet Meagles accepts Gowan's proposal, our hero's narrative immediately sags into a slough of middle-aged despond. "At that time . . . he first finally resigned the dying hope that had flickered in nobody's heart . . . [and] he became in his own eyes, as to any similar hope or prospect, a very much older man who had done with that part of life" (326). As in Andersen's story, Nobody "disappears," running away from an overly sedentary master. Clennam, now abandoned by his desiring self, loses his sense of purpose and direction. During the novel's extended middle period, his low points begin to merge into a lengthy lull. Mourning the loss of his fantasy about Pet, he "softly opened his window, and looked out upon the serene river," contemplating that "it might be better to flow away monotonously, like the river, and to compound for its insensibility to happiness with its insensibility to pain" (200). The narrative, achieving sympathy between form and content, also seems to "flow away monotonously." Nevertheless, flowing away "monotonously" must be differentiated from completely standing still. Clarifying the difference between these two states proves to be of utmost importance in distinguishing between the stasis of Little Dorrit's inset story and the subtle progress of the novel.

Perhaps, then, we have an explanation for why Dickens finally abandoned Nobody, despite the usefulness of his counterfactual storyline. After all, Nobody effectively absorbed the displaced action from Clennam's story, Nobody made the protagonist's unrealized yearnings manifest, and Nobody kept the narrative fueled with desire—the quality, as previously stated, that many narratologists stipulate as being necessary for forward movement. By all these accounts, Nobody did his job well, which makes his dismissal particularly perplexing. From the hundreds of pages that follow Nobody's disappearance, one can only conclude that Dickens deliberately departed from using this counterfactual folkloric model to immerse his readers more fully in Clennam's lugubrious midlife woes. If Nobody is ousted, his exile corresponds with Dickens's investment in another kind of shadow story that unfolds alongside this first one, ultimately redeeming it in the novel's conclusion. This second shadow story is the narrative of a protagonist's journey to purgatory, a familiar trope in nineteenth-century fictions of maturity, and one that Dickens reinvents to offer a vision of progressive maturation that contrasts with the stasis found in shadow folklore. This purgatorial vision of progress provides Amy's bleak tale with its own meaningful afterlife in the novel as a whole.

The Two Scrooges: Dickens and Purgatory on Earth

Clennam's story begins, accordingly, in what might be considered the opening to the realm of Judgment, or purgatory. Immediately before presenting his protagonist for the first time, Dickens closes the preceding chapter, "Sun and Shadow," with an image of Judgment Day, figured as the long stare of Marseille and the sea: "The wide stare stared itself out for one while; the sun went down in a red, green, golden glory; the stars came out in the heavens, and the fire-flies mimicked them in the lower air, as men may feebly imitate the goodness of a better order of beings; the long dusty roads and the interminable plains were in repose—and so deep a hush was on the sea, that it scarcely whispered of the time when it shall give up its dead" (28). From this opening onward, Clennam is akin to a shade, or a shadow cast under the glaring stare of purgatorial Judgment, but existing in a hopeful state nonetheless also characteristic of purgatory. Not coincidentally, this purgatorial image corresponds with Clennam's introduction as a tourist detained in quarantine, a state of incubatory existence that doubles the metaphor of uneventful but crucial inward development. Clennam may physically leave this quarantine, moving on to vast bacterium-laden London, but he is not released from his holding pattern until the novel's ending; only with Amy's final Beatrice-like intervention is he lifted out of the long, purgatorial existence that Dickens presents as the novel's own middle life.

Lionel Trilling's well-known remark that "we understand Little Dorrit to be the Beatrice of the Comedy" speaks to this purgatorial motif running throughout the novel, a motif that, in turn, dually reflects a larger Victorian preoccupation with Dante and with reading narratives of the afterlife.[26] The years of Dickens's ascent to unprecedented heights of popularity were characterized by fascination with eschatology and with redefining Judgment, the debate over purgatory being a part of larger cultural trends in how Victorians thought about change and redemption as explored in chapter 1. The extent to which Dickens engaged in theological debates of his time has been much discussed in critical literature and remains an elusive topic, given his well-known resistance to making overt religious statements. Yet despite his reticence on the subject of faith, Dickens was well aware of contemporary religious movements and controversies, as well as of the bourgeoning religious life surrounding him, including the Oxford Movement.[27] Although he once questioned, in a dream, "[P]erhaps the Roman Catholic [religion] is the best? Perhaps it makes one think of God oftener, and believe in him more steadily?" and was, in turn, advised by a dream "spirit" to convert, as John Forster relates in his biography, Dickens opposed Catholic religious practices.[28] It is generally agreed that Dickens identified himself as a form of liberal Christian, expressing open approval of many Unitarian practices and open disapproval of Catholic and Evangelical proselytizing. Scholars intent on discerning Dickens's religious views have turned to two of the only explicitly religious texts penned by the author: *The Life of Our Lord*, a religious educational text intended for the private use of his children, and his writing on the Sabbatarian controversy.

If Dickens eschewed overt religious discourse, many of his era's religious preoccupations appear at their most interesting and explorative in his fiction, and not necessarily in disguised form. It is in "A Christmas Carol," written in 1842 during the height of the Oxford Movement, that we first see a Dickensian model of the journey of a purgatorial shade. Freed from the bonds of earthly chronological time, Scrooge's disembodied spirit undergoes what Newman described as a "school-time of contemplation" in his sermon on the intermediate state.[29] Later, in *Little Dorrit*, Amy's whole life appears to arise as a purgatorial afterlife from the grave of the Marshalsea Prison. Upon regarding the vista of incarceration before her, "she looked down into the living grave on which the sun had risen, with her father in it, three and twenty years" (229), figuring herself as a baby born into limbo, never having been baptized into the world. More humorously, John Chivery imagines his entire life as a form of purgatorial "fore-death," picturing his autobiography as a sequence of imagined tombstones, the markers of his "plot."[30] Purgatorial images including these and the opening vision of Judgment in Marseille appear throughout Dickens's writing and are evidence of how theological metaphors common to the period found their way into his work. These metaphors reveal Dickens's place in the larger cultural pattern of Victorian interest in purgatory I identify in this book, for his writing provides a mirror of many of the popular social, religious, and cultural preoccupations of his time.

Yet while Dickens's invocation of eschatology has been approached in studies of his religious frame of reference, critics display a predilection for discussing his work only in relation to hell, leaving out other realms of the afterlife altogether.[31] To be sure, Dickens invokes both hell and purgatory as common metaphors, but he does not invoke these two realms of the afterlife indiscriminately. The difference between them speaks to a larger conceptual distinction in his work, a difference between two models of "arrested development" that he represents: a folkloric model that is terminally end-stopped and a theological model that presents a productive, if understated, kind of growth. The studies that connect Dickens with Victorian notions of hell would seem to seize upon the more negative and static of these two models of arrested development, refraining from considering redemptive eschatology in his texts. Although it may appear static or suspended, the work performed in purgatory is not to be mistaken for an absence or termination of development. Understanding the difference between these forms of arrested development, one in which a character develops during an incubatory period in adult life, and another in which a character has ceased to mature and merely molders, proves important in attempting to understand the purgatorial development of the novel as distinguished from Amy Dorrit's hellish folktale.

Of all Dickens's works, *Little Dorrit* perhaps most extensively showcases the phenomenon of adult-onset arrested development in both its purgatorial and its hellish forms, although the condition is by no means rare in the Dickens corpus as a whole. Mature characters such as Scrooge, Miss Havisham in *Great Expectations*, and Richard Carstone in *Bleak House* all display the severe effects of stagnation in adult life. To this panoply of arrested characters, *Little Dorrit* adds both its protagonist, Clennam, and its heroine, prison attendant *cum laude* Amy, as well as Clennam's variously paralyzed mother. Although the novel houses an unusual plenitude of stalled characters, not all of these personages suffer from the same predicament. For example, Scrooge, Miss Havisham, and Richard Carstone each represent different types of arrested development found in *Little Dorrit*. Only Scrooge experiences positive change while he resides in a seemingly arrested state. Conversely, Miss Havisham and Richard Carstone exhibit fixity without change. They suffer from the condition that Frederick Dorrit's coworkers in *Little Dorrit* jestingly identify as being "dead without being aware of it" (234), also providing a cautionary example of Mr. Rugg's warning, "[M]ay you never outlive your feelings!" (292). Judged from the outside, a slumbering Scrooge and Dickens's two "Sleeping Uglies,"[32] as Stone labels Miss Havisham and Mrs. Clennam, appear similarly inert and indistinguishable. Likewise, the Circumlocution Office and the Marshalsea Prison might easily be confused for the more positive, if similarly uneventful, space of quarantine in which the novel opens. The former two places do not present the redemptive potential of incubation, instead appearing as hellish examples of circular repetition and terminal blockage. They are the places where one goes to discover "HOW NOT TO DO IT" (110), a dispiriting mantra that Dickens hangs over the Circumlocution Office like a signpost when he first introduces this "most important Department under government," an inscription that might as well mark the gateway to the Inferno.

Rather than abandoning all hope as one about to enter the netherworld, Clennam becomes a figure of persistent hope in the face of both depressing midlife prospects and equally depressing retrospections. As readers early learn of his character, "[I]t had been the uniform tendency of this man's life—so much was wanting in it to think about, so much that might have been better directed and happier to speculate upon—to make him a dreamer, after all" (52). As with Dantean shades in purgatory as well as Scrooge's earlier purgatorial example, Clennam's "school-time of contemplation" cannot be measured in chronological time or by clear linear events, just as in Victorian models of purgatory, duration cannot be used to precisely map and track the soul's development. Any attempts at "counting," as Mr. Meagles erroneously and irritatingly suggests as a method to quantify the amount of time it takes to feel better, fail to help Clennam propel himself through his long, dark, and uneventful journey. When Pet tells Clennam of her engagement, Clennam seems to embark upon Mr. Meagles's futile prescription to count to twenty-five to regain his composure, advice previously directed at Tattycoram to little effect:

"Five-and-twenty, Tattycoram, five-and-twenty!" (313). Clennam accordingly "counted the trees between them, and the fading light as they slowly diminished in number" (327). Later he explains to Little Dorrit what happened with Pet and why Amy should subsequently regard him as being "very old": "Being wiser, I counted up my years, and considered what I am, and looked back, and looked forward, and found that I should soon be grey" (371–72). This method of counting, whether it involves counting the shadows of trees or years gone by, does not help Clennam move forward or measure his progress. In the opening of the novel, Clennam similarly recounts and details his series of disappointments in life to Mr. Meagles: "Trained by main force; broken, not bent . . . shipped away to the other end of the world before I was of age, and exiled there until my father's death there, a year ago; always grinding in a mill I always hated; what is to be expected from *me* in middle-life? Will, purpose, hope?" (33). The proleptic quality of hope, a quality that is difficult to *account* for given Clennam's history, is what provides the positive force that guides purgatory as a concept and redeems Clennam as a middle-aged protagonist. This same quality of hope is notably absent in Little Dorrit's fairy tale, making for a sad little round of circumlocution, an unproductive "spinning" and stasis that the larger novel seems to partake of, but which it eventually moves beyond.

In thus using eschatological metaphors to illustrate "arrested development" in its varied forms, Dickens extends the possibility for a new consideration of narrative continuation that breaks with our accepted studies of closure. The trend has been to assume that "the narratable inherently lacks finality" and that the "tendency of a narrative would therefore be *to keep going*."[33] Desire-driven theories of narrative postulate either that endings must be forced upon stories that continue ad infinitum or, alternatively, that narratives drive themselves toward predetermined ends. These dominant ways of framing closure both take something important for granted: narrative development. What if, far from overflowing the constraints of closure or rushing toward finality, stories are in constant danger of arrest? This arrest can manifest itself as the sudden death of narrative, as the conclusion of Amy's tale evidences, or as a condition wherein stories return upon themselves in an infinite, unprogressive circumlocution. Both negative variations of arrested development—one befitting the dead, the other the undead, but neither appropriate to the living—are present in Amy's story. Instead of showing that you can never go home again, her story illustrates a threat of circular return that pervades the novel, underlying Clennam's anxious homecoming, Amy's sense of the Marshalsea following her abroad, and the Father of Marshalsea's final breakdown and regressive outburst. The tiny woman's dilemma speaks to this omnipresent fear that after years of spinning one's wheels, one might circle back to the same place, unchanged and unfulfilled. But amid this "usual uproar" of adult struggle, Dickens offers readers a more positive purgatorial example that contrasts with Amy's hellish tale. By casting Clennam as a shade, Dickens calls upon eschatological metaphors to enact a subtle shift from one kind of arrested development to another, revitalizing a terminal Fairy Story that haunts the novel as the corpse of an already moribund Peter Schlemihl folktale. Purgatory, as a state of hoping amid perceived stasis, becomes a metaphor for Clennam's gradual renewal, a story of change that reaches its climax at the place of his greatest immobility: the Marshalsea Prison.

Gathering Substance

In moving beyond stasis, Clennam's final release from purgatory comes only after he has reached his darkest point of incarceration in the Marshalsea penitentiary, the site of his earthly repentance. Existing in a lull for much of the novel—a time of aborted romantic encounters, failed job prospects, and generalized loneliness—Clennam is described as leading all through the second book "a life of slight variety. Regular visits to his mother's dull sick room, and visits scarcely less regular to Mr. Meagles at Twickenham, were its only changes during many months. He sadly and sorely missed Little Dorrit" (498). This monotony composes a large part of Clennam's journey, but only during his imprisonment in the Marshalsea does he clearly become a shade. "Imprisonment began to tell upon him. He knew that he idled and moped. After what he had known of the influences of imprisonment within the four small walls of the very room he occupied, this consciousness made him afraid of himself. Shrinking from the observation of other men, and shrinking from his own, he began to change very sensibly. Anybody might see that the shadow of the wall was dark upon him" (703). In no uncertain terms, Dickens depicts Clennam as a shadow of his former self. Like a shade in the intermediate state, he appears to lose his earthly senses, including his awareness of time passing and of the progression of his days, until a breakthrough comes with Amy's divine intervention:

> Dozing and dreaming, without the power of reckoning time, so that a minute might have been an hour and an hour a minute—some abiding impression of a garden stole over him—a garden of flowers, with a damp warm wind gently stirring their scents. . . . Beside the tea-cup on his table he saw, then, a blooming nosegay: a wonderful handful of the choicest and most lovely flowers. Nothing had ever appeared so beautiful in his sight. He took them up and inhaled their fragrance, and he lifted them to his hot head, and he put them down and opened his parched hands to them, as cold hands are opened to receive the cheering of a fire. (722)

Clennam's final release from purgatory and prison alike comes in the form of his own Little Beatrice. Visiting the prison in her old worn garb, Amy helps Clennam literally to return to his senses after the sensory deprivation of his time in Judgment. In this pivotal scene, Dickens imagines Clennam's inward changes and his maturation throughout the course of the novel as a metaphorical reembodiment, a literal gathering of substance.

This metaphorical reembodiment, while providing the novel with one of its great turning points, does not describe the heavenly climax of Beatrice lifting Dante out of purgatory but instead reveals

Dickens's radical departure from using the Dantean epic as a model. Dickens does not complete his exploration of Clennam's purgatorial journey in *Paradiso*—an ascent that *Little Dorrit*'s last sentence clearly denies by insisting that the couple "[w]ent down into a modest life of usefulness and happiness. Went down to give a mother's care, in the fulness of time, to Fanny's neglected children no less than to their own.... Went down to give a tender nurse and friend to Tip.... They went quietly down into the roaring streets, inseparable and blessed; and as they passed along in sunshine and in shade, the noisy and the eager, and the arrogant and the froward and the vain, fretted, and chafed, and made their usual uproar" (787). In all this uproar, Dickens returns to the more humble folkloric mode of Little Dorrit's Fairy Story only to provide a different model of descent than Amy first describes in her tale of the tiny woman and the shadow both "sunk quietly into her own grave." The novel's ending—with its inclusion of the froward and the vain, the fretted and the chafed, Tip's decline and Fanny's maternal neglect—shows a surprising acceptance of the darker side of life. Instead of effacing these more sinister constants in the blazing sunshine of a happy ending, Dickens incorporates them into the novel's conclusion, thereby creating a final union between sun and shadow.

Although shadow is not banished to the margins in this conclusion, it is also not allowed to dominate as it does in Amy's bedtime story. In the miserable ending of Amy's tale, death brings an unsatisfying and mismatched merging of body and shade, the tiny woman co-opting and taking Nobody's bodiless shadow to the grave with her. Andersen's and Chamisso's earlier models similarly end on a negative note of descent, with the man and his shadow concluding in an alarming state of alienation. It is only in *Little Dorrit* the novel, if not in Little Dorrit's Fairy Story, that Dickens uniquely reunites the man with the shadow, the body with the shade, thereby rejuvenating Amy's unhappy tale and the original folkloric sources as well. The novel that emerges as Clennam's story of a purgatorial No-body is consequently not a "counterpoint to Little Dorrit's tale," as Carlisle argues, but instead a continuation of it, a form of narrative resuscitation. Rather than abandon Amy's story as terminally arrested, this strategy recuperates her tale as merely unfinished. If, in her initial telling, the tiny woman and the man's shadow are brought together prematurely, before the shadow has regained his body, in the novel Amy and Arthur can become a happy couple only when both parts of Clennam are restored, and restored by Little Dorrit's hand.[34] The novel thus ends by escaping the insularity of the tiny woman's hoarding—her tale appearing as a tiny hoard itself that only yields its wealth most fully in the conclusion of the novel. With her gift of a blooming nosegay, Amy breaks through the hermetic seal of her previous fiction, opening up both the story and the novel to greater possibilities of restoration and release. Returning Clennam's senses to him, she reunites the lost man's body and spirit, a gift of self that he chooses to share with her, the grown woman who has not only given but also gathered substance.

II. Dickens, James, and the "Poor, Sensitive Gentleman"

The story of a bachelor's midlife renewal finds its own remaking in the works of Henry James, an author whose favored leading man, the "poor, sensitive gentleman," inherits Arthur Clennam's self-questioning mantra, "[W]hat is to be expected from *me* in middle-life?" (*LD*, 33). Like Dickens, James received criticism for the ruminative quality of his novels, especially *The Ambassadors*, his favorite work. As Arnold Bennett commented, "I asked myself: 'What the dickens is this novel about, and where does it think it's going to?' Question unanswerable! I gave up. To-day I have no recollection whatever of any characters or any events."[35] In creating his own "subtle" approach to plot, James adopts Dickens's methods for capturing the bachelor's slow progress, making references to purgatory as a trope and likewise renovating doppelganger stories in a realist framework. In doing so, he uses Dickens's counterfactual methods of storytelling to drive the story of the middle-aged bachelor further inward, an effect he achieves by uniquely effacing beginnings, depicting the bachelor's moments of renewal as severely delayed, and also by eliding final epiphanies, leaving readers in medias res. In evolving this approach to forestalling beginnings and forgoing epiphanies, James occupies a pivotal place, echoing Dickensian techniques from *Little Dorrit* and, simultaneously, setting the precedent for twentieth-century writers such as Virginia Woolf.

The method James employs in *The Ambassadors* appears in compressed form in his short fiction starring middle-aged bachelors, including "The Altar of the Dead," "The Beast in the Jungle," and "The Jolly Corner." One of the most economical of examples of purgatorial plotting, "The Altar of the Dead" (1895), is a short story that achieves the remarkable effect of seeming, at times, as though it were four hundred pages long. At fifty-five years of age, its protagonist, George Stransom, dedicates himself to building an altar for deceased friends in a Catholic church, a curious decision given that he is professedly not Catholic. Instead, he practices a religion he terms his "religion of the Dead."[36] Candles representing dead friends comfort him, and he reflects on how his perpetual mourning makes it seem "as if their purgatory were really still on earth" (451). What becomes clear is that the altar more accurately represents Stransom's own "purgatory . . . on earth," a period of waiting that spans the remaining years of his life. As the altar takes shape, James increasingly ironizes Stransom's mission, describing the undertaking using free indirect discourse as a "great charity" (451), as a work that gives "employment to his piety" (452), and as the product of a "liberal heart" (452). The altar becomes an outgrowth of less charitable motivations, revealing a collector's compulsion: "There were hours at which he almost caught himself wishing that certain of his friends would now die, that he might establish with them in this manner a connection more charming than, as it happened, it was possible to enjoy with them in life" (460).

Like *Silas Marner*, this story follows the accretive pattern of a miser. Altar maintenance as a form of collecting increasingly absorbs Stransom, holding him in a ritualized deadlock that proves detrimental to relationships with the living. In a rare turning point in the narrative—an unmistakable "event" that stands out from the morass of middle-aged melancholia—Stransom pulls away from his one remaining friend, a female mourner and potential romantic partner who urges him to forgive an old foe. The source of Stransom's one abiding grudge is, by inconvenient coincidence, also her former lover. They part ways until the end of the story, which finds Stransom alone and sick, his years of spiritual hoarding culminating in the lighting of a single candle, a flame that ambiguously represents the expiation of this last grudge and his own death—an appropriately cathartic ending to any purgatorial tale. His second chance is deferred as late as possible, coming at the point of his and the story's mutual expiration.

In this vision of middle-aged latency, Catholic imagery and references to purgatory do more than simply reveal a Jamesian belief system or an effort to redeem sacred art, as some critics have claimed.[37] Instead, allusions to purgatory fulfill an important narrative function: they metaphorically stand in for a longer process of suspension, allowing James to capture his protagonist's gradual development over many years in the condensed form of short fiction. "The Altar of the Dead" signals James's familiarity with popular models of purgatory that infused nineteenth-century literature in England, but it also reveals a broader Victorian inheritance, an approach to plotting stories of midlife that owes its methods, dominant tropes, and frame of reference to writers before him, such as Dickens.[38] James was a great admirer of Dickens, and in James's autobiographical writing he often discusses how difficult it was to separate his authorial viewpoint from readings of his favorite writers. In *The Middle Years*, James's last transcribed autobiography, he reflects on the inescapable quality of this "particular ancient piety embodied in one's private altar to Dickens."[39] This "private altar" to Dickens found public expression in "The Altar of the Dead" and other works in which Jamesian protagonists share Clennam's bifurcated sense of being a "very old man" (*LD*, 371) while surreptitiously entertaining a contrary impulse, a barely understood excitement over having "detected in his cup the dregs of youth" (*Amb.*, 114).[40] The split he envisions between youthful impulses and middle-aged resignation erupts, as in *Little Dorrit*, in shadow stories. In "The

Altar of the Dead," the "mountain of fire" (457) Stransom creates effectively provides him with a form of "altar" ego, for the altar functions like a doppelganger in James's subsequent stories in serving as the emblem of years spent waiting, a representation of foreclosed possibilities displaced outside of himself and given shape.

These lost opportunities are given a supernatural body in two of James's subsequent works, "The Beast in the Jungle" (1903) and "The Jolly Corner" (1908). The "beast" of the title in "The Beast in the Jungle" takes shape as a growing manifestation of John Marcher's chronic hesitation. We first meet Marcher in the process of pondering why his encounter with May Bertram "affected him as the sequel of something of which he had lost the beginning. He knew it, and quite welcomed it, as a continuation, but didn't know what it continued."[41] Marcher's first impression of May Bertram is memorable precisely for not seeming like one at all. This technique, which James later expands in *The Ambassadors*, is one of rendering a protagonist's "first impressions" through the form of the afterthought. The story's opening is presented as "a sequel," a decoy beginning to a more authentic introduction that does not in fact exist. As Marcher reflects, if it is a sequel, he "didn't know what it continued," an amnesiac approach to beginning in medias res. This sense of having "lost" the beginning allows James to expand the sense of being stalled in a vast narrative middle, even in short works of fiction, and to devastating effect in longer novels. If Eliot reflects in the opening epigraph in *Daniel Deronda* that beginnings are always understood retrospectively as having started before the first moment of recognition, she pursues the first moments of growth that elude witnessing, and her novels emerge as heroic acts of excavation that seek to recuperate our earliest stirrings. James takes a different approach. In his representational hierarchy, first stirrings prove secondary to belated reflections. This delayed process of understanding is what James embodies and gives weight to in his stories starring middle-aged bachelors. Giving a physical form to years as they pass in this way allows for an act of compression verging on symbolism, valuable in the tight economies of short stories. The beast that springs at Marcher is the consolidated realization that "he had been the man of his time, *the* man, to whom nothing on earth was to have happened" (540). As in "The Altar of the Dead," this delayed beginning, now given a "monstrous" (540) shape, comes to mark both a second chance and an "arid end" (539). The protagonist's beginning is so delayed that it barely arrives before the end of the story, for James withholds the awakening necessary for a second chance so far as to render this second chance itself almost null, converting the "lost" beginning into a suddenly found conclusion instead.

Of all James's stories featuring sensitive bachelors, "The Jolly Corner" can be said to establish the clearest continuity with Dickens's methods of shadow storytelling in *Little Dorrit*, in being a doppelganger story that centers on the dormant half of a split personality. Spencer Brydon's hard-living double is relegated to the periphery of the story, configured spatially as the dark corridors of his childhood home, now empty except for "the impalpable ashes of his long-extinct youth, afloat in the very air like microscopic motes."[42] When James finally introduces the alter ego as an embodied representation of "what might have been" (706), he follows Dickens's model in declining to relate the alter ego's more eventful storyline. This alternative history is suggested in the physical scars Brydon's double bears—he "had lost two fingers, which were reduced to stumps, as if accidentally shot away. . . . The face, *that* face" (725)—but rather than give readers the story behind these injuries, these physical markers stand in for the events that caused them in an inaccessible, alternative past. James instead keeps the focus on Brydon's contemplation of "what might have been" as the main event, building suspense toward the final confrontation between his protagonist and his double, an altercation that James, in the end, elides. Brydon faces his double and faints, awakening to discover, "'Ah, I've come to myself now'" (730), an ending that marks the reunion of his two halves.

The conclusion echoes Dickens's finale in *Little Dorrit* in which Clennam, in a similar state of fainting passivity, is likewise restored to himself, with the aid of a female attendant. It is a climax that resembles

Jonah's time in the whale in being, simultaneously, an anticlimax: "The apprehension of knowing it must after a little have grown in him, and the strangest moment of his adventure perhaps, the most memorable or really most interesting, afterwards, of his crisis, was the lapse of certain instants of concentrated conscious *combat*.... The state of 'holding-on' was thus the state to which he was momentarily reduced" (715). Brydon's final "apprehension" is buried in a multiplicity of Jamesian clauses and qualifications that dispel immediacy. First impressions, once again, become afterthoughts, refracted through an array of addenda: they come "after a little," "afterwards," as a "lapse." The epiphany is therefore muted in being described from a slight temporal distance. We are not privy to the thoughts that accompany Brydon's transformation in real time. Instead, readers occupy the perspective of the event's aftermath, the period when he has already begun processing and reflecting on what happened, clothing the experience in retrospection. The crucial moment, the realization that marks a fulfillment of Brydon's waiting, is itself absented. Instead of an epiphany, we encounter a lapse, a signature move in James's writing that allows him to channel suspense into continued (and often concluding) suspension.

This technique receives its fullest treatment in *The Ambassadors*, his novel of mature "adventure," a word James uses no less than thirty times to describe Lambert Strether's Parisian experience. *The Ambassadors* at once evolves from novels like *Little Dorrit* and breaks with such earlier fictions of maturity largely by dispensing with a staple element of contemplative plots: the epiphany. The epiphany, with its origin in Christian models of revelation, is an event that registers as inward and, at the same time, as a major plot point. Herbert Tucker, seeking to "revive *epiphany* for academic inquiry," traces the origins of modern concepts of epiphany in nineteenth-century works, showing how Wordsworth's "spots of time" and Browning's dramatic monologues are evidence of a historical shift in which the concept of the epiphany as a literary device becomes apparent.[43] As Tucker says, "epiphany arises at a major narrative juncture of modernity, the place where the story of the essential self meets the accidents of historical contingency" (1211). In revealing

Clennam's awakening love for Amy Dorrit, Dickens gives readers the satisfaction that "some marked stop in the whirling wheel of life brings the right perception with it" (*LD*, 689). Clennam's right perception, the pinnacle of his mature marriage plot, centers on understanding Amy Dorrit's proper place in his personal cosmology: "Looking back upon his own poor story, she was its vanishing-point" (702). The epiphany is presented as a contemplative climax that is both within the bounds of plot—its very end point—and excluded from its frenzied activity, the eye of the storm.[44] One might say that it is a telos that functions, ultimately, as a novelistic plot's own vanishing point.

James drives toward this same vanishing point of the epiphany in his plots of maturity but then, unlike Dickens, withholds the crucial moment of awakening. In *The Ambassadors*, a slight delay in perception becomes a feature of each of Strether's awakenings, conveyed via James's repeated use of phrases such as "he was to remember" and "he was to reflect," a grammatical strategy that resembles the one we find in his doppelganger stories such as "The Jolly Corner." In one turning point for Strether, his transformative encounter with Gloriani, his experience of the importance of this moment appears to expand, to dilate, to take on the fullness of an adventure as defined by Georg Simmel in being "completely torn out of the inclusive context of life and that simultaneously the whole strength and intensity of life stream into it."[45] This new, crucial susceptibility to his experiences is described as a feeling of "opening . . . all the windows of his mind":

> Strether, in contact with that element as he had never yet so intimately been, had the consciousness of opening to it, for the happy instant, all the windows of his mind, of letting this rather grey interior drink in for once the sun of a clime not marked in his old geography. He was to remember again repeatedly the medal-like Italian face, in which every line was an artist's own, in which time told only as tone and consecration, and he was to recall in especial, as the penetrating radiance, as the communication of the

illustrious spirit itself, the manner in which, while they stood briefly, in welcome and response, face to face, he was held by the sculptor's eyes. He wasn't soon to forget them, was to think of them, all unconscious, unintending, preoccupied though they were, as the source of the deepest intellectual sounds to which he had ever been exposed. He was in fact quite to cherish his vision of it, to play with it in idle hours; only speaking of it to no one and quite aware he couldn't have spoken without appearing to talk nonsense. (120–21)

The "happy instant" reaches superlative pitches (it was "the source of the *deepest* intellectual sounds to which he had *ever* been exposed"), but its real force, as James implies, lies in its indelibility, how it impresses itself on Strether's memory. The glory of Gloriani is thus expressed only from a nostalgic vantage point, represented retrospectively from a series of unspecified moments in the future in which Strether looks back on the sculptor's impact: it was an experience he "was to remember again repeatedly."[46] These repeated brief forays into the future undermine the urgency of Strether's realization in his lived present, making this momentous occurrence less *of the moment*. His urgent imperative to Little Bilham, an injunction to embrace youth and "Live!" uttered but a few pages later, is advice that he, himself, will fail to follow fully in the future. He will continue his previous pattern: a tendency to "lapse" out of the present and look back nostalgically.

This tendency to interrupt the moment with retrospection is even more apparent in the epiphany that concludes the novel, Strether's final perception of the open secret of Chad's affair with Madame de Vionnet. He "almost blushed, in the dark, for the way he had dressed the possibility in vagueness, as a little girl might have dressed her doll" (468). Yet the understanding that makes him almost blush is a long time coming, taking days for Strether to process after the first instant of accidentally discovering the couple together on an amorous vacation. After this chance encounter, Strether "scarce went to bed till morning. . . . He then knew more or less how he had been affected—he but half knew at the time" (465). The cogitations take all night: "Strether didn't quite see what else they could have done. He didn't quite see *that* even at an hour or two past midnight, even when he had, at his hotel, for a long time, without a light and without undressing, sat back on his bedroom sofa and stared straight before him" (465–66). As far as epiphanies go, this one needs a good deal of mental midwifery to be coaxed out before dawn, and the image of his realization is one that is labored to the point of evoking the birth process: "[H]is consciousness, though muffled, had its sharpest moments during this passage" (465). James manages to efface and pass over his hero's first "sharp" awareness by muffling it with layers of retrospective phrasing: "Strether was to remember afterwards further that this had had for him the effect of forming Chad's almost sole intervention; and indeed he was to remember further still, in subsequent meditation, many things that, as it were, fitted together" (464). The more momentous the revelation, the more James distances Strether from the force of first realizations, insisting that he "was to remember," "afterwards," "further," "further still," "in subsequent meditation." The grand long-awaited reveal, the vanishing point of Strether's mature fiction, is swallowed up in James's rendering of a middle-aged hero's "belated vision."

The belated quality of Strether's realization is especially pronounced in *The Ambassadors*, but in its inwardness his great turning point resembles other Jamesian scenes of realization, for example, Isabel Archer's "meditative vigil" (14) in *The Portrait of a Lady* after she perceives with a "flicker" (343) of shock Madame Merle's and Osmund's extramarital intimacy.[47] James describes this scene in the preface as being a "landmark" (14) event although "it all goes on without her being approached by another person and without her leaving her chair," stating that he tried to capture "all the vivacity of incidents and all the economy of picture" (14). This description recalls Eliot's treatment of narrative movement and visual stasis in the tableau vivant in *Daniel Deronda*; pictorial art again stands in for developments so inward that they defy being understood as action, being presented metaphorically as still images instead. Like Eliot before him, James reclaims these motionless occurrences as major events, saying that they reveal "what an 'exciting' inward life may do"—without, conveniently, requiring any *doing* (one need not leave one's chair). Despite their lack of outward flair, these unconventional epiphanies are, in his estimation, "as 'interesting' as the surprise of a caravan or the identification of a pirate" (15), a description that brings the adventure topos inside, as James does repeatedly in Strether's story of mature rejuvenation in *The Ambassadors*.

That Strether's series of revelations—his grand inward "adventure"—is belated both in occurring in midlife and in being characterized by a series of small, delayed realizations—has prompted critics to label *The Ambassadors*, as a whole, a "belated bildungsroman."[48] The implication of this categorization is that the mature bachelor's story is simply a bildungsroman deferred and translated into middle age, or rather, a classic bildungsroman with "poor fine melancholy, missing, striving, Strether" dropped into it. Whether this formulation yields a middle-aged bildungsroman or, as others have asserted, an "anti-bildungsroman" makes little difference. In either case, the tendency is to read this novel within the bildungsroman tradition, in particular, within the European bildungsroman tradition established by Goethe, Balzac, and Stendhal. However, it becomes clear that in telling Strether's retrospective story, James manages to elude certain conundrums in the bildungsroman, a form that many have identified as the novel of compromise, or as Franco Moretti asserts, the novel in which the protagonist's desire for individuality and freedom is either absorbed into the social fabric (marriage, work, family) or, alternatively, preserved by the hero's death and his refusal to conform. Strether, in his conclusion, meets neither a matrimonial nor a fatal end. He seemingly renounces these two options, taking a third route: that of remaining indefinitely in medias res. In being left at loose ends, he is granted possibilities that even Isabel as a married woman is denied. She returns to her ill-fated marriage, a willing captive to what Eliot calls in *Daniel Deronda* "the ordinary wirework of social forms" (53). In James's account of the poor sensitive gentleman's adventure, Strether alone eludes this "wirework."

Curiously, his last bold act of renunciation has been viewed in a negative light as a denouncement of pleasure, the signature stoical move of the closeted Victorian bachelor. It is nevertheless possible to regard Strether's finale as a liberating event. In short, rather than considering what Strether gave up, we might admire what he got away with.[49] Marriage or death—the Scylla and Charybdis of the bildungsroman—are endings that Strether eludes in his mature odyssey to achieve an open-ended finale not typically available to his youthful counterparts. This state of being left in medias res is one that, upon examination, characterizes many novels of maturity, becoming a feature of these works as they compose a larger genre. As Moretti notes, "A *Bildung* is truly such only if, at a certain point, it can be seen as *concluded:* only if youth passes into maturity, and comes to a stop there" (26). One notable feature of many novels of maturity is that they resist conclusions altogether. It is perhaps fitting that novels that represent middle age tend to conclude by upholding a continuing sense of a middle instead. Such endings include not only Gwendolen Harleth's "humdrum" homecoming but also the perversely unresolved endings of novels including *Villette*, a work in which the heroine exits the novel as a trenchantly middle-aged woman, enjoining readers in the last pages, "Here pause: pause at once," and tempting us to "picture union and happy succeeding life" (496). Instead, she leaves us with a vision of frustratingly unconfirmed wreckage. These midlife endings, be they calmly prosaic or perversely unfulfilling, extend the possibility of a different kind of plotting in Victorian fiction than the bildungsroman affords. *The Ambassadors* vitally contributes to this alternative tradition in both using techniques pioneered by Dickens and in finding new ways to tell inward, uneventful adventure stories. Where James uniquely succeeds is in pushing the novel of maturity even further as the genre that defiantly, and ingeniously, manages to remain in medias res—a midlife "state of holding-on" that prefigures Woolf's subsequent innovations in her works that seek to capture a quality of Victorian retrospection.

CHAPTER FOUR

Odd Women and Eccentric Plotting

Maturity, Modernism, and Woolf's Victorian Retrospection

Maturity and midlife, far from being a realm of "general lost freshness," as Henry James describes his own "middle years," carry a freight of subversive potential for writers experimenting with new methods for resisting plot—those "gig lamps" of eventful storytelling that Virginia Woolf protested in "Modern Fiction."[1] The familiar literary history is that this resistance to plot arose in the modernist era contemporaneously with Woolf's imperative that writers strive to represent the "luminous halo" of lived experience. Yet in exploring nineteenth-century novels that deviate from the bildungsroman, we see an early strain of this defiance already at work. From short fiction like *Silas Marner* and "The Beast in the Jungle" to sprawling multivolume novels like *Little Dorrit* and *The Ambassadors*, a suspended approach to plot can be found in works oriented around middle-aged characters, those figures clustered eccentrically around the edges of the Austenian dance floor earlier in the nineteenth century: confirmed bachelors, aging parents and grandparents, widows and widowers, and lastly, that figure of cheerful abjection, Miss Bates, the "old maid" or "odd woman."

The threat at the heart of Jane Austen's *Emma*, a threat that goes unrealized in her narrative of formation, is that Emma's own plot will veer toward this margin. At Harriet's concern that Emma "will be an old maid! and that's so dreadful," the heroine insists that the term does not apply to wealthy unmarried women, only poor ones, and she instead envisions an alternative life story that marks a radical departure from both the bildungsroman and the marriage plot as the available trajectories for female protagonists: "If I know myself, Harriet, mine is an active, busy mind, with a great many independent resources; and I do not perceive why I should be more in want of employment at forty or fifty than one-and-twenty. Woman's usual occupations of eye, and hand, and mind, will be as open to me then, as they are now; or with no important variation."[2] Emma's fantasy of her life "at forty or fifty" as an unmarried and fulfilled woman—the continuing heroine of a life characterized by "some of the best blessings of existence" (7) if not by marriage—is a plot that would take many decades to be realized as a common central story line in British fiction. Even Austen's eldest heroine, twenty-eight-year-old Anne Eliot from *Persuasion*, evades this fate. The eight years Anne waits to reencounter Captain Wentworth, her interlude of suspension, is handled elliptically, the narrative commencing only with the renewed onset of their interrupted romance. *Persuasion* may be an unconventional marriage plot, telling of first love delayed until the heroine has self-consciously come of age, but it is not the account of the unmarried older woman that Emma fictively envisions. Miss Bates would have to wait until later in the century to receive fuller treatment. The elevation of the "odd woman" from part of the melancholic decor to George Gissing's central, albeit often unkindly represented, focus for his novel *The Odd Women* would eventually meet with a more lyrical treatment at the hands of writers including Sylvia Townsend Warner and Virginia Woolf.

I. Woolf's Odd Women

Following the "eccentric" plots of midlife into the early twentieth century enables us to see how a focus on the "odd woman" as a visionary protagonist developed in relation to precedents established by writers of the latter half of the nineteenth century. Many accounts of the bildungsroman see a marked disjunction with the onset of World War I. Franco Moretti, for example, discusses the bildungsroman's dominance waning at this historical moment. However, by tracing an alternative tradition, fictions of maturity, we can perceive continuity in the resistance to eventful plotting that Woolf made one of the key facets of her fiction. Such an approach stresses continuity over rupture and experimentation, in distinct contrast with foundational discussions of the novel's development that present its literary history as a story of *bildung* writ large. Accounts as disparate as Moretti's and Hugh Kenner's prize a disjunction that defines modernist innovation at the expense of a broader understanding of the persistence of Victorian methods of representation in the twentieth century.[3] In contrast, the formal approach under consideration—that of novelists adopting the marginalized vantage of middle age as grounds for innovation—is one that Woolf and other modernist writers developed by engaging with a Victorian precedent rather than by rejecting nineteenth-century novelistic conventions. In other words, Woolf sought to "make it new" by also, in her novels of midlife and maturity, "making it old" at the same time.

From Miss Bates to Mrs. Brown

Beginning in the wake of Austen's fictions, in the latter half of the nineteenth century, we find Miss Bates playing a crucial role in works that imagine, at once, social and economic alternatives for women and, concomitantly, new formal approaches to novelistic plotting. This coincidence of form and content is borne out in a variety of novels that imagine a new strain of radically uneventful, meditative, suspended, and lyrical plotting through the figure of the single middle-aged woman—works ranging from *Villette, Cranford,* and *Washington Square,* which exemplify this trend in its incipient form, to twentieth-century novels that develop this strain more fully, such as *Lolly Willowes, To the Lighthouse,* and *The Years.* The "odd woman" increasingly appears as a figure of resistance, one who defies, as Catherine Sloper does in *Washington Square*, the expectation that she was "made to do the usual thing."[4] Catherine instead becomes an "admirable old maid" who "developed a few harmless eccentricities" (226), her "eccentric" stance amounting to a rejection of the masterplot of parental expectations as well as the closural pressures of the novel. For writers, adopting this position of eccentricity, that of being outside the conjoined plotlines of the bildungsroman and marriage plot, provides a generic foundation for defying the expectation that they too are "made to do the usual thing" on a formal level as storytellers. This resistance to doing "the usual thing" is precisely what Woolf identifies in "Modern Fiction" as a vital approach for writers seeking to break new ground.

The approach she urges was being taken up by contemporaries, notably Sylvia Townsend Warner, whose *Lolly Willowes* tells of a spinster aunt's conversion to witchcraft. This supernatural event, occurring a remarkable two-thirds of the way through the novella, comes as slowly and gently as her earlier transition from a girl named Laura into "Aunt Lolly," a middle-aged, unmarried woman shuffled between her brothers' houses along with bequeathed furniture. In imagining Lolly's liberating transformation, Warner's political message on the state of odd women in England emerges distinctly but not stridently; no violent acts of sorcery punctuate Laura's burgeoning self-awareness. As in Newman's account of his mature conversion, Warner's vision is surprisingly lacking in *sturm* and *drang*. Instead, the heroine's gradual conversion appears as a practical stance against the current state of affairs: "When I think of witches, I seem to see all over England, all over Europe, women living and growing old, as common as blackberries, and as unregarded."[5]

Woolf, too, imagines the conversion of the middle-aged "unregarded" woman in her fiction and essays. In her prose manifesto "Mr. Bennett and Mrs. Brown" she provocatively suggests that "all novels begin with an old lady in the corner opposite."[6] The unregarded "Mrs. Brown" of the essay's title embodies the need for writers to capture character rather than the "fabric" of modern existence, the latter being a failing Woolf attributes to the Edwardians and Georgians. In Woolf's playful anthropomorphizing of literature, Mrs. Brown is an older woman, "over sixty." She is not, in the guise Woolf gives her, someone resembling Austen's Emma or James's Isabel Archer. As Woolf insists, "Mrs. Brown is eternal, Mrs. Brown is human nature, Mrs. Brown changes only on the surface, it is the novelists who get in and out—there she sits and not one of the Edwardian writers has so much as looked at her" (16). It is interesting that in choosing a representative for the novel, for literature in its "eternal" essence and for "human nature," Woolf chooses a woman who is past the prime of youth, who sits like Mrs. Gummidge, a "lone lorn creetur." Mrs. Brown, in being universal, is also an emblem of marginalization, an exile from the plots of youth who exhibits the kind of eccentricity that Catherine Sloper made into a principled stance years earlier. She is a widow or an odd woman, someone who for Woolf, as for her literary predecessors, could provide the decentered perspective necessary to perform new experiments in prose. As Woolf insists, "we are trembling on the verge of one of the great ages of English literature. But it can only be reached if we are determined never, never to desert Mrs. Brown" (24).

To ask, "Why Mrs. Brown?" is to ask, in another form, "Why focalize a novel through Lily Briscoe? Or center a prose elegy on Mrs. Ramsay? Why give Eleanor Pargiter the thread of continuity to carry across *The Years*?" Exploring fictions of maturity requires tracing these narratives of midlife and adulthood from the Victorian period into the twentieth century to show how an older (and odder) female protagonist becomes a thoroughly modern figure—the older woman as "new woman"—even as she provides continuity with Victorian methods of representation. The mature odd woman as a protagonist bridges the nineteenth and twentieth centuries, offering retrospection and insight and playing a connective role in Woolf's novels, as Eleanor Pargiter does in the sprawling family chronicle *The Years* and as Lily Briscoe does in *To the Lighthouse*.

Centering on *The Years*, this final chapter briefly considers an earlier work, *To the Lighthouse*, for its purgatorial interval, "Time Passes," a central interlude that seemingly expiates the novel of "story." This famed narrative middle sets a precedent for Woolf's longest novel, *The Years*, which emerges in its gentle pacing as an expansive literary interlude—the interlude being defined as a period of suspended plotting and uneventful development. This interlude writ large is stretched over five decades and hundreds of pages. In both of these literary works, Woolf extends a cultural pattern identified in previous chapters by invoking eschatological metaphors as a model for plotting suspension and progression simultaneously. She begins *The Years* in 1880, framing the Victorian era as purgatorial itself and Eleanor's journey from her childhood to a "Present Day" in the 1930s as one guided by a reading of Dante's *Purgatorio*. As in the works of writers like George Eliot before her, the *Purgatorio* provides a touchstone for Woolf in representing a gentler, transformative model of personal and historical change, as well as a narrative model for experimenting with gradualist plotting in her postwar fictions of maturity.

Lily Briscoe, the Interlude, and the Decentered Modernist Plot in To the Lighthouse

On the surface, to compare "Time Passes" and *The Years* as interludes may seem counterintuitive, for "Time Passes" is upheld as the hallmark of Woolf's formal radicalism while *The Years*, which Woolf professedly modeled on Victorian fiction, is considered by many to be her most conservative work.[7] Yet in both we see a fascination with suspending plot and exploring the novel's limits for encompassing lyrical and descriptive stasis at the expense of narrative movement. This quality of suspension is achieved in predominantly different ways: in *To the Lighthouse*, through a jolting, sublime shift into lyricism, and in *The Years*, through an immersion in daily life, the "the cotton wool" of habitual existence.[8] Whereas *To the Lighthouse* enacts its own formal violence in presenting the interlude as a break with the narrative that antecedes and follows it, further punctuating the air of suspension with bracketed intrusions, in *The Years* Woolf prioritizes continuity as a means of achieving one of her goals: that of realizing historical change "without death or violence,"[9] a goal accomplished by way of Eleanor's reflections on a purgatorial potential for slow progress over the course of several decades. In both works, Woolf's most overt experiments in plot suspension coincide with her representations of the disjunction and the trauma of historical violence. The trope of descent into the afterlife, a descent presented as internalized and contemplative—a true journey into the whale—surfaces in both works at key moments when Woolf represents scenes from the war. These rare and disjunctive war scenes, which include the eerily muted deaths and bombings presented in "Time Passes" and the air raid in *The Years*, in both works are brought back into a larger progression and narrative arc through a single character's reflections; in *To the Lighthouse* this important role is played by Lily Briscoe and in *The Years* by Eleanor Pargiter, odd women who abide to offer retrospection and a renewing vision of the future.

The peripheral status of these women proves crucial in both novels. Lily's spatial introduction in *To the Lighthouse* establishes, and at once privileges, her point of view as fundamentally decentered. In a scene of shared looking, Lily is first observed through Mrs. Ramsay's dominating line of vision. Turning "apprehensively" to see whether anyone has heard her husband chanting "The Charge of the Light Brigade," Mrs. Ramsay is relieved that it was "[o]nly Lily Briscoe . . . ; and that did not matter. But the sight of the girl standing on the edge of the lawn painting reminded her; she was supposed to be keeping her head as much in the same position as possible for Lily's picture. Lily's picture! Mrs. Ramsay smiled. With her little Chinese eyes and her puckered-up face, she would never marry; one could not take her painting very seriously; she was an independent little creature, and Mrs. Ramsay liked her for it; so, remembering her promise, she bent her head" (17). Lily emerges as dually eccentric, to the family as well as to the marriage plots that Mrs. Ramsay generates, for she is at once introduced as a fringe artistic observer, glimpsed through a window outside the domestic sphere, and also as someone who is, in Mrs. Ramsay's estimation, unmarriageable and "independent" of her favored reproductive storylines. Lily's fringe status is made clear through Woolf's asymmetrical treatment of the women's mutual act of observing each other. What is in actuality a scene of shared looking—Mrs. Ramsay at Lily, and Lily with even greater constancy at Mrs. Ramsay—is skewed toward Mrs. Ramsay, whose vision dominates this scene. Lily's thoughts are not rendered at this specific point in the narration, and her point of view is at first diminished, not only in Mrs. Ramsay's slights but also in Woolf's spatial slighting of her character.

Ultimately, the eccentric position afforded by Lily becomes invaluable, allowing Woolf to create a cohesive yet crucially decentered form for her fiction. Lily bridges the chasm of "Time Passes," and this decentered middle—the interlude in which the central maternal authority of Mrs. Ramsay is displaced and Lily's eccentric perspective emerges as a new governing and shepherding sensibility—corresponds with Woolf's larger experiment in purgatorial plotting. "Time Passes" is the novel's own purgatory, its descent into the afterlife and Hades, a place of shadow and absence that Pericles Lewis characterizes as a sublime "post-messianic interlude."[10] This purgatorial middle section simultaneously stages Mrs. Ramsay's death and that of the marriage plot as a genre, for her loss is presented as a dropping away of narrative forms, a cleansing of the marriage plot with the elegy. The loss of the mother-goddess Demeter, the keeper of the hearth and of fertility, is rendered into a new, lyrical form for capturing absence and its inexpressibility. In presenting "Time Passes" as a sublime interlude, Lewis contrasts Woolf's writing with the work of nineteenth-century realists, instead aligning Woolf with Romantic writers in her approach to the sublime. He makes the case that Victorian realists rarely had recourse to representing the sublime, except in the form of a holdover from the gothic romance (159). His account, like many others, frames Woolf's fiction as a break from the preceding Victorian literature, yet his discussion of the sublime and religious experience in modernist fiction potentially has greater implications for understanding Woolf's approach to plot suspension—and how it developed in continuity with Victorian realist fiction.

In the Victorian novel, the gothic moments Lewis discusses as remnants of the sublime pervade stories of adult *bildung*, often helping to shape a novelistic approach to gradual plotting. In novels like *Villette* and *Daniel Deronda*, these seemingly gothic interruptions prove to be part of a larger approach to capturing suspension, for they crystallize the gradual, accretive stretches of the "humdrum" into moments. We see these punctuated gothic scenes given instantaneous shape in images, for example the picture of the dead face that leaps out at Gwendolen (a holdover from Ann Radcliffe's school of interior decorating) and in the convention of pathetic fallacy that blasts through *Villette* as a series of storms. At work in these scenes, as in Woolf's fiction, is a tension between the moment versus the duration—the moment serving to illustrate and give weight to a preceding duration. Indeed, in Eliot's tableaux and Brontë's storms, we find a precursor for Woolf's methods for revealing the conflict between her signature "moments of being" and "moments of non-being" that compose her literary interludes. We see this tension between the moment and the duration most urgently represented in "Time Passes," with the dark span of ten years being punctuated, periodically, by sudden revelations; it is also captured in more-subtle ways in *The Years*, the novel Woolf presents in its entirety as a suspended interlude of uneventful development. How Woolf uses the Victorian novel to craft this new quotidian sublime proves central to understanding her purgatorial approach to plot both in her most overtly experimental works, such as *To the Lighthouse*, and even more interestingly in her late work of extreme gradualism spanning several decades, *The Years*. It is in this subsequent novel that Woolf develops her overarching vision of gradual maturation in midlife, adulthood, and old age, realizing most fully the story of Mrs. Brown and her sisters.

II. *The Years* and the Victorian Novel

Woolf openly emulated Victorian novelists for their ability to capture a quality of prosaic life. This emulation guided her approach to writing *The Years*, her longest work and the first to become a "best seller" in the United States.[11] She spoke of making *The Years* "objective, realistic, in the manner of Jane Austen: carrying on the story all the time."[12] This goal was reiterated in her autobiographical writing when she described *The Years* as her attempt to evoke the "real novelists," identifying nineteenth-century writers as models, including Austen, Thackeray, Trollope, Dickens, and Tolstoy.[13] These writers were, according to Woolf, the true masters of preservation, unequalled in their ability to capture the details of the daily. Their methods of preservation would inform Woolf's approach to creating a narrative of continuity between the Victorian era and the "Present Day" in *The Years*, a work that looks back even as it rises from the Pargiter childhood through World War I to the rosy-fingered dawn.

The continuity of this vision resulted in part from Woolf's professed mission of "[c]arrying on the story," which seemed to jar with her open call to experimentalism in *To the Lighthouse* and *The Waves*.[14] *The Waves* is famed for Woolf "not trying to tell a story,"[15] as well as for being the novel that, even more than *To the Lighthouse*, exemplifies her manifesto in "Modern Fiction" that "if a writer were a free man and not a slave, if he could write what he chose, not what he must, if he could base his work upon his own feeling and not upon convention, there would be no plot, no comedy, no tragedy, no love interest or catastrophe in the accepted style, and perhaps not a single button sewn on as the Bond Street tailors would have it."[16] If *The Waves* has been deemed the fulfillment of this rallying cry, *The Years*, as evidenced often by its best-seller status, has been framed as a capitulation to pressures to provide readers with a greater degree of probability, a linear model of development, and other "clear-cut features" that lead to accessibility, often at the expense of avant-garde poetics; in a word, *The Years* provides readers with what many consider to be the most traditional of novelistic staples: plot.

The move toward a model of plot that more closely resembles the "loose baggy monsters" of the previous era has been viewed with considerable suspicion as being both formally and politically regressive.[17]

Originally Woolf wanted to incorporate past methods of representation into her novel but to do so while simultaneously creating a new kind of political writing. *The Years* was to be "a terrific affair . . . bold & adventurous," taking in the past but giving "the whole of the present society—nothing less: facts, as well as the vision. And to combine them both."[18] To achieve this balance between "facts" and "vision," she sought to create a hybrid genre of political fiction that would bring together the novel and the essay. Woolf planned for this "Essay-Novel, called the Pargiters . . . to take in everything, sex, education, life, &c; & come, with the most powerful & agile leaps, like a chamois across precipices from 1880 to here & now."[19] *The Pargiters* was to have six essays alternating with five fictional pieces, a structure that she eventually dropped in favor of pursuing a more outwardly old-fashioned form of plotting. In its finished state, *The Years* would maintain the structure of leaping between 1880 and the "Present Day," likewise leaving temporal chasms between separate chapters. But even with these preserved divisions, the novel moved beyond the compact ecosystems of individual essays, sprawling into an interwoven network of facts and fiction.

Reviewers almost universally acknowledged that the resulting "precipices" of the novel are often overshadowed by narrative plateaus, or long stretches of prosaic observation that, at times, partake more of the Victorian novel than of Woolf's signature modernist poetics. It would seem that Woolf was getting criticism from both sides. As when George Eliot derided religious novels for being an ungainly hybrid genre that should be killed off, the underlying hybridity of *The Years* has created rifts and critical discomfort. Reviewers claimed that the novel had both too much plot and also too little, disagreeing on whether its lengthy reflections could be considered an outgrowth of Victorian nostalgia or a development in keeping with Woolf's iconoclastic experiments in resisting plot. One of the most positive assessments from 1937 declared *The Years* to be "Woolf's Richest Novel," citing its uneventful structure as its strongest point: it is "long-drawn-out lyricism in the form of a novel."[20] This "long-drawn-out lyricism" drew only frustration from other quarters; another review, published the day before, cautioned that readers must have "patience" and forecasted that "many people will wonder what on earth Mrs. Woolf is trying to say in so many uneventful pages."[21]

These uneventful vistas in prose, or narrative lulls, have become the central feature under scrutiny in contemporary studies too, several of which present *The Years* as having an escapist politics when compared to the more overtly political agenda of *The Pargiters*. Recent studies of *The Years* preserve a division over how to regard Woolf's aversion to "story," but in the 1980s criticism shifted to focus on whether the novel's uneventful structure is a successful vehicle for Woolf's politics. As Pamela Transue asserts, it is "nearly impossible . . . to remember who did what and when," and Transue argues that plot vagaries hinder Woolf's attempt to achieve larger political goals of writing about the war and addressing the interplay between public policy and women's private lives.[22] Jane Marcus contrastingly makes the case that Woolf displays a pacifist politics in *The Years*, what Susan Friedman further describes as an "anti-authoritarian" form in fiction that privileges "lyricism" over "narrative."[23] Again we see the dual tendency to link the novel's "many uneventful pages" either with modernist "lyricism" (claiming plotlessness as a formal innovation) or with the vast rambling form of the nineteenth-century novel (thereby claiming plotlessness as a move *away* from innovation and as a diffusion of Woolf's previous vision in *The Waves*).[24]

Yet contrary to the interpretations in these studies and others that pose modernism as the movement that unmoored the novel from its obsession with plot, Woolf's most interesting innovations in *The Years* do not always result from distancing herself from Victorian fiction; instead, many of her lauded technical achievements evolved from adopting and renovating aspects of nineteenth-century encounters with the prosaic. James's inverted epiphanies, Dickens's accumulated daily detail, and Eliot's methods of revealing introspection in fictions of maturity all find a corollary and an extension in Woolf's gradualist vision of a family's development over five decades. In creating a family chronicle with myriad shifting perspectives and no single protagonist,

Woolf cast Eleanor Pargiter, a spinster aunt and early twentieth-century "odd woman," as a central figure whose perspective guides the novel. Like the bachelor and the widow, she is a character who has eluded, and been eluded by, the marriage plot. Rather than exist outside of the web of marital and reproductive plotlines that Woolf weaves together, Eleanor's maturation consistently shapes the story's development from its Victorian beginning to its festive finish in the 1930s. The vast middle of the novel corresponds with Eleanor's own middle age. During this extended period, her reading features centrally as a way of invoking the past as part of a larger vision of historical progress. In particular, Dante's *Purgatorio*, a book Eleanor casually picks up at bedtime one night alongside her Victorian reading matter, becomes a continual source of reflection in the novel, recurring most pressingly in a scene of literal descent in which Eleanor travels underground during an air raid. Woolf alludes to the *Purgatorio* in this and other scenes to achieve two effects: first, she does so at moments when she seeks to capture a Victorian approach to purgatorial plotting, or rather, when she seeks to depict Eleanor's experience of prosaic and gradual change as she ages; and second, she makes references to Dante when imagining possibilities for gradual historical progress in the future by way of a descent into the literary past.

Like each of the other writers in this study, then, Woolf offers readers a vision of the journey to the afterlife, thereby extending a cultural pattern of purgatorial plotting shaped by Victorian writers and Victorian theological debates alike. These debates were simultaneously experiencing a resurgence after World War 1, a phenomenon discussed in this book's first chapter as part of the legacy of Oxford Movement theology in the twentieth century, when gentler progressive models of the afterlife increasingly appealed to those mourning the many youths who had died during the war. Ultimately, by tracing purgatory's plots from Victorian novels into the realm of Woolf's postwar modernism, we can view *The Years* in continuity with a nineteenth-century tradition of fictions of maturity. At the same time, this approach allows for a new consideration of the seemingly conservative structure of *The Years* as deceptive, concealing as it does a radicalism of form more subtle and less recognized than her overtly experimental works *The Waves* and *To the Lighthouse*.

Purgatorial Plotting in The Years *and the Descent of Midlife*

Describing the "joy" of reading as an inspiration in her early stages of writing, Woolf spoke of being "in sublime reading fettle . . . encouraged to read by the feeling" that she was "on the flood of creativeness in The Pargiters—what a liberation that gives one—as if everything added to that torrent—all books become fluid and swell the stream."[25] In addition to revisiting nineteenth-century novels, Woolf was reading Dante's *Purgatorio* for the entire duration of writing and revising *The Years*. Dante and Victorian fiction proved to be an important reading combination in Woolf's life as in her novel *The Years*. The connection between Dante's *Purgatorio* and *The Years* has been traced in accounts of Woolf's reading notebooks, most notably Brenda Silver's scholarship, although it is rarely explored in light of Woolf's formal approach to plot in the novel—an approach to plot that she openly stated partakes of Victorian fiction.[26]

Woolf reread the *Purgatorio* on several occasions, dating back as early as 1917, when in her diary she discusses reading Dante between accounts of air raids, an association I explore in greater detail when examining the air raid scene in the 1917 chapter of *The Years*. In the decades between the wars, Woolf would return to Dante many times, and in a prescient moment in 1930 she summed up what would become her relationship to the *Divine Comedy* over the course of the next decade: "I am reading Dante; & my present view of reading is to elongate immensely. I take a week over one canto. No hurry."[27] Accordingly, we find her recording as late as October 1940, "But I will read Dante," as part of her continued regimen,[28] and as early as 1930 she notes beginning Dante's *Inferno* while writing *The Waves*. Woolf moved on to rereading the *Purgatorio* during her work on *The Years*, and in commencing the second volume of *The Divine Comedy* she mentions "trying to start the nameless book again," the nameless book being a reference to her work on *The Pargiters*.[29]

Taken all together, individual entries spanning the course of a decade reveal that Dante informed Woolf's earliest conception of *The Years*, and continued to influence her writing through to her novel's completion and publication. Thus, Dante's *Purgatorio*, *The Years*, and the Victorian fiction that inspired Woolf's longest novel were all inseparably intertwined. Woolf's diary often speaks to the slippage between her reading inspiration and her writing, with many of her more anxious entries attesting to how the pace of Dante's penitents seemed to govern both endeavors.[30] "At this rate I shall never finish the *Purgatorio*. But whats [sic] the use of reading with half ones [sic] mind running on Eleanor & Kitty."[31] Other entries frame Dante's *Purgatorio* as the force lifting Woolf out of the "grind" of her novel: "Isn't it odd? Some days I cant [sic] read Dante at all after revising the P.s [*The Pargiters*]: other days I find it very sublime & helpful. Raises one out of the chatter of words."[32] Looking back on *The Years* after its publication, Woolf makes a final connection between her extended reading of Dante and how *The Years* also seemed to "elongate immensely" to become her longest work of fiction:

> What can I do with the last hour of my morning? Dante again. But oh how my heart leaps up to think that never again shall I be harnessed to a long book. No. Always short ones in future. The long book still wont [sic] be altogether downed—its rever[b]erations grumble. Did I say—no the London days were too tight, too hot, & distracted for this book—that H. Brace wrote & said they were happy to find that The Years is the best selling novel in America? This was confirmed by my place at the head of the list in the Herald Tribune. They have sold 25,000—my record, easily.[33]

It would appear that Woolf was "harnessed" to not one but several "long books"—Dante's, her own, and the Victorian novels she sought to emulate—all yoked together in occupying the same duration of "London days," of pages written and read, and of progress made by leaps and lulls. Interestingly, the *Purgatorio* and *The Years* would come to share not only the same literal duration in Woolf's timeline for completing her novel but also the same sense of the duration as a central temporal mode, with Woolf at the same time employing methods from Victorian writing to extend a pattern of gradualist plotting in fiction.

In *The Years*, Eleanor begins reading the *Purgatorio* in the 1911 section of the novel alongside an assortment of nineteenth-century texts. If *The Years* shows the "nineteenth century going to bed," as one of Woolf's characters exclaims in the final chapter, in this scene Eleanor, our most constant representative from the Victorian era, is herself going to bed.

> She lay looking at the ceiling. A faint water mark appeared there....
>
> She opened the book that lay on the counterpane. She hoped it was *Ruff's Tour*, or *The Diary of a Nobody*; but it was Dante, and she was too lazy to change it. She read a few lines, here and there. But her Italian was rusty; the meaning escaped her. There was a meaning however; a hook seemed to scratch the surface of her mind . . .
>
> > For by so many more there are who say "ours"
> > So much the more of good doth each possess.
>
> . . . [T]he words did not give out their full meaning, but seemed to hold something furled up in the hard shell of the archaic Italian. I'll read it one of these days, she thought, shutting the book. When I've pensioned Crosby off, when . . . Should she take another house? Should she travel? . . . No, I don't mean to take another house, not another house, she thought, looking at the stain on the ceiling . . . Things can't go on forever, she thought. Things pass, things change, she thought, looking up at the ceiling. And where are we going? Where? Where? . . . she mused; made an effort; turned round, and blew out the candle. Darkness reigned.

Woolf gives a detailed, almost Victorian account of Eleanor's bedtime rituals, her reaching for a book, her staring at the ceiling, further evoking nostalgia for Victorian writing by displaying Eleanor's reading preferences: *Ruff's Tour* or *The Diary of a Nobody*. *The Diary of a Nobody*, a work that harkens back to a Dickensian model of caricature, is the fictional diary of an ordinary man named Charles Pooter, written by George and Wheedon Grossmith in 1892. It is characterized by a knowingly mundane sense of humor, and its equivalent today, in effect, would be the experience of reading a stranger's blog. The work spawned the term *pooter* or *pooterish*, which the *Oxford English Dictionary* defines as a "person resembling or reminiscent of the character Charles Pooter, esp. in displaying parochial self-importance, over-fastidiousness, or lack of imagination." Although no exact title matches *Ruff's Tour*, two possibilities exist. Woolf could be referring to either *Ruff's Beauties of Cheltenham*, a travel book published in 1806, or *Ruff's Guide to the Turf and the Sporting Life Annual*.[34] Both would be excellent literary equivalents to Ambien or another soporific of choice. Yet after taking pains to introduce these two literary possibilities, Woolf almost mischievously dismisses them. Instead of grabbing a book about turf or Cheltenham, or a fictional Victorian diary about the most ordinary of "ordinary people" (another title Woolf contemplated for *The Years*) Eleanor is disappointed to find that she has grasped Dante. We are then given two lines from the *Purgatorio* that emerge in compact and cryptic form: "For by so many more there are who say 'ours'/ So much the more of good doth each possess."

The scene raises several questions. Why does Woolf trouble to mention two Victorian books, only to displace these works with Dante? And why must Eleanor peruse these two lines from the *Purgatorio*, presented under the guise of being randomly chosen? Again, Woolf's contradictory goals for the novel—her attempt to both emulate and renovate nineteenth-century novels—may shed some light on Dante's cameo in this scene, for her method of capturing the prosaic combines the "objective, realistic . . . manner of Jane Austen" with "haze & dream & intoxication."[35] In other words, this scene bears out

Woolf's struggle to combine "fact" and "vision," binary terms that she would reframe in retrospectively assessing the novel as a struggle to represent "moments of non-being" and of "being."

In her memoir "A Sketch of the Past," Woolf introduces the elusive term "moments of non-being" to explain the quality of Victorian fiction that she wanted to capture in *The Years*:

> Often when I have been writing one of my so-called novels I have been baffled by this same problem; that is, how to describe what I call in my private shorthand—"non-being." Every day includes much more non-being than being. Yesterday, for example . . . I have already forgotten what Leonard and I talked about at lunch; and at tea; although it was a good day the goodness was embedded in a kind of nondescript cotton wool. This is always so. A great part of every day is not lived consciously. One walks, eats, sees things, deals with what has to be done; the broken vacuum cleaner; ordering dinner; writing orders to Mabel; washing; cooking dinner; bookbinding. When it is a bad day the proportion of non-being is much larger. I had a slight temperature last week; almost the whole day was non-being. The real novelist can somehow convey both sorts of being. I think Jane Austen can; and Trollope; perhaps Thackeray and Dickens and Tolstoy. I have never been able to do both. I tried—in Night and Day; and in The Years. But I will leave the literary side alone for the moment. (69)

The term "moments of non-being" would seem to describe our most ghostly experiences in daily life, those passing and forgettable periods of time that are both repetitious and accretive. The difficulty for Woolf in capturing these moments seems to be that once she illuminates the prosaic instants that we live unconsciously, they bloom into meaningful moments of perception instead. "Non-being" disappears, and we discover, in its place, the match alight in a crocus. If Woolf claims to have failed to capture "moments of non-being," it is perhaps because the idea of the "moment of non-being" is itself oxymoronic, the act of isolating a moment being more conducive to epiphanies than to lulls. Non-being would seem to be better illustrated over a stretch of time. One would almost expect Woolf to speak of "stretches of non-being" instead of "moments of non-being." Yet Woolf insists that this evanescent quality can be represented, that fiction extends the possibility of finding a valence at which non-being registers without converting itself into epiphanic significance. Judging by her "private shorthand," Woolf clearly wanted to accomplish two very different goals at once: to give readers her signature moments of introspection and revelation, and to show how these moments cohere to form a narrative of prosaic continuity. This seeming contradiction between suspension and progression lies at the heart of many afterlife conversion stories, including those of Dante and Newman. Woolf's concept of "moments of non-being" captures the same purgatorial paradox that each of these other works illustrates: a temporality that strives to be both the moment and the duration, both suspension and progression. Though Woolf asserts that she found these moments of non-being impossible to capture, leading to her professed "failure" to extend the techniques of "real novelists," these moments of prosaic importance nonetheless register in several of the more slippery epiphanies in *The Years*, including Eleanor's drowsy contemplation of Dante's *Purgatorio*.

If we are briefly presented with *Ruff's Tour* and *The Diary of a Nobody* as options, only to see them disappear from the novel, it is because these works represent and even parody the kind of prosaic Victorian writing that Woolf wanted to emulate in *The Years*. Their inclusion is a self-identification on Woolf's part but also a rejection. Woolf expressed wanting to transmute the prosaic into a larger political vision, and Dante's *Purgatorio* offers a hinge on which the prosaic turns into the progressive. Like the two unread Victorian books, the *Purgatorio* depicts travels and travails over extensive and monotonous turf, but in the *Purgatorio* alone monotony, repetition, and plodding are translated into a larger vision of redemption and conversion. Woolf consequently uses Dante to stage a small intervention in this bedtime scene, for the introduction of the *Purgatorio* immediately counters the pooterish quality of Eleanor's 1911 family visit. Her day of chatting with relatives is capped off by another relatively unexciting finale: Eleanor is going to sleep and staring at a stain on the ceiling. Yet this scene of the prosaic, the unremarkable, and the forgettable immediately flashes into a tentative "moment of being" when Eleanor reads from Dante. In other words, Victorian models of suspension are converted, via Dante, to Woolf's more sublime approach to the quotidian.

If, as Woolf wrote of the *Purgatorio* in her diary, Dante "[r]aises one out of the chatter of words," this is exactly the effect his *Purgatorio* has upon Eleanor, leading her away from the chatter of her internal monologue—her thoughts about her maid, Crosby, and the stain on the ceiling—to a moment of questioning that dramatically telescopes outward. And the questions Eleanor asks about the future, "where are we going?" echo Dante's quoted lines from the *Purgatorio*:

> For by so many more there are who say "ours"
> So much the more of good doth each possess.

In the *Purgatorio*, this quotation comes in Canto XV when Virgil tries to explain that in heaven there is no "fear of sharing."[36] But Virgil's explanation confuses Dante, who immediately asks,

> "How can it be that a good, distributed,
> can enrich a greater number of possessors
> than if it were possessed by few?"[37]

To which Virgil replies,

> "Because you still
> have your mind fixed on earthly things,
> you harvest darkness from the light itself."[38]

Like Dante, Eleanor harvests darkness from Virgil's abstract explanation of heavenly cooperation, the chapter concluding with Eleanor falling asleep to the words "[d]arkness reigned." She drops off before consciously grasping what she has read, only to wake in subsequent chapters onto the war years. Nevertheless, despite her foggy comprehension, the quoted lines from Dante's *Purgatorio* continue to dawn upon Eleanor as the novel progresses, appearing repeatedly in different forms as a choral refrain. The *Purgatorio* thereby comes to play a Virgilian role in the novel, guiding characters as they think about the potential for utopian change.

In reabsorbing Dante's *Purgatorio* into a novelistic model of purgatorial plotting based on Victorian fiction, Woolf places this first Dantean revelation on the borders of sleeping and waking. These are not Woolf's signature moments of being, a sublime approach to suspension. They recede into non-being quickly and without sufficient lyrical pause, defying recognition as tangible narrative "events." As opposed to the punctuated Joycean epiphanies of *Dubliners* or Clarissa Dalloway's lark and plunge, these revelations are forgotten even as they come into being. In this, they more closely resemble James's muted epiphanies, revelations swallowed up in retrospection, here reimagined as moments of transcendence that never escape from the context of normal life; Eleanor's visionary moments arise from the surrounding cotton wool but never fully differentiate themselves from its texture. Instead, it is the accumulation of characters pondering the future that begins to gather the force of an event in the novel, a group movement that Woolf spans over generations rather than isolating in moments. Dante, as Hermione Lee has noted, provides a "philosophical centre" for this movement, and Woolf uses the *Purgatorio* to capture a paradoxical temporality—a progression that is also a suspension—at the same time that she invokes specific Dantean images of redemption to create a more expansive secular and novelistic vision of the afterlife: a "New World" and "another life" that partakes of both Victorian retrospection and prophetic hopes for the future.[39]

Descent into the Underworld: The Air Raid

"Here's to the New World!" toasts Sara in the 1917 chapter of the novel, and her festive call to action gives an inchoate shape to Eleanor's thoughts on Dante from 1911. While writing this pivotal scene in 1935, Woolf records that she was searching for "some bridge" between her novel and the *Purgatorio:* "I see I am becoming a regular diariser. The reason is that I cannot make the transition from the Pargiters to Dante without some bridge. And this cools my mind. I am rather worried about the raid chapter: afraid if I compress & worry that I shall spoil. Never mind. Forge ahead, & see what comes next."[40] In forging ahead, what came next was a vision of a dinner party interrupted by an air raid. The prosaic form of the diary (her own this time rather than that of a "Nobody") not only helped Woolf transition between her two daily activities, reading and writing, but may have given her a template for her 1917 chapter in *The Years.* Woolf's diary from almost two decades earlier in December 1917 records an earlier reading of the *Purgatorio,* and she mentions being "past the middle" of it just before describing an air raid. The depiction of the dark winter night, of waking to sirens and going downstairs, contains many of the same images Woolf would include in her 1917 chapter in *The Years:*

> Nothing was further from our minds than air raids; a bitter night, no moon up till eleven.... [W]e went down stairs to sit with the servants.... Lottie having said she felt bad, passed on to a general rattle of jokes & comments which almost silenced the guns. They fired very quickly, apparently towards Barnes. Slowly the sounds got more distant, & finally ceased.... Servants apparently calm & even jocose. In fact one talks through the noise, rather bored by having to talk at 5 A.M. than anything else. Guns at one point so loud that the whistle of the shell going up followed the explosion. One window did, I think, rattle. Then silence. Cocoa was brewed for us, & off we went again.[41]

In *The Years,* Woolf would similarly focus on the overlap between the prosaic and the disruptive. The mixture of cocoa and whistling shells would become "pudding" and "gunfire" in the novel (290), and Woolf would similarly use conversation to create a sense of comfort and continuity, thereby overlaying the "rattle" of windows with the "general rattle of jokes." This scene in the novel also redoubles Eleanor's previous somnabulescent reading of Dante, for Eleanor philosophizes only as she wavers on the threshold of lucidity. This time, it is the effects of alcohol that both blur and dilate her focalizing lens: "She had not drunk wine for months. She was feeling already a little blurred; a little light-headed. It was the light after the dark; talk after silence; the war, perhaps, removing barriers" (284).[42] Wine, war, and conversation are grouped together as mind-altering substances, a trio that Woolf returns to when the dinner party guests discuss Eleanor's nephew North joining the war efforts as a soldier: "A little blur had come round the edges of things. It was the wine; it was the war. Things seemed to have lost their skins; to be freed from some surface hardness; even the chair with gilt claws, at which she was looking, seemed porous; it seemed to radiate out some warmth, some glamour, as she looked at it" (287). Objects provide a measure of what Eleanor calls "the space of time" (294), altering in her perception as the air raid intensifies. Eleanor suddenly feels "as if some dull bore had interrupted an interesting conversation. The colours began to fade. She had been looking at the red chair. It lost its radiance as she looked at it, as if a light had gone out" (288). The chair loses and regains its "surface hardness," coming in and out of focus in sync with time crystallizing into a moment defined and demarcated by gun booms: "'One, two, three, four,' she counted. 'On top of us,' said Nicholas" (291). Eleanor, her family, and their guests crouch together, their evening interrupted and descent proving to be the only option.

In this moment of waiting as the guns boom, any sense of "removing barriers" is accompanied by a heightened awareness of enclosure and separation. Far from dissolving boundaries altogether, the war centers Eleanor's thinking on the proliferation of barriers around her: "'Oughtn't we to ask people in?' she said, turning round.

But when she looked back the old woman had disappeared. So had the men. The street was now quite empty. The houses opposite were completely curtained. She drew their own curtain carefully. The table, with the gay china and the lamp, seemed ringed in a circle of bright light as she turned back" (289). Objects expose the ringing round of the moment, revealing a "space of time" that is limited and confining rather than revelatory. Woolf's "luminous halo" and "semi-transparent envelope" from "Modern Fiction" meet the resistance of a small circle of lamplight, a space curtained against the German planes above but also against neighbors across the street. Enclosure in all its forms dominates this scene—the cellar as a "cave of mud and dung," the circle of light against the dark, the moment counted down between bomb drops ("the moment" as a temporal unit here defined par excellence). As critics including Marcus and Levenback claim, Woolf's resistance to war and her resistance to the hierarchical structuring of plot do converge in *The Years*, nowhere more so than in this scene. The violently inscribed spot of time becomes the medium by which to critique a condition that Nicholas protests using spatial terms: the state of living with "each . . . his own little cubicle." If the "space of time" can open onto transcendence, as Eleanor experiences in wanting to "enclose the present moment; to make it stay; to fill it fuller and fuller, with the past, the present and the future" (428) in the "Present Day," it can also be constricted, denoting isolation and a failure of a Dantean imperative to "say ours," an imperative that Woolf shows her characters pursuing when they resurface.

When Eleanor finally ascends to consider the possibility of a "New World," Woolf continues to resist recurring to her usual arsenal of techniques for "removing barriers" as a writer. Stream of consciousness does not supersede conversation, and Eleanor and Nicholas must continue to fumble in the dark, at least metaphorically, groping their way toward a shared understanding by way of halting, if hopeful, discussion:

> "It is only a question," he said—he stopped. He drew himself close to her—"of learning. The soul . . . The soul—

> the whole being," he explained. He hollowed his hands as if to enclose a circle. "It wishes to expand; to adventure; to form—new combinations? . . . Whereas now . . . this is how we live, screwed up into one hard little, tight little—knot? . . . Each is his own little cubicle; each with his own cross or holy books, each with his fire, his wife . . ."
>
> When, she wanted to ask him, when will this New World come? When shall we be free? When shall we live adventurously, wholly, not like cripples in a cave? He seemed to have released something in her; she felt not only a new space of time, but new powers, something unknown within her . . . We shall be free, we shall be free, Eleanor thought. (297)

The two jointly reread Virgil's critique of the earthly "fear of sharing," performing the idea presented in the lines quoted from the *Purgatorio* in 1911: "For by so many more there are who say 'ours' / So much the more of good doth each possess." The form of their conversation can be said to enact Virgil's recommendation of coming together to say "ours"; by completing each other's sentences and piecing together fragmented and elliptical statements, they arrive at a collective if incomplete understanding. And although their conversation is framed in religious language, including a discussion of the nature of the "soul," this growing vision of what will be termed "another life" is not confined to holy books and crosses or to a religious sense of the afterlife. As Woolf questioned in a letter, "After all, does Dante's religion make any difference, or Milton's? No I think all convictions, if honestly held . . . strengthen the brew. . . . It works itself into the fibre, and one can't exclude it, isolate it, or criticise it. It becomes part and parcel of the whole."[43] Dante's journey to the afterlife becomes part and parcel of a larger secular vision in *The Years*, a possibility for utopia that her characters will continue to build upon and articulate as a group as the novel moves toward the "Present Day."

In the meantime, in 1917, the idea of a "New World" is interrupted,[44] unfinished, barred such that North will consider how to "down barriers" (410) more than a decade later in a "Present Day" in the 1930s, when he has returned from the front and established himself as a farmer. In 1917, he is about to descend into the trenches just as Eleanor descends into the cellar.[45] Woolf's signature method of fluidly shifting between perspectives deliberately does not play out here with the same formal panache exhibited in *Mrs. Dalloway*, *To the Lighthouse*, *The Waves*, and the final party scene of *The Years*. Instead, we are held more firmly than ever within the space of Eleanor's mind, this hardening of surfaces corresponding with the physical entrenchment of Woolf's characters. Woolf draws our attention to the interiority of characters outside of Eleanor, but she does so to show that she leaves these reservoirs untapped. From across the drawing room Eleanor observes that another character, Renny, "hoarded immense supplies of emotion that he could not express." When Eleanor says, "I'm glad I'm alive . . . Is that wrong Renny?" he at first "did not answer" and then gives a sudden reply: "I have spent the evening in a coal cellar while other people try to kill each other above my head" (295). Woolf never returns to give a privileged view into the fullness of what Renny "could not express," and the prophecy of Nicholas's opening proclamation—"'We all think the same things; only we do not say them"—will not find its formal equivalent until the 1930s, when characters share unspoken thoughts about "another life"—an extension of Eleanor's thinking about a "New World" in 1917.

Why does Woolf leave us, comparatively speaking, in the dark in 1917, with only Eleanor as our guiding point of view? Is this curtaining of consciousness a formal function of writing the only scene in the novel to explicitly portray the war? And why does Woolf select Eleanor, a middle-aged and at times "unregarded" woman, as the medium for understanding the events as they unfold? Reflecting upon the task of representing World War I, Woolf wrote of being "bored to death by war books,"[46] and she explained in a letter why she refused to give readers scenes of fighting in *The Years*: "I couldn't bring in the Front as you say partly because fighting isnt [*sic*] within my experience, as a woman; partly because I think action generally unreal. It's the thing we do in the dark that is more real; the thing we do because peoples [*sic*] eyes are on us seems to me histrionic, small boyish."[47] Instead of depicting fighting, Woolf presents this air raid scene as a series of musings made by the novel's spinster aunt, omitting other perspectives to an unusual degree. In thus plunging readers into a scene of darkness, she immerses us more fully in Eleanor's journey "into the whale."

The dark would appear to be Woolf's favored condition in *The Years*, judging by her tendency to deliver revelations on the thresholds of sleep, inebriation, and cellars. Her assessment of literary trends in "Modern Fiction" further confirms that she regarded "the dark" as the appropriate condition for contemporary writing: "The tendency of the moderns and part of their perplexity is no doubt that they find their interest more and more in [the] dark region of psychology." In subsequently praising Dostoevsky as the master of these "dark regions," Woolf gives what appears to be a road map for the shadowy techniques she would strive to employ in *The Years*. According to Woolf, Dostoevsky captures the

> labyrinth of the soul through which we have to grope our way. . . . Alone among writers Dostoevsky has the power of reconstructing those most swift and complicated states of mind, of rethinking the whole train of thought in all its speed now as it flashes into light, now as it lapses into darkness; for he is able to follow not only the vivid streak of achieved thought, but to suggest the dim and populous underworld of the mind's consciousness where desire and impulses are moving blindly beneath the sod. Just as we awaken ourselves from a trance of this kind by striking a chair or a table to assure ourselves of an external reality, so Dostoevsky suddenly makes us behold, for an instant, the face of his hero, or some object in the room.[48]

In *The Years*, Woolf also makes us behold "some object in the room," the red chair with its passing air of distinction and indistinction that defines the "instant" for us; she gives us an at once literal and metaphoric train of thought that "flashes into light . . . [and] lapses into darkness" as we follow Kitty to London (270–71). And even when Woolf resists floating between multiple points of view in the 1917 chapter, "impulses" and "desires" that never see the light of day come as small revelations, "moments of *non-being*" that resist the designation of "achieved thought," let alone of achieved "action," before slipping into darkness:

> "D'you mind air raids?" Nicholas asked. . . .
> "Not at all," she said. She would have crumbled a piece of bread to show him that she was at her ease; but as she was not afraid, the action seemed to her unnecessary. (289)

This is a curious vision of the mental action behind inaction, and perhaps as close to glimpsing a true "moment of non-being" as one finds in Woolf's fiction. The impulse to crumble bread follows a circuitous maze of conditions before becoming "unnecessary" as Woolf captures a remarkably complex and roundabout set of motives in a short space. The swift path of a contemplated act as it moves toward evanescence can be considered the real action of the moment, an example of how thinking is tantamount to acting in a novel in which "events" can be constituted by "impulses . . . moving blindly beneath the sod."

In rendering dim impulses that move beneath the sod in the 1917 chapter, Woolf would seem to be guided by her own praise of Dostoevsky, further incorporating underworld images into her novel that she used to characterize his fictions. In *The Years*, the "dark region of psychology" that she identifies as the terrain for modern fiction meets the "populous underworld" of a vast literary tradition: epic and sacred voyages to the afterlife. After Eleanor's first reading of Dante, darkness will reign many times before Woolf finally concludes the novel with the dawn, the entire work following the descent model that characterizes the 1917 chapter on a smaller scale. Taken in isolation, Woolf's air raid scene bears the same formal structure as the underworld interludes of Odysseus and Aeneas, as well as Jonah's journey inside the whale, the tension in Jonah's story between his two descents finding one of its most precise articulations in this scene. Over the course of the evening, Eleanor, our mature guide and figure of continuity from the Victorian age to the present, comes to identify a central conflict: the problem of craving safety and "immunity" while also seeking political participation, transformation, and a prophetic vision of a "New World":[49]

> Eleanor came into the drawing-room.... She lay back in the chair. Everything seemed to become quiet and natural again. A feeling of great calm possessed her. It was as if another space of time had been issued to her, but, robbed by the presence of death of something personal, she felt—she hesitated for a word—"immune"? (293–94)

> "They're only killing other people," said Renny savagely....
> "But you must let us think of something else," Eleanor protested. (293)

The something else Eleanor thinks of is the New World, but the question and conflict have already been framed: can the New World ever come into being alongside the desire for "immunity"? The need for action, the call to action, has been issued, but what form this action should take—both politically and in terms of a narrative plotting—remains cloudy, indeterminate, as incipient as Sara's rousing toast. The New World can never arise from a search for self-preservation above all else or from other forms of indifference, but a question lingers as to what kind of action might be demanded and how this action can itself be represented. Clearly, the action must take a different form than the militaristic movements that North recalls in the "Present Day" when he reflects upon the possibility for "another life; a different life. Not halls and reverberating megaphones; not marching in step after leaders, in herds, groups, societies caparisoned. No; to begin inwardly, and let the devil take the outer form. . . . Why not down barriers and simplify? . . . To keep the emblems and tokens of North Pargiter . . . but at the same time spread out, make a new ripple in human consciousness, be the bubble and the stream, the stream and the bubble—myself and the world together" (410). In this concluding "Present Day," Woolf opposes militaristic action to a method of "beginning inwardly" that she captures by renovating stories of descent. Eleanor's dream of a "New World" returns when she too thinks about "another life," this repeated wording also recalling the "afterlife" as a model for imagining inward change:

> There must be another life, she thought, sinking back into her chair, exasperated. Not in dreams; but here and now, in this room, with living people. . . . There must be another life, here and now, she repeated. This is too short, too broken. We know nothing, even about ourselves. We're only just beginning, she thought, to understand here and there. . . . [S]he felt that she wanted to enclose the present moment; to make it stay; to fill it fuller and fuller, with the past, the present and the future, until it shone, whole, bright, deep with understanding. (427)

Here we finally begin to see how the purgatorial idea of time as an apparent stasis that involves progression is justified for what Eleanor seeks to understand: over time it might be possible to attain a different state of being, one that can only ever be conceived of in accumulated present moments that form a duration. As in the 1917 chapter, the wording returns us to Dante's quotation, for Eleanor's reveries continue to take the plural form, being framed in terms of "we" and "ourselves." But unlike in 1917, this vision of positive group psychology emerges throughout the party scene on a formal level as well. Characters share phrases and overlap in their internal monologues, with Eleanor and North "beginning inwardly" by sharing thoughts about "another life." And, as when Eleanor and Nicholas muddle through their discussion of a "New World," Woolf's concept of "another life" is not limited to religious conceptions of the hereafter but includes the earthly present as well—what Eleanor calls the "here and now."

The phrase "here and now" holds special significance in the novel. Woolf had great trouble in selecting a title before settling upon *The Years*, "Here and Now" being one of her many early titles for the work. In total, the novel went through more than ten titles, including "The Next War," "The Pargiters," "Here and Now," "Time Passes," "In the Flesh," "Music," "Dawn," "Uncles and Aunts," "Sons and Daughters," "Daughters and Sons," "Ordinary People," "The Caravan," "Other People's Houses," and finally "The Years." It could be said that if one put all these titles together it would allow for a better sense of the scope of *The Years*, its constellated concerns, and its vast, almost Dickensian population of characters than its present title admits. The fact that Woolf almost chose "here and now" but then settled upon another unit of time—*The Years*—reveals in part how she was struggling to accommodate different temporal registers at once: both the moment and the duration, the very tension at the heart of her term "moments of non-being," and a tension inherited from Victorian novels. This insistence on simultaneously representing suspension and progression is what defines Woolf's purgatorial project of envisioning change on a grand scale but without the militancy of megaphones, marching, and societies caparisoned.

If Woolf presents us with a story that lacks revolutionary events and instead offers readers a gentle progression, she does so because this model of storytelling, which harkens back to Victorian fictions of midlife suspension, also allows her to create a vision of change without violent rupture, aiding her refusal to make wartime events the building blocks for her storyline. In Woolf's original conception of *The Years*, she set forth to write about the war, but as she stated, with the express goal of doing so "without death or violence." Like critics before me, I also see Woolf thinking about nonviolence on the level of literary form but view her references to the *Purgatorio* and to Victorian accounts of mature descent as her method for accomplishing this goal.

Woolf's vision of the journey to the underworld speaks to her interest in placing herself within the continuity of a literary tradition while at the same time renovating this tradition from the inside. Indeed, immersing oneself in tradition informs each legend of descent, for the communion with the past is allegorized in the hero's immersion in the realm of the dead—this place of death becoming a generative space: the birthplace of prophecy. In *The Years*, Woolf shows an understanding that for change to happen, something must be lost and old ways of life purged, but she frames the novel in her "contradictory" opening vision as one of renovation through preservation. This may explain why the act of reading, both Victorian literature and Dante's *Purgatorio*, figures so prominently in numerous scenes as a way to draw the past and the future together. Reading becomes a way to "enclose the present moment; to make it stay; to fill it fuller and fuller, with the past, the present and the future," and in one of the final scenes of the novel, Eleanor's niece Peggy echoes her aunt's earlier action by opening an unknown book at random in the novel's conclusion: "Peggy, marooned when the dance started, over by the book-case, stood as close to it as she could. In order to cover her loneliness she took down a book. . . . But I can't stand here admiring the binding, she thought. She opened it. He'll say what I'm thinking, she thought as she did so. Books opened at random always did" (383). As in the mystery of Eleanor's bedtime reading, a small detail about a character opening a book at random has much larger implications. In *The Years*, books opened at random always do.

CODA

Descent and Tradition

This is no deception sent by Queen Persephone,
this is just the way of mortals when we die.
Sinews no longer bind the flesh and bones together—
the fire in all its fury burns the body down to ashes
once life slips from the white bones, and the spirit,
rustling, flitters away . . . flown like a dream.
But you must long for the daylight. Go, quickly.
Remember all these things
So one day you can tell them to your wife.

—Homer, *The Odyssey*[1]

They went quietly down into the roaring streets, inseparable and blessed; and as they passed along in sunshine and in shade, the noisy and the eager, and the arrogant and the froward and the vain, fretted, and chafed, and made their usual uproar.

—Charles Dickens, *Little Dorrit*[2]

It had begun to snow again. He watched sleepily the flakes, silver and dark, falling obliquely against the lamplight. The time had come for him to set out on his journey westward.

Coda: Descent and Tradition

> Yes, the newspapers were right: snow was general all over Ireland. It was falling on every part of the dark central plain, on the treeless hills, falling softly upon the Bog of Allen and, farther westward, softly falling into the dark mutinous Shannon waves. It was falling, too, upon every part of the lonely churchyard on the hill where Michael Furey lay buried. It lay thickly drifted on the crooked corpses and headstones, on the spears of the little gate, on the barren thorns. His soul swooned slowly as he heard the snow falling faintly through the universe and faintly falling, like the descent of their last end, upon all the living and the dead.
>
> —James Joyce, "The Dead," in *Dubliners*[3]

Descending through caverns measureless to man, each of the authors in this study goes down to a sunless underworld in fictions about mature protagonists. The cadence of these downward voyages—calming, quieting, softly falling—guides readers into a realm of contemplative action. In this realm, conclusions resonate and the world's events, the strivings of war and romance, yield to the lull of the dead. But this time of retrospection, reflection, and stillness witnesses important stirrings as well: the beginnings of ascent and of journeys westward, plans of reclamation, and above all else, the injunction to tell future stories.

Visiting the Kingdom of the Dead, Odysseus finds that his mother cannot embrace him. In their mutual yearning she can only tell her story and his, leaving her son with words as the only possible connection: "Remember all these things / So one day you can tell them to your wife." The souls, each in turn, tell Odysseus their tales as the truths they must share, the individual histories becoming part of a larger insistence that he incorporate their narratives into his own. History and prophecy dwell close together in the underworld, for while Odysseus hears his future from Tiresias, the histories of the dead become an equal part of the "truths" he receives, and it is the communion with these shades that inspirits his future storytelling. His journey onward consequently entails retrospection and preservation as much as creativity, ingenuity, and iconoclasm. Whereas Orpheus may be punished for looking back to Hades, in Odysseus's trip to the underworld, he is enjoined to keep looking back even as he ascends and looks forward.

As a writer, Woolf understood the benefits of descending into the past as part of her ongoing creative project. To bring unseen actions to light, Woolf returns us to the underworld as a realm through which modern writers can perform afresh "the thing we do in the dark that is more real." As Woolf's mission of renovation through preservation reveals, for every account of the "anxiety of influence" there exists a counter story of the reassurance and refreshment that comes from immersing oneself in tradition: the vast kingdom of the dead. From the *Odyssey* to *Little Dorrit* to *Dubliners*, each descent becomes part of a torrent, a sacred river, whose origin and final destination lie together in an interior realm that storytellers seek out to find "a truth which this world will not give," as John Henry Newman wrote.[4] This truth is not one that can be rushed or extracted quickly, and just as Odysseus must listen to each shade with patience, absorbing their lessons one by one, so must Newman's Gerontius undergo an unhurried "school-time of contemplation" in his journey to the afterlife. This process, which Newman characterized as a "strange introversion," appears repeatedly in the different imagined descents in this study: Silas Marner's years as a miser, Gwendolen Harleth's purgatory on earth, Arthur Clennam's sentence in the Marshalsea, Stransom's years of altar building, and Eleanor Pargiter's contemplation of immunity and a New World during an air raid. The story of descent surfaces again and again, from Newman to Woolf, as the age-old quest story of maturity, a literary touchstone for imagining the most demanding feats of introspection and the transformations these feats enact.

In seeking a renewal born of conclusions, novels such as *The Years*, *Little Dorrit*, *Silas Marner*, and *Daniel Deronda* are consequently fed by the same archetypal wellspring. Dickens escorts readers downward while opening onto a vista, albeit sloping, of Amy and Arthur's shared life together, and the novel parts with a prophecy: the promise of their stories continuing to unfold in sunshine and in shade. This prophecy of gradual development is taken up in a variety of future fictions, the modest plot of uneventful development—at once prosaic and profound—being realized afresh in works devoted to the subtle and surprising adventures of mature life. In *Daniel Deronda*, Gwendolen's purgatory on the green earth awakens her burgeoning desire to "live to be one of the best of women, who make others glad that they were born," and Gwendolen concludes by looking forward to changes that can only be accomplished at a continued purgatorial pace. Gazing across vistas likewise dappled by sunshine and shade, Eleanor repeatedly descends into reflection in *The Years* and rises again to face the dawn, becoming a figure of retrospective prophecy in recurring to Dante to envision a "new world."

As the wellspring of history and prophecy, the underworld becomes a place for new beginnings as much as for the sense of an ending. Yet, as we have seen, these descents and the contemplative lulls they entail are not commonly recognized as adventures—or tales of advent—for according to Simmel, adventures are necessarily constrained to youth. This insistence that adventuring precedes and precludes maturity has been echoed in criticism that prizes the bildungsroman as the "symbolic form of modernity": "Achilles, Hector, Ulysses: the hero of the classical epic is a mature man, an adult. . . . This paradigm will last a long time . . . but with the first enigmatic hero of modern times, it falls apart. . . . Youth, or rather the European novel's numerous versions of youth, becomes for our modern culture the age which holds the 'meaning of life.'"[5] The argument has been that adventures of yore may have involved Achilles, Hector, and Ulysses but with the rise of the novel a critical change occurred, the "adventure" becoming the property of youthful figures such as Telemachus and Stephen Daedalus. When we leave Stephen in James Joyce's *A Portrait of the Artist* with the cry, "Welcome, O Life! I go to encounter for the millionth time the reality of experience and to forge in the smithy of my soul the uncreated conscience of my race,"[6] it is with the expectation that much of his story is yet to be told and that he has reserve adventures in abundance. Yet for all of Stephen's adventuring potential, Joyce approaches him only obliquely in *Ulysses*, leaving the youth still hammering away at the smithy of his soul by the novel's conclusion. It is Bloom, already formed and facing the external hammering of the world, Bloom with his ability to "pass on" from desolation and to continue relishing the world around him, that Joyce ultimately chooses for his grand experiment. But one may ask, why Leopold Bloom and not Stephen Hero?

In Moretti's argument, the choice of a mature hero in *Ulysses* provides evidence of a historical shift, a change in literary form corresponding with the violent rupture of historical events:

> If one wonders about the disappearance of the novel of youth, then, the youth of 1919—maimed, shocked, speechless, decimated—provide quite a clear answer. . . . If history can make cultural forms necessary, it can make them impossible as well, and this is what the war did to the *Bildungsroman*. (*Way*, 229–30)

> Stephen Hero—could hardly survive in the new context, and in an epoch-making change the decentered subjectivity of Leopold Bloom—this more adaptable, more "developed" form of bourgeois identity—set the pattern for twentieth-century socialization. (*Way*, 244)

Leopold Bloom marks the end of an era in this conception, coming into the spotlight at a time when "youth has become more vulnerable, and reluctant to grow," and the young protagonist faces "a world that is thoroughly indifferent to his personal development" (Moretti, *Way*, 233). This reading upholds a traditional division between the postwar modernist novel and the nineteenth-century bildungsroman, *Ulysses* signaling the death of the bildungsroman rather than serving as the continuance of another literary tradition that could equally vie for symbolic status: the story of mature life. This common account of the novel's history seems to follow the structure of the bildungsroman itself, ending with World War I in the same violent and abrupt manner that Maggie Tulliver and Julien Sorel conclude their stories. But the history of the novel could also be said to follow a different line of progression: a narrative of continuity exemplified in the mature fictions examined in this study.

To make a claim for continuity, as Woolf did, I follow the development of fictions of maturity through the twentieth century to offer a new way of viewing the historical development of the novel as a whole as being continuous across the wars. The story of maturity appears continuously in visions as varied as Newman's *The Dream of Gerontius* and Dickens's *Little Dorrit*, extending forward in time to more-recent novels such as *The Years*, a constancy existing between these narratives but also being thematized within them, for in each experience of purgatory, protagonists and their guiding authors recur to the past as a crucial source for future inspiration. This tale of renovation through preservation is another possible way of framing the history of the novel, for the story of maturity—with its rich history of descent and renewal—is an important literary tradition in the period between Newman and Joyce. These mature voyages, moreover, critically have come to inform our sense of the novel's most important features and developments: its ability to capture both suspension and progression at once, as well as its unique methods for representing the inner life as active, not simply as a passive state of reflection. From the nineteenth century onward, these novels offer an unbroken vision of the benefits of journeying "inside the whale," to where introspection is an important form of action. Considering the history of the novel as a mature progression in this manner allows for readings that acknowledge the differences that arise between works over time, even while it allows for a greater understanding of continuity that exists between works that—swooning, inseparable, and blessed—reveal the adventures of maturity.

Notes

Introduction: The Belly of Sheol

1. George Orwell, "Inside the Whale," in *George Orwell: A Collection of Essays* (New York: Harcourt, 1981), 244.

2. For useful working definitions of the differences between Sheol, hell, Hades, and purgatory, see Stephen Greenblatt, *Hamlet in Purgatory* (Princeton: Princeton University Press, 2001), 7; Jacques Le Goff, "Ancient Imaginings," in *The Birth of Purgatory*, trans. Arthur Goldhammer (Chicago: University of Chicago Press, 1981), 17–51; and David Lawrence Pike, *Passage through Hell: Modernist Descents, Medieval Underworlds* (Ithaca, NY: Cornell University Press, 1997). Zachary Hayes also offers useful definitions in *Visions of a Future: A Study of Christian Eschatology* (Wilmington, DE: Michael Glazier, 1989). In my considerations of nineteenth-century theological and literary texts, I use the terms *Hades, Sheol,* and *purgatory* interchangeably in cases where the primary sources under consideration also do so.

3. Jonah 2:2, in *The New Oxford Annotated Bible*, ed. Bruce M. Metzger and Roland E. Murphy (New York: Oxford University Press, 1994).

4. Robert Caserio's *Plot, Story and the Novel: From Dickens and Poe to the Modern Period* (Princeton: Princeton University Press, 1979) proves helpful in tracing a history of critical discomfort with plot lulls in the nineteenth and twentieth centuries.

5. In his essay, Orwell designates Henry Miller the prime example of Jonah-authorship, deeming him a writer who embodies lethargy between the wars and a "feminine" style of writing ("Inside the Whale," 243). Given this designation, it is not surprising that for Orwell the stomach becomes interchangeable with the womb only to remain, at best, a retentive digestive tract. This feminine gendering of uneventful literature raises problematic questions that are pursued throughout this book.

6. Anne-Lise François, *Open Secrets: The Literature of Uncounted Experience* (Stanford: Stanford University Press, 2008); Stefanie Markovits, *The Crisis of Action in Nineteenth-Century English Literature* (Columbus: Ohio State University Press, 2006), 4, 7. Markovits states that although she is "interested in passivity (and its relationship to passion)," she "often refer[s] instead to *inaction* . . . to stress the link between not doing and inner doings, between inaction and character" (6).

7. For an explication of *yarad*, see James S. Ackerman, "Jonah," in *The Literary Guide to the Bible*, ed. Robert Alter and Frank Kermode (Cambridge, MA:

Belknap Press of Harvard University Press, 1987), 234–44. Ackerman notes that *yarad* translates as "descent," and specifically as the descent into the afterlife.

8. Aristotle famously draws a boundary between action and character in the *Poetics* in stating, "Tragedy is not an imitation of persons, but of actions and of life. Well-being and ill-being reside in action, and the goal of life is an activity, not a quality; people possess certain qualities in accordance with their character, but they achieve well-being or its opposite on the basis of how they fare.... [T]here could not be a tragedy without action, but there could be one without character" (11–12). In this hierarchy, "Plot is the source and (as it were) the soul of tragedy; character is second" (12). See Aristotle's *Poetics*, trans. Malcolm Heath (New York: Penguin Classics, 1997).

9. Henry James, *The Middle Years* (New York: C. Scribner's Sons, 1917), 1. *The Middle Years* is James's incomplete and posthumously published autobiography, which opens with an anecdotal account of how his twenty-sixth year "was to mark the end of his youth" (1). Of course, no sooner does James delineate this clear end to youth and beginning of midlife than he qualifies his (or anyone's) ability to draw such a firm dividing line: "Everything depends in such a view on what one means by one's youth—so shifting a consciousness is this, and so related at the same time to many different matters. We are never old, that is we never cease easily to be young, for *all* life at the same time: youth is an army, the whole battalion of our faculties and our freshnesses, our passions and our illusions, on a considerably reluctant march into the enemy's country, the country of the general lost freshness" (1–2). James's fluid definition of "the middle years" serves as a useful guide for my own exploration of adulthood and midlife in literature of the nineteenth and early twentieth century in this study. Although including set ages as parameters for a definition of "maturity" is not productive, I take this period of adulthood construed broadly to range from a character's late teens and early twenties (as in the case of George Eliot's Gwendolen Harleth) to a character's experience of being in his or her fifties and sixties (to use Henry James's George Stransom and Lambert Strether as an upper end in terms of age). I thus use the term *maturity* to include both early adulthood—the period in which most bildungsromane conclude—and midlife or middle age, "middle age" being a concept that sociologists and, more recently, literary critics trace back to having originated in the Victorian era. See Kay Heath, *Aging by the Book: The Emergence of Midlife in Victorian Britain* (Albany: SUNY Press, 2009); and Patricia Cohen, *In Our Prime: The Invention of Middle Age* (New York: Scribner, 2012).

10. This tendency to marginalize novels of maturity holds true even for studies devoted to Victorian representations of "middle age." Scholars such as

Heath and Cohen compellingly argue for the rise of "middle age" as a concept originating in the Victorian era, but the broad formal implications of this Victorian preoccupation with midlife have yet to be considered. Instead, novels that represent middle age are often framed as a minor subgenre, having little influence on our sense of novelistic plotting when compared to the bildungsroman.

11. For examples, see Jed Esty, "The Colonial Bildungsroman: *The Story of an African Farm* and the Ghost of Goethe," *Victorian Studies* 49, no. 3 (2007): 407–30; Esty, *Unseasonable Youth: Modernism, Colonialism, and the Fiction of Development* (Oxford: Oxford University Press, 2012); and Susan Fraiman, "*The Mill on the Floss*, the Critics, and the Bildungsroman," *PMLA* 108, no. 1 (January 1993): 136–50.

12. Henry James, "*Daniel Deronda*: A Conversation," *Atlantic Monthly* 38 (December 1876): 684; George Gissing, *Collected Works of George Gissing on Charles Dickens*, vol. 2, ed. Simon J. James (Surrey, UK: Grayswood Press, 2004), 54; H. G. Wells, *Boon* (1915), vol. 13 of *The Works of H. G. Wells* (London: Unwin, 1925), 456.

13. My insistence on framing narrative lulls as productive places of development and inward action owes much to Caroline Levine's recuperation of suspense as a productive mode in nineteenth-century writing, one that engenders active inquiry rather than passivity and submission. See Levine, *The Serious Pleasures of Suspense* (Charlottesville: University of Virginia Press, 2003).

14. Charles Dickens, *David Copperfield* (New York: Penguin Classics, 2004), 703.

15. Ellen Wood, *East Lynne* (Oxford: Oxford University Press, 2008).

16. William Makepeace Thackeray, *Vanity Fair* (New York: Penguin Classics, 2003), 677.

17. Franco Moretti, *The Way of the World: The Bildungsroman in European Culture*, trans. Albert Sbragia (New York: Verso, 1987), 5.

18. The novel is directly pitted against the epic in Bakhtin's account, for it is "the sole genre that continues to develop, that is as yet uncompleted," while the epic is presented as a "genre that has not only long since completed its development . . . [but also] is already antiquated." Mikhail Bakhtin, *The Dialogic Imagination* (Austin: University of Texas Press, 1981), 4.

19. Georg Lukács, *The Theory of the Novel*, trans. Anna Bostock (Cambridge, MA: MIT Press, 1971), 86.

20. Esty maintains Moretti's fundamental assertion that the bildungsroman is the form that expresses the individual's struggle with (and eventual integration into) modern capitalist society, although he shows how "colonialism disrupts the bildungsroman and its humanist ideals" ("Colonial Bildungsroman," 411), leading to stories of arrested development and perpetual immaturity. This concept of arrested storytelling is very much in keeping with previous discussions of plot extrapolated from the bildungsroman—discussions

that likewise preclude theorizing extreme gradualism as a distinctly novelistic narrative mode.

21. See Virginia Woolf, "George Eliot," *Times Literary Supplement*, November 20, 1919. For Woolf, this novel was not only *for* grown-up people but also *about* grown-up people and their interests and dilemmas. As she makes clear, Woolf believed that Eliot's novels were uniquely the product of a woman who "never wrote a story until she was thirty-seven," and consequently, even her bildungsroman, *The Mill on the Floss*, is about the problems of adulthood and not simply of girlhood: "[B]efore George Eliot knows what has happened she has a full-grown woman on her hands demanding what neither gipsies, nor dolls, nor St. Ogg's itself is capable of giving her."

22. Marianne Hirsch, "Defining Bildungsroman as a Genre," *PMLA* 91, no. 1 (January 1976): 122.

23. The marginalization of novels about maturity is especially evident in desire-driven theories of plot that combine structuralist and psychoanalytic approaches, like Peter Brooks's *Reading for the Plot: Design and Intention in Narrative* (New York: A. A. Knopf, 1984), 5.

24. Ian Watt, *The Rise of the Novel: Studies in Defoe, Richardson, and Fielding* (Berkeley: University of California Press, 1957), 22. Watt makes this point by way of citing T. H. Green's "Estimate of the Value and Influence of Works of Fiction in Modern Times" (1862), in *Works of Thomas Hill Green*, ed. R. L. Nettleship (London: Longmans, 1888), 3:36.

25. George Levine, *The Realistic Imagination* (Chicago: University of Chicago Press, 1981), 146.

26. Amanpal Garcha, *From Sketch to Novel: The Development of Victorian Fiction* (Cambridge: Cambridge University Press, 2009).

27. Critics positing the existence of "female" plots of desire and formation gesture at alternative ways of framing the event as a narrative unit that are useful to this study. Susan Winnett responds to Brooks's work by suggesting that "female pleasure might have a different plot" ("Coming Unstrung: Women, Men, Narrative, and Principles of Pleasure," *PMLA* 105 [1990]: 507). The cyclical view of plot and reader pleasure that Winnett describes opens room for discussions of gradual plotting as a form of narrative pleasure. Indeed, her focus on George Eliot's *Romola*, a notoriously uneventful novel featuring a mature heroine, speaks to the central place of mature fictions in rethinking desire-based theories of plot. Scholars who set out to define a separate "female" bildungsroman (as in *The Voyage In: Fictions of Female Development*, ed. Elizabeth Abel, Marianne Hirsch, and Elizabeth Langland [Hanover, NH: Dartmouth University Press, 1983]) likewise chafe against eventful models of plotting based on male ambition and

arousal, though they continue a longstanding tradition of using the bildungsroman as the generic touchstone for all discussions of plot.

28. George Eliot, *Daniel Deronda* (New York: Penguin Classics, 1995), 705.

29. George Eliot, *Middlemarch* (New York: W. W. Norton, 1999), 305.

30. Henry James, *Literary Criticism: French Writers, Other European Writers; The Prefaces to the New York Edition* (New York: Library of America, 1984), 1250.

31. G. K. Chesterton, *The Victorian Age in Literature* (New York: Henry Holt, 1913), 17.

32. John Stuart Mill, "The Spirit of the Age," in *The Spirit of the Age: Victorian Essays*, ed. Gertrude Himmelfarb (New Haven, CT: Yale University Press, 2007), 53.

33. Caroline Levine and Mario Ortiz-Robles invite "subtler, more fine-grained and gradualist accounts of political and cultural experience," stating that these studies are "needed in order to address critically the discourse of 'crisis' we all too often leave unexamined." Levine and Ortiz-Robles, introduction to *Narrative Middles: Navigating the Nineteenth-Century British Novel*, ed. Levine and Ortiz-Robles (Columbus: Ohio State University Press, 2011), 2. This book strives, like several of the essays that compose that recent volume, to provide a new way of understanding both an emergent sense of Victorian historical consciousness and the ways that this consciousness was reflected in, and developed through, the art of fictional representation.

34. Walter Pater, *Plato and Platonism: A Series of Lectures* (London: Macmillan, 1895), 15.

35. William Wordsworth, *The Prelude: The Four Texts (1798, 1799, 1805, 1850)* (New York: Penguin Classics, 1995), 441, lines 108–9.

36. Gillian Beer, *Darwin's Plots: Evolutionary Narrative in Darwin, George Eliot and Nineteenth-Century Fiction* (Cambridge: Cambridge University Press, 2000); George Levine, *Darwin and the Novelists* (Cambridge, MA: Harvard University Press, 1988).

37. Geoffrey Rowell, *Hell and the Victorians: A Study of Nineteenth-Century Theological Controversies Concerning Eternal Punishment and the Future Life*, Oxford Scholarly Classics (Oxford: Clarendon Press, 1974), 31.

38. See Erich Auerbach, "Odysseus's Scar," in *Mimesis: The Representation of Reality in Western Literature* (Princeton: Princeton University Press, 1953), 3–23. Scholarly sources indicate that the lyric was most likely interpolated later and added to the prose narrative, a theory that helps explain the rapid tense shifts and the juxtaposition of a retrospective perspective with the immediacy of the thanksgiving prayer.

39. See John Henry Newman, "The Intermediate State," Sermon 25, in *Parochial and Plain Sermons* (London: J. G. and F. Rivington, 1891), 3:377.

40. Charlotte Brontë, *Villette* (Oxford: Oxford World's Classics, 2008), 413.

41. Dante Alighieri, *Inferno*, trans. Robert Hollander and Jean Hollander (New York: Anchor Books, 2000), 2, line 1.

CHAPTER ONE
"Strange Introversions"
Newman, Mature Conversion, and the Poetics of Purgatory

1. John Henry Newman, *Apologia Pro Vita Sua*, ed. David J. DeLaura (New York: W. W. Norton, 1968), 16.

2. Critics often tie Newman's writing to Romantic concepts of *bildung*, but his fiction and autobiographical writing reveal a uniquely Victorian approach to gradual development. For discussions of Newman's channeling of Romantic ideas of *bildung*, see G. B. Tennyson, *Victorian Devotional Poetry: The Tractarian Mode* (Cambridge, MA: Harvard University Press, 1981), 192; Gregory H. Goodwin, "Keble and Newman: Tractarian Aesthetics and the Romantic Tradition," *Victorian Studies* 30, no. 4 (Summer 1987): 475–94; Philip C. Rule, *Coleridge and Newman: The Centrality of Conscience* (New York: Fordham University Press, 2004).

3. Stephen Prickett, *Romanticism and Religion: The Tradition of Coleridge and Wordsworth in the Victorian Church* (Cambridge: Cambridge University Press, 1976), 153; George Levine, *The Boundaries of Fiction* (Princeton: Princeton University Press, 1968), 173.

4. In *Aging by the Book*, Heath "explores the rise of midlife in Victorian Britain as a new way of understanding the human life span" (3), urging that the onset of midlife, as she construes it, starts, approximately, in the forties for men, the age at which Newman converted to Catholicism, a period of midlife conversion captured in the *Apologia*.

5. Nicholas Wiseman, "Loss and Gain," *Dublin Review* 24, no. 47 (March 1848): 218.

6. The first two quotations are from Newman, "Intermediate State," 377. He delivered this sermon as an Anglican minister before his conversion to Catholicism but published it most widely in 1868, long after he had abandoned the Church of England (in 1845). The third quotation, "strange introversion," is from *The Dream of Gerontius* (14). The poem was initially published in May and June 1865 in the Catholic periodical *The Month* in two installments. The first edition was subsequently published in 1866 (London: Burns, Lambert and Oates, 1866). Pagination from this first edition is hereafter cited parenthetically in the text.

7. For one such study that explores Newman's changing public life and the rise of liberal tolerance in the 1860s, see Erik Sidenvall, *After Anti-Catholicism?*

John Henry Newman and Protestant Britain, 1845–c. 1890 (London: T and T Clark International, 2005). Mark Knight and Emma Mason survey the scope of ritualism in Victorian poetry in *Nineteenth-Century Religion and Literature: An Introduction* (Oxford: Oxford University Press, 2006), 106–19.

8. Sidenvall, *After Anti-Catholicism*, 90 and 99.

9. Michael Wheeler, *Death and the Future Life in Victorian Literature and Theology* (Cambridge: Cambridge University Press, 1990), 305.

10. Algernon Charles Swinburne, *Miscellanies* (London: Chatto and Windus, 1886), 146, reprinted from *The Nineteenth Century*, May 1884.

11. Francis Hastings Doyle, *Dr. Newman's* Dream of Gerontius *Lectures Delivered before the University of Oxford, 1868* (London: Macmillan, 1869), 122.

12. Charles Kingsley and Frances Eliza Grenfell Kingsley, *Charles Kingsley: His Letters and Memories of His Life* (New York: Scribner, Armstrong, 1877), 270.

13. Charles Kingsley, "The Irrationale of Speech," *Fraser's Magazine* 60 (July 1859): 13.

14. Charles Kingsley, review of *The Dream of Gerontius*, by John Henry Newman, *Independent* 24, no. 1214 (March 7, 1872): 3.

15. As Andrew H. Miller notes in *The Burdens of Perfection: On Ethics and Reading in Nineteenth-Century British Literature* (Ithaca, NY: Cornell University Press, 2010), the "hazard in studying Newman lies in his apparent distance from current critical concerns" (143). Works as varied as Miller's *Burdens of Perfection*, Gauri Viswanathan's *Outside the Fold: Conversion, Modernity, and Belief* (Princeton: Princeton University Press, 1998), and James Eli Adams's *Dandies and Desert Saints: Styles of Victorian Masculinity* (Ithaca, NY: Cornell University Press, 1995) offer compelling arguments for Newman's influence on contemporary thought and his continued interest to literary critics. Although these studies recuperate Newman's prose, they exclude his poetry for still being, it would seem, too distant from current critical concerns, a trend this chapter addresses.

16. This emphasis on consolation appears frequently in scholarly work on Tractarian poetry. In reading John Keble's *Lectures on Poetry*, Knight and Mason show how for Tractarian poets, "Poetry does not simply offer relief, but is actually defined *as* relief, soothing the harried individual by producing tender feelings within the heart and guiding and composing the mind to worship and prayer" (*Nineteenth-Century Religion*, 101). See also G. B. Tennyson's analysis of the limitations of the "soothing" quality of Tractarian poetry (*Victorian Devotional Poetry*, 190).

17. Brontë, *Villette*, 413.

18. Alison Milbank's *Dante and the Victorians* (Manchester: Manchester University Press, 1998) and David Moldstad's "The Dantean Purgatorial Metaphor in

Daniel Deronda" (in *Papers on Language and Literature: A Journal for Scholars and Critics of Language and Literature* 19, no. 2 [1983]: 183–98) present a wealth of Dantean allusions to purgatory in Victorian fiction. However, many of these allusions to Dante's *Purgatorio* were infused with a uniquely Victorian model of Judgment found in Tract 90 and *The Dream*.

19. Newman, "Intermediate State," 408.

20. As early as 1825, Newman had proposed a tempered vision of Judgment that he called the "Intermediate State." Newman's early work on the intermediate state can be found in unpublished sermons housed at the Birmingham Oratory. The earliest sermon on the subject, Sermon No. 110, "On the Feelings Produced in Common by All Revelation" was delivered on October 16, 1825. Also see Sermon No. 266, delivered on November 1, 1830, and subsequently on November 1, 1833, and November 1, 1838. For a brief discussion of these unpublished sermons, see Colm McKeating, *Eschatology in the Anglican Sermons of John Henry Newman* (Lampeter, UK: Mellen Research University Press, 1992), 224–37.

21. Newman, "Intermediate State," 377; Newman, *An Essay on the Development of Christian Doctrine* (South Bend, IN: Notre Dame University Press, 2005), 393. Also see Newman's 1853 poem "The Golden Prison," *Verses on Various Occasions* (London: Burns, Oates and Co., 1880), 299–300.

22. Rowell, *Hell and the Victorians*, 178–79.

23. See Greenblatt, *Hamlet in Purgatory*; and Le Goff, *Birth of Purgatory*.

24. For more religious historical background, see Rowell, *Hell and the Victorians*; and Wheeler, *Death and the Future Life*. For an early twentieth-century reflection on Victorian literature and religious history, see Joseph Ellis Baker's *The Novel and the Oxford Movement* (Princeton: Princeton University Press, 1932).

25. For historical background on anti-Catholic movements in England and the Catholic Emancipation, see D. G. Paz, *Popular Anti-Catholicism in Mid-Victorian England* (Stanford: Stanford University Press, 1992).

26. Newman, *Tract XC: On Certain Passages in the XXXIX Articles* . . . (London: Walter Smith, 1866), 25. The model presented in Tract 90 extended Saint Catherine of Genoa's conception of the afterlife as a place for gentle growth rather than punishment. See also Saint Catherine of Genoa (1447–1510), *Purgation and Purgatory: The Spiritual Dialogue*, trans. Serge Hughes (New York: Paulist Press, 1979).

27. Arthur Williamson, B.D., late scholar and theological prizeman of Christ's College, Cambridge, vicar of St. James's Norlands, *The Intermediate State: An Essay upon the Relation of Prayer to a Conscious and Progressive Life in the Intermediate State.* (London: Wells Gardner, Darton, 1890), 37–38.

28. In *The Writing of History* (trans. Tom Conley [New York: Columbia University Press, 1988]), Michel de Certeau discusses how *parousia* structures historical narratives.

29. As Lawrence remarked: "You see, it was really George Eliot who started it all. . . . It was she who started putting all the action inside. Before, you know, with Fielding and the others, it had been outside." *D. H. Lawrence: A Personal Record*, ed. Jessie Chambers (Cambridge: Cambridge University Press, 1980), 105.

30. Karel Hanhart (te Telburg), "The Intermediate State in the New Testament" (PhD diss. in theology, University of Amsterdam, 1966), 1.

31. John Thomas Pickering, *When a Man Dies Where Does He Go? or, Some Things about the Intermediate State, by a Priest of the Church of England* (London: Skeffington and Son, 1902), 89. Additionally, numerous sermons from the period emerge as defensive justifications of the intermediate state as a state differing from models of Catholic purgatory. For example, as one clergyman named R. E. Sanderson wrote in 1896, "What the Twenty-second Article condemns is not any and every conceivable doctrine concerning Purgatory, but the Romish doctrine only." See R. E. Sanderson, D.D., vicar of Holy Trinity, Hastings, canon residentiary of Chichester Cathedral; formerly head master of Lancing College, *The Life of the Waiting Soul in the Intermediate State* (London: Gardner, Darton, 1896), 81.

32. For further considerations of "soul sleep" in a nineteenth-century literary context, see Milbank, *Dante and the Victorians* for a discussion of its Swedenborgian and Calvinist roots (167, 171); and Jerome McGann, "The Religious Poetry of Christina Rossetti," *Critical Inquiry* 10, no. 1 (September 1983): 127–44.

33. Richard Whately, D.D., archbishop of Dublin, *A View of the Scripture Revelations Concerning a Future State* (Philadelphia: Lindsay and Blakiston, 1856), 80.

34. Sophia L. Scott, *Catholic Views as Held by Our Church in All Ages, on Praying for the Departed Soul in the Intermediate State, and Communion of Saints* (London: James Ivison, Printer, 1876), 1–21; for the quotations, see pages 10 and 9 respectively.

35. William Ince, D.D., canon of Christ Church, *The Future Life—The Intermediate State—Heaven: Two Sermons Preached in the Cathedral Church of Christ, Oxford, in September, 1895* (London: James Parker, 1895), 29.

36. Edward Henry Bickersteth, vicar of Christ Church, Hampstead, and bishop of Exeter, *The Shadowed Home and the Light Beyond* (London: Sampson Low, Marston, Low, and Searle, 1875), 193. Bickersteth also wrote a vision of Judgment that was published shortly after Newman's *The Dream of Gerontius*. See Bickersteth's 1866 *Yesterday, To-day, and Forever, in Twelve Books* (New York: Robert Carter and Brothers, 1875) as well as his treatise *The Blessed Dead: What Does Scripture Reveal of Their State before the Resurrection?* (London: John F. Shaw, 1863). Michael Wheeler examines Bickersteth's life and works in relation to

Newman. See Wheeler, *Heaven, Hell and the Victorians* (Cambridge: Cambridge University Press, 1994), 40.

37. John Henry Newman, *Poetry with Reference to Aristotle's* Poetics, ed. Albert S. Cook (Boston: Ginn, 1891).

38. Reflecting on critical trends in 1957, Norman Friedman wrote of how Newman's essay on Aristotle set forth an assessment that governed modern takes on the *Poetics*. In "Newman, Aristotle, and the New Criticism: On the Modern Element in Newman's Poetics" (*PMLA* 81, no. 3 [June 1966]: 261–71), Friedman sees modern readings failing to move past Newman's approach: "Newman, then, is with the moderns both in how he takes Aristotle and in how he mistakes him" (264).

39. Alan G. Hill traces the influence of Romantic predecessors on Newman in "Three 'Visions' of Judgement: Southey, Byron, and Newman," *Review of English Studies*, n.s., 41, no. 163 (August 1990): 334–50.

40. Newman, *Poetry*, 10.

41. As Hannah Arendt writes, "This unchangeable identity of the person, though disclosing itself intangibly in act and speech, becomes tangible only in the story of the actor's and speaker's life; but as such it can be known, that is, grasped as a palpable entity only after it has come to its end. In other words, human essence—not human nature in general (which does not exist) nor the sum total of qualities and shortcomings in the individual, but the essence of who somebody is—can come into being only when life departs, leaving behind nothing but a story. Therefore whoever consciously aims at being 'essential,' at leaving behind a story and an identity which will win 'immortal fame,' must not only risk his life, but expressly choose, as Achilles did, a short life and premature death. Only a man who does not survive his one supreme act remains the indisputable master of his identity and possible greatness." Arendt, *The Human Condition* (Chicago: University of Chicago Press, 1998), 193.

42. Newman, *Poetry*, 4.

43. Isobel Armstrong, *Victorian Poetry: Poetry, Poetics and Politics* (New York: Routledge, 1993), 175.

44. See Monique R. Morgan, *Narrative Means, Lyrical Ends: Temporality in the Nineteenth-Century British Long Poem* (Columbus: Ohio State University Press, 2009). For further discussions of narrative lulls and poetic suspension, also see Markovits, *Crisis of Action*; and François, *Open Secrets*.

45. For a brief comparison of the two, see Wheeler, *Heaven, Hell*, 223.

46. T. S. Eliot famously found the presentation of doubt to be the hallmark of *In Memoriam*'s greatness and likewise found the speaker's journey toward faith to be unconvincing. See Eliot, *Essays Ancient and Modern* (London: Faber and

Faber, 1936). For a few exemplary passages in which Hallam's potential existence after death is questioned, see stanzas XXXVIII, "But in the songs I love to sing / A doubtful gleam of solace lives. / If any care for what is here / Survive in spirits render'd free / Then are these songs I sing of thee / Not all ungrateful to thine ear"; XLIII, "If Sleep and Death be truly one / And every spirit's folded bloom / Thro' all its intervital gloom / In some long trance should slumber on"; and LIV, "So runs my dream: but what am I? / An infant crying in the night: / An infant crying for the light: / And with no language but a cry" in *Tennyson: A Selected Edition*, ed. Christopher Ricks (Berkeley: University of California Press, 1989), 331–484.

47. Herbert F. Tucker, "From Monomania to Monologue: 'St. Simeon Stylites' and the Rise of the Victorian Dramatic Monologue," *Victorian Poetry* 22 (1984): 124.

48. Esther R. B. Pese attributes the popularity of the *Dream* to a surge in midcentury death poetry, citing Tennyson's *In Memoriam* as a main contributing factor ("A Suggested Background for Newman's 'Dream of Gerontius,'" *Modern Philology* 46, no. 2 [November 1949]: 110). One could also cite Bickersteth's *Yesterday, To-day, and Forever* as part of this trend, though Bickersteth's epic poem bypasses purgatory in favor of a millennial vision.

49. Ian Ker, *John Henry Newman: A Biography* (Oxford: Oxford University Press, 2009), 741; Wilfrid Phillip Ward, *The Life of John Henry Cardinal Newman*, vol. 2 (London: Longmans, Green, 1912), 514.

50. See William E. A. Axon, "The 'Dream of Gerontius.'" *The Library: A Quarterly Review of Bibliography and Library Lore*, n.s., 6 (1905): 281–87. Gordon Tidy additionally gives a publication history of *The Dream* in his introduction to *The Dream of Gerontius* (London: John Lane, Bodley Head, 1916), 42.

51. Ward, *Life of . . . Cardinal Newman*, 357. Before Newman received Gordon's copy, several of its keepers copied the general's markings into multiple other editions and shared these copies with other people. See Axon, "The Dream of Gerontius," 285–86, and Ker, *John Henry Newman*, 741. Eventually, Gordon's original copy ended up in the Manchester Free Library, at which point Axon encountered it and gave a paper on it in 1888, subsequently printing this lecture and making available all the passages General Gordon marked. Axon's account of the history of the poem was later published in his piece "On General Gordon's Copy of Newman's *Dream of Gerontius*," *Manchester Quarterly: A Journal of Literature and Art* 8 (January 1889).

52. See Knight and Mason, *Nineteenth-Century Religion*, 107.

53. See Christina Rossetti's "The General Assembly and Church of the Firstborn" (line 7), "The Joy of Saints" (lines 1–2) and "Advent Sunday" (line 19),

respectively, in *The Complete Poems*, ed. R. W. Crump and Betty S. Flowers (New York: Penguin, 2001).

54. On the subject of lyrical suspension, see Northrop Frye, "Approaching the Lyric," in *Lyric Poetry: Beyond New Criticism*, ed. Chaviva Hošek and Patricia Parker (Ithaca, NY: Cornell University Press, 1985), 31–37. Frye identifies lyric with meditation, describing "the lyric of mental focus" as a "kind of meditative intensity" in which "the mind is identified with what it contemplates" (33). Morgan further defines lyric against narrative movement: "Lyric creates a timeless present, an indefinitely suspended moment, which contrasts with narrative's past progression of events" (*Narrative Means, Lyrical Ends*, 9).

55. Jonathan Culler, *The Pursuit of Signs: Semiotics, Literature, Deconstruction* (Ithaca, NY: Cornell University Press, 1981), 152.

56. Wheeler discusses this passage and identifies Newman's central technique as an ability to represent an "eternal now within the limits of language" (*Death and the Future Life*, 319–20). George Levine views Newman's overall approach as a drive toward stasis and permanence: "Newman insisted on change only to get as close as possible to the unchanging" (*Boundaries of Fiction*, 187). Unchanging as *The Dream* may appear, the poem seeks to capture gradual development, not stasis. As Gerontius's Soul observes: "I hear no more the busy beat of time / .... Nor does one moment differ from the next" (*Dream*, 14).

57. Robert Browning, "Johannes Agricola in Meditation," in *Selected Poems by Robert Browning*, ed. Daniel Karlin (New York: Penguin, 1989), 19; Alfred Lord Tennyson, "St. Simeon Stylites," in *Tennyson: A Selected Edition*, 124–35. Line numbers are cited parenthetically in the text.

58. Tucker, "From Monomania to Monologue," 132.

59. *Tennyson: A Selected Edition*, 245.

60. Tucker, "From Monomania to Monologue," 124.

61. G. B. Tennyson, *Victorian Devotional Poetry*, 187.

62. Newman's waning popularity coincided with a twentieth-century surge in scholarly work on two other poets influenced by Tractarianism and by Newman: Christina Rossetti and Gerard Manley Hopkins. Yet Newman's poems are rarely considered alongside even the works of these two poets. G. B. Tennyson (in *Victorian Devotional Poetry*, 197–211) and Jill Muller (in *Gerard Manley Hopkins and Victorian Catholicism: A Heart in Hiding* [New York: Routledge, 2003]) offer insight into Newman's declining literary critical trajectory, as well as the curious omission of his poetry over time despite his influence. We learn from Diane D'Amico and David A. Kent's "Rossetti and the Tractarians" (*Victorian Poetry* 44, no. 1 [2006]: 93–103) that Rossetti owned a copy of *The Dream of Gerontius* and wrote a poem for Newman after his death. Muller further claims, "Hopkins draws

on Newman's imagery of purgatorial suffering to describe the spiritual agonies that laid waste to his earthly life during the Dublin years" (*Gerard Manley Hopkins*, 128). Consolation and influence have been posed as the twentieth-century legacies of Newman's poetry. I propose that Newman's poetic conciliation—wrought a generation after Tract 90—shaped the critical discourse about religion and literature in ways that make the poem a valuable subject of attention itself. One reason that Newman's *Dream* may have slid into obscurity is that it fostered poetic conciliation so effectively that its achievement in this understated art went largely unrecognized, even as its effects laid the groundwork for a new generation of Tractarian poets.

63. Doyle, *Dr. Newman's . . . Lectures*, 108–9.

64. John Henry Newman, "John Keble," in *Essays Critical and Historical*, vol. 2 (London: Basil, Montagu, Pickering, 1871), 442–43.

65. Rowell, *Hell and the Victorians*, 6. In discussing the poem's achievements, Rowell further quotes a friend of Newman's, J. M. Capes, who wrote in the *Fortnightly Review* that the poem put into "shape the conviction of innumerable men and women who are as fervently Protestant as can be conceived but who find in some such relief as is here embodied, the only possible solution to the mysteries of life and death" (ibid., 159).

66. Margaret Oliphant, "The Land of Darkness" (313–62) and "A Beleaguered City" (1–106), collected in *A Beleaguered City and Other Tales of the Seen and the Unseen*, edited by Jenni Calder, Canongate Classics (London: Birlinn, 2000); C. S. Lewis, *The Great Divorce: A Dream* (San Francisco: Harper San Francisco, 1946).

67. George Bernard Shaw completely erases the boundary between heaven and hell in *Man and Superman: A Comedy and a Philosophy* (New York: Brentano's, 1903), sinking these distinctions in murkiness and reversibility both comical and disorienting. His vision of the afterlife occurs in the play as an imbedded dream manifesto—an interpolated form that exculpates Shaw from "the importance of being earnest" that characterizes the works of Lewis and Oliphant.

68. Quoted in Richard Schweitzer, *The Cross and the Trenches: Religious Faith and Doubt among British and American Great War Soldiers* (Westport, CT: Praeger, 2003), 147. Schweitzer gives a counternarrative to accounts of the war marking a decline in organized religion, and he discusses the widespread expectation for a religious revival that immediately accompanied the war.

69. Excerpted in Schweitzer, *The Cross and the Trenches*, 150.

70. Michael Snape details a rise in Catholicism between 1914 and 1945 in *God and the British Soldier: Religion and the British Army in the First and Second World Wars* (New York: Routledge, 2005): "Whereas there were 2,389,000 Roman Catholics in 1914, by 1946 their numbers had risen to 3,094,000, this growth being assisted

by continuing immigration from Ireland" (21). In surveying what he terms a kind of "diffusive Christianity" during the war, he charts the common wearing of rosaries as good luck amulets by non-Catholics (Snape, *God and the British Soldier*, 35). For further information on Anglican practices during World War I, see Alan Wilkinson, *The Church of England in the First World War* (London: SCM Press, 1996); and Albert Marrin, *The Last Crusade: The Church of England in the First World War* (Durham, NC: Duke University Press, 1974).

71. R. E. Hutton, chaplain of St. Margaret's, East Grinstead, *The Life Beyond: Thoughts on the Intermediate State and the Soul in the Unseen World* (London: Robert Scott Roxburghe House, 1916), 92.

72. Popular fiction of the time also reflected this increased acceptance of purgatory as a consolatory model, as evidenced by works such as W. Tudor-Pole's spiritualist fantasy, *Private Dowding: A Plain Record of the After-Death Experiences of a Soldier Killed in Battle, and Some Questions on World Issues Answered by the Messenger Who Taught Him Wider Truths* (London: J. M. Watkins, 1917), in which the soldier protagonist finds himself in a kindly afterlife devoted to growth. This purgatory for veterans proves to be so gentle that Private Dowding recounts that he did not know he was dead for quite some time—despite having been fatally shot. These literary visions of purgatory ranging from Oliphant in the nineteenth century to Tudor-Pole and Lewis in the twentieth century illustrate how controversial Oxford Movement theology continued to inform depictions of the afterlife after several decades and across denominations.

CHAPTER TWO
George Eliot's Winter Tales

1. In James's "*Daniel Deronda*: A Conversation," one of the two interlocutors reflects that if *Daniel Deronda* is "lacking current," it "has almost as little as *Romola*" (685).

2. Robert A. Colby's "An American Sequel to *Daniel Deronda*," *Nineteenth-Century Fiction* 12, no. 3 (December 1957): 231–35. Gwendolen by Anna Clay Beecher was "published in Boston in 1878 by the firm of Ira Bradley . . . with the intention no less 'to remedy the chief defect' of George Eliot's last novel." Colby, "American Sequel," 231.

3. "Her observation of matrimony had inclined her to think it rather a dreary state, in which a woman could not do what she liked, had more children than were desirable, was consequently dull, and became irrevocably immersed in humdrum." Eliot, *Daniel Deronda*, 33. Hereafter cited parenthetically in the text with the abbreviation *DD*.

4. Sarah Gates makes this point in "'A Difference of Native Language': Gender, Genre, and Realism in *Daniel Deronda*" (*ELH* 68, no. 3 [2001]: 699–724),

offering a reading of how Daniel's plot of Jewish nationhood completes the marriage plot but also coopts it from Gwendolen. See also Rosemarie Bodenheimer, "Ambition and Its Audiences: George Eliot's Performing Figures," *Victorian Studies* 34 (Autumn 1990): 7–33; and John Stokes's assertion of Gwendolen's "final stasis"—"Gwendolen is left to confront alone the doubtful possibilities of an independent female life" (789)—in "Rachel's 'Terrible Beauty': An Actress among the Novelists." *ELH* 51, no. 4 (Winter 1984): 771–93.

5. Gates, "Difference of Native Language," 720.

6. This trend is apparent in recent work on Eliot's "failed" reform plots. See Evan Horowitz, "George Eliot: The Conservative," *Victorian Studies* 49, no. 1 (Autumn 2006): 7–32.

7. Amy M. King explores Eliot's interest in depicting maturity over youth when discussing heroines who have a "second bloom." As King writes, "In both *Adam Bede* and *Middlemarch*, Eliot is formally innovative in exploring 'second blooms,' thereby making the associations of bloom with virginity or youth less hard." King, *Bloom: The Botanical Vernacular in the English Novel* (Oxford: Oxford University Press, 2003), 46.

8. Georg Simmel, *On Individuality and Social Forms* (Chicago: University of Chicago Press, 1971), 197–98.

9. Woolf, "George Eliot."

10. George Eliot [Mary Ann Evans] to Maria Lewis, March 16, 1839, in *The George Eliot Letters*, ed. Gordon S. Haight (New Haven, CT: Yale University Press, 1954–78), 1:23.

11. George Eliot to Sara Sophia Hennell, London, November 25, 1853, in *Letters*, 2:128. For further reference to *The Idea of a Future Life*, see George Eliot to John Chapman, May 13, 1853, in *Letters*: "You may put down 'The Idea of a Future Life' on your list if you will put it far enough on" (2:100).

12. Gillian Beer notes, "The book of 'the further life' would always have been premature, since the topic continued to preoccupy George Eliot throughout her working life and found its intensest form in *Daniel Deronda*" (*Darwin's Plots* 171). Neil Hertz also explains that "echoes of her title survive scattered throughout her writings" and makes brief example of *The Lifted Veil* and *Romola* in "George Eliot's Life-in-Debt" (*Diacritics: A Review of Contemporary Criticism* 25, no. 4 [1995]: 60).

13. Hertz, "George Eliot's Life-in-Debt," 60.

14. In addition to the earlier cited works by Beer and Hertz, see Levine, *Darwin and the Novelists*; Sally Shuttleworth, *George Eliot and Nineteenth-Century Science* (Cambridge: Cambridge University Press, 1984); Catherine Gallagher, "Sexing Culture: Malthusian Echoes in George Eliot's Early Fiction," *Feminist Studies*

in English Literature 10, no. 2 (2002): 77–96; Eileen Cleere, "Reproduction and Malthusian Economics: Fat, Fertility, and Family Planning in George Eliot's *Adam Bede*," in *On Your Left: The New Historical Materialism*, ed. Ann Kibbey, Thomas Foster, Carol Siegel, and Ellen Berry (New York: New York University Press, 1996), 150–83; and David Carroll, "'Janet's Repentance' and the Myth of the Organic," *Nineteenth-Century Fiction* 35, no. 3 (1980): 331–48, which complements Hertz's attention to the importance of germination and botanical imagery in Eliot's writing. Mary Wilson Carpenter uniquely combines religious philosophy and narrative theory, invoking Frank Kermode's *The Sense of an Ending* in her study of Eliot's use of apocalyptic thought. See Carpenter, *George Eliot and the Landscape of Time: Narrative Form and Protestant Apocalyptic History* (Chapel Hill: University of North Carolina Press, 1986). While Carpenter's work probes Victorian eschatology, it does not touch upon the active debate surrounding the realm of Judgment and the possibility of an Anglican purgatory.

15. Various critical works explore Eliot's religious beliefs at greater length. For examples, see Elisabeth Jay, *The Religion of the Heart: Anglican Evangelicalism and the Nineteenth-Century Novel* (Oxford: Clarendon Press, 1979); U. C. Knoepflmacher, *Religious Humanism and the Victorian Novel: George Eliot, Walter Pater, and Samuel Butler* (Princeton: Princeton University Press, 1965); Bernard Paris, "George Eliot's Religion of Humanity," *ELH* 29, no. 4 (1962): 418–43; Martha S. Vogeler, "George Eliot and the Positivists," *Nineteenth-Century Fiction* 35, no. 3 (1980): 406–31; Peter C. Hodgson, *The Mystery beneath the Real: Theology in the Fiction of George Eliot* (London: SCM Press, 2001); and Barry Quails's overview "George Eliot and Religion," in *The Cambridge Companion to George Eliot*, ed. George Levine (Cambridge: Cambridge University Press, 2001), 119–37.

16. George Eliot's first actual published work, a poem entitled "Knowing That Shortly I Must Put Off This Tabernacle," published in *The Christian Observer* (January 1840), depicts a soul's departure for either "heaven's sunshine or hell's moan." Later, she would reflect on the subject of personal immortality in her essay critiquing Edward Young's model of afterlife reward and punishment. See "Worldliness and Other-Worldliness: The Poet Young," in *Essays of George Eliot*, ed. Thomas Pinney (New York: Columbia University Press, 1963), 336.

17. See Ludwig Feuerbach, *The Essence of Christianity*, specifically, chapter 18, "The Christian Heaven or Personal Immortality." Eliot's translation of this text was published in 1854. Joseph Butler's *Analogy of Religion* (1736) was a religious text known to many Victorians. Eliot quotes from the text as early as 1842 in her letters. Later her friend and correspondent Sara Sophia Hennell would publish her *Essay on the Sceptical Tendency of Butler's "Analogy"* in 1859, a work that became the subject of several letters between Hennell and Eliot (Eliot, *Letters*, 2:377).

18. Rowell, *Hell and the Victorians*, 6. George Eliot read Isaac Taylor's *Physical Theory of Another Life* (New York: D. Appleton, 1836) in 1841 and recorded "rapture . . . as intense as any schoolgirl over her first novel" (*Letters*, May 21, 1841, 1:93).

19. Eliot to Sara Sophia Hennell, London, November 2, 1851: "I am reading with great amusement (!) J. H. Newman's Lectures on the Position of Catholics. They are full of clever satire and description" (*Letters*, 1:372).

20. Beer, *Darwin's Plots*, 172.

21. Eliot, December 5, 1859, in *Letters*, 3:227.

22. This claim characterizes Hodgson's approach in his study of each of Eliot's novels, in *Mystery beneath the Real*.

23. Beer, *Darwin's Plots*, 99.

24. John Blackwood to Eliot, February 19, 1861, in Eliot, *Letters*, 3:379–80.

25. As Kate E. Brown observes, these fits are a state akin to death. Brown's work provides a rare example of criticism that gestures toward the productive and regenerative potential of Silas's sequestered hoarding. See Brown, "Loss, Revelry, and the Temporal Measures of *Silas Marner*: Performance, Regret, Recollection," *NOVEL: A Forum on Fiction* 32, no. 2 (Spring 1999): 222–49.

26. George Eliot, *Silas Marner: The Weaver of Raveloe* (New York: Modern Library, 2001), 10, 11.

27. Susan Stewart, *On Longing: Narratives of the Miniature, the Gigantic, the Souvenir, the Collection* (Durham, NC: Duke University Press, 1993), 152.

28. Jean Baudrillard, *The System of Objects*, trans. James Benedict (London: Verso, 2005), 100.

29. Stewart, *On Longing*, 54.

30. For a perspective on the closed circuit of Silas Marner's onanism, see Jeff Nunokawa, *The Afterlife of Property: Domestic Security and the Victorian Novel* (Princeton: Princeton University Press, 1994), 100–122. Also see Donald E. Hall, "The Private Pleasures of Silas Marner," in *Mapping Male Sexuality: Nineteenth-Century England*, ed. Jay Losey and William D. Brewer (Cranbury, NJ: Associated University Presses, 2000), 178–96. Rather than view Silas Marner's coin fondling and weaving as similarly ungenerative activities, we might view these daily doings as a precursor to future gains, or rather, as "make-believe" beginnings.

31. Baudrillard, *System of Objects*, 97.

32. George Eliot, "Janet's Repentance," in *Scenes of Clerical Life* (New York: Penguin, 1998), 237.

33. Richard Whately, *A View of the Scripture Revelations*, 69–70.

34. E. H. Bickersteth, *The Shadowed Home and the Light Beyond*, 114–15.

35. George Eliot, review of *The Progress of the Intellect*, by Robert William Mackay, *Westminster Review* 54 (January 1851): 353–68. Reprinted in *Essays*, ed. Thomas Pinney, 29.

36. See Neil Hertz, *George Eliot's Pulse* (Stanford: Stanford University Press, 2003): "*Pulse*—as well as its cognates, *pulsing, pulsation, impulse, compulsion, repulsion*—turns up at telling moments in Eliot's fiction, and does some of the same work as the word *seed*. Each refers to a small, replicable unit of vitality, and as such is a sign of life.... Indeed, at two moments in Eliot's writings, *pulse* and *seed* merge" (13).

37. Lee Edelman's reading of *Silas Marner* is pertinent to my discussion of circularity versus linear progression; in his analysis of Silas Marner's bachelor plotline, he reveals how the novel "offers us Eppie, in her relation to Marner, as the material embodiment of futurism" (58), her introduction enacting a shift away from "the closed economy of the backward gaze" (53–54). Edelman, *No Future: Queer Theory and the Death Drive* (Durham, NC: Duke University Press, 2004).

38. George Eliot, *Romola* (Oxford: Oxford University Press, 1998), 119.

39. Anthony Trollope, *Barchester Towers* (Oxford: Oxford University Press, 2008), 14.

40. Elizabeth Gaskell, *Cranford* (Oxford: Oxford University Press, 2011), 64.

41. For information about how George Eliot saw Rossetti's *Pandora*, *Beatrice*, and *Cassandra* and the Jane Morris paintings, *Mariana* and *La Pia de' Tolomei*, see Joseph Nicholes, "Dorothea in the Moated Grange: Millais's *Mariana* and the *Middlemarch* Window-Scenes," *Victorian Institute Journal* 20 (1992): 104. Sophia Andres further argues that "Eliot captures all of the elements and qualities of Rossetti's *Pia de' Tolomei* in her representation of Gwendolen at the opening of chapter 54, where we find her a pitiful prisoner, 'a galley-slave' in her husband's yacht." Andres, *The Pre-Raphaelite Art of the Victorian Novel: Narrative Challenges to Visual Gendered Boundaries* (Columbus: Ohio State University Press, 2005), 113.

42. In sum, Lessing argues that painting is a spatial art and poetry a temporal one that unfolds sequentially (Lessing, 99–100, 109). He describes their relation as follows: "Painting and poetry should be like two just and friendly neighbors, neither of whom indeed is allowed to take unseemly liberties in the heart of the other's domain, but who exercise mutual forbearance on the borders" (10).

43. G. E. Lessing, *Laocoön*, trans. Ellen Frothingham (Boston: Roberts Brothers, 1874), 13.

44. This medusa fascination leads many scholars to frame Gwendolen's conclusion as punitive and terminally arrested—as a medusa's finale—thereby overlooking Eliot's insistence on her heroine's future growth. See also Robin Riley Fast, "Getting to the Ends of *Daniel Deronda*," *Journal of Narrative Technique* 7, no. 3 (Fall 1977): 200–217; and Nancy Pell, "The Fathers' Daughter in *Daniel Deronda*," *Nineteenth-Century Fiction* 36, no. 4 (1982): 424–51. Other critics who read the painting of the dead face as a mirror invoke W. J. T. Mitchell: "Medusa is the image that turns the tables on the spectator and turns the spectator into an

image: she must be seen through the mediation of mirrors (Perseus' shield) or paintings or descriptions.... Medusa is the perfect prototype for the image of the dangerous female other" (Mitchell, *Picture Theory: Essays on Verbal and Visual Representation* [Chicago: University of Chicago Press, 1994], 172). In one such reading of Eliot's mirroring, Nina Auerbach insists that the "dead face Gwendolen sees in the tableau is a mirror of her own face" (Auerbach, "Alluring Vacancies in the Victorian Character," *Kenyon Review*, n.s., 8, no. 3 [Summer 1986]: 47).

45. George Eliot, "Art and Belles Lettres," *Westminster Review*, n.s., 10 (July and October 1856): 566–82.

46. When Eliot refers to this passage in her Art and Belles Lettres review, she relates Lessing's point that the sculptor of the statue of *Laocoön and His Sons* did not capture the full range of physical agony described by Virgil, "because he could have given us nothing else than the distorted mouth, which would merely have been rigid ugliness, exciting in us no tragic emotion" (566).

47. Lessing, *Laocoön*, 13.

48. See Joseph Wiesenfarth, "*Middlemarch:* The Language of Art," *PMLA* 97, no. 3 (1982): 363–77; and Hugh Witemeyer, *George Eliot and the Visual Arts* (New Haven, CT: Yale University Press, 1979).

49. The Medusa quotation is from Andres, *Pre-Raphaelite Art*, 127, and the second quotation is from Gates, "Difference of Native Language," 720.

50. Kenneth Gross, *The Dream of the Moving Statue* (Ithaca, NY: Cornell University Press, 1992), 32. Gross shows how "[e]kphrastic writing turns on statues, makes metaphors out of statues' peculiar mode of being" (167).

51. In discussing "Gwendolen's dangerous striking energies," Gates aptly notes Eliot's pun on the word *striking* ("Difference of Native Language," 713), as describing both Gwendolen's ambiguous good looks and her serpentine tendencies. Tellingly, the injunction *to strike* is what activates *The Winter's Tale* tableau vivant in the first place, when Mrs. Davilow, playing Paulina, utters her line, "Music, awake her, strike!" (Eliot, *Daniel Deronda*, 55).

52. See Abigail Rischin, "Besides the Reclining Statue: Ekphrasis, Narrative, and Desire in *Middlemarch*," *PMLA* 111, no. 5 (1996): 1121–32; see also Wiesenfarth, "*Middlemarch*"; and Witemeyer, *George Eliot*, 42.

53. Rischin, "Besides the Reclining Statue," 1122.

54. George Eliot, "The Natural History of German Life," in *Selected Essays, Poems and Other Writings* (New York: Penguin, 1990), 110.

55. If the lack of beauty can bar sympathy, in both verbal and visual works, Eliot makes this point most aggressively in chapter 17 of *Adam Bede*, which includes her well-known commentary on Dutch painting: "But bless us, things may be lovable that are not altogether handsome, I hope? I am not at all sure that the majority of the human race have not been ugly.... I have seen many an

excellent matron, who could have never in her best days have been handsome" (New York: Penguin Books, 2008; orig. pub. 1859), 196.

56. Eliot, "Natural History," 107.

57. Eliot depicts Dorothea's postnuptial trials as purgatorial in *Middlemarch*. As a married woman, Dorothea aids Casaubon in his tedious stockpiling of knowledge, joining him in his "labourious uncreative hours" that are crowded with "the vaporous pressure of Tartarean shades" (55). In choosing this desiccated paramour, Dorothea is likened to a Persephone figure, prematurely stolen down to Hades. As Joseph Wiesenfarth has noted in "*Middlemarch:* The Language of Art," "[T]he epigraph to ch. 19, from Dante, makes it clear that Dorothea's marriage *is* her purgatory" (364).

58. In collecting George Eliot's Dante references, Andrew Thompson's "George Eliot's Borrowings from Dante: A List of Sources," *George Eliot–G. H. Lewes Studies* 44–45 (September 2003): 26–74, provides a useful guide to Eliot's novels, notebooks, and letters, as does his *George Eliot and Italy: Literary, Cultural, and Political Influences from Dante to the Risorgimento* (New York: St. Martin's Press, 1998). On *Daniel Deronda* specifically, see Moldstad, "Dantean Purgatorial Metaphor in *Daniel Deronda*." Also see Joseph Wiesenfarth's notes on purgatorial references in *Daniel Deronda* in *George Eliot: A Writer's Notebook, 1854–1879*, ed. Joseph Wiesenfarth (Charlottesville: University Press of Virginia, 1981).

59. John Cross gives an account of how he and Eliot met by reading Dante's *Divine Comedy* together in Italian, and then how they later reread *Purgatorio* out loud together on their honeymoon. Earlier, Lewes's letters include multiple accounts of Eliot staying in bed to read Dante. "I get up at 6, and before breakfast take a solitary ramble, which I greatly enjoy but which I can't get Madonna to share. Instead of this, she sits up in bed and buries herself in Dante or Homer." See Cross, *Life of George Eliot* (New York: T. Y. Crowell, 1884); and July 10, 1878, in Eliot, *Letters*, 7:39.

60. All quotations from Dante Alighieri's *Purgatorio* are taken from the translation by Jean Hollander and Robert Hollander (New York: Anchor Books, 2003). The original Italian text is as follows:

> "[Q]uando sarai di là da le larghe onde,
> dì a Giovanna mia che per me chiami
> là dove a li 'nnocenti si risponde.
> Non credo che la sua madre più m'ami,
> poscia che trasmutò le biache bende,
> le quai convien che, misera!, ancor brami.
> Per lei assai di lieve si comprende

> quanto in femmina foco d'amor dura
> se'occhio o 'l tatto spesso non l'accende.
> Non le farà sì bella sepultura
> la vipera che Melanesi accampa,
> com' avria fatto il gallo di Gallura."
> Così dicea, segnato de la stampa,
> nel suo aspetto, di quel dritto zelo
> che misuratamente in core avvampa.
>
> (Alighieri, *Purgatorio*, Canto VIII, lines 70–84)

61. Thomas Carlyle, *On Heroes, Hero-Worship, and the Heroic in History: Six Lectures* (New York: Wiley and Putnam, 1846), 85–86.

62. Eliot quotes from this canto of *Purgatorio* in her notebooks. Thompson, in his summary of her Dante citations, includes three passages from Canto VIII of *Purgatorio:* lines 1–6, recorded in the Beineke Notebooks; lines 13–15 in her notebooks residing at the Bodleian Library; and lines 76–78, also from the Beineke Notebooks. All three entries include Eliot's own translation. Her translation of lines 76–78, which concern us here, reads as follows: "By her it is easy indeed to know how long love's fire endures in woman if sight and touch do not often kindle it." See Thompson, "George Eliot's Borrowings," 45.

63. In Hollander and Hollander's translation of Dante's *Purgatorio*, La Pia says,

> [P]lease remember me, who am La Pia.
> Siena made me, in Maremma I was undone.
> He knows how, the one who, to marry me,
> first gave the ring that held this stone.
>
> (Alighieri, Canto V, lines 133–36)

Many translations render the critical line as "Siena made me, Maremma unmade me." In the original Italian, this reads

> [R]icorditi di me, che son la Pia;
> Siena mi fé, disfecemi Maremma:
> salsi colui che 'nnanellata pria
> disposando m'avea con la sua gemma.

64. The "late-repenters" in Dante's ante-purgatory captured the imagination of numerous Victorian and twentieth-century artists. In addition to Doré and

Rossetti, see Samuel Beckett's *More Pricks Than Kicks*, featuring Belacqua, Dante's slacker-penitent par excellence.

65. In the notes to their translation, Jean and Robert Hollander clearly define ante-purgatory: "Purgatory thus has three places: the mountain of purgation itself, ante-purgatory, and 'pre-ante-purgatory' located somewhere never described but at or near Ostia" (Alighieri, *Purgatorio*, 42). They also comment on the movement of the late-repenters: "Our first glimpse of the souls of ante-purgatory marks them as unexcited and slow moving, attributes that will gain in meaning as we learn more about them" (61).

66. For a further consideration of the eroticization of the female figure, see Griselda Pollock, *Vision and Difference: Femininity, Feminism, and Histories of Art* (New York: Routledge, 1988).

67. Tennyson, "Mariana," in *Tennyson: A Selected Edition*, 3–6.

68. Dante Gabriel Rossetti, *The Blessed Damozel* (New York: Thomas Bird Mosher, 1905).

69. Milbank's *Dante and the Victorians* touches upon intermediate state theology in relation to Victorian references to Dante, though she views the intermediate state simply as an extension of earthly existence.

70. Moldstad, "Dantean Purgatorial Metaphor," 195.

71. Ibid., 192.

72. Eliot, *Daniel Deronda*, 751; Alighieri, *Purgatorio*, Canto IV, lines 88–90.

73. Alighieri, *Purgatorio*, Canto IV, lines 128–34.

74. Eliot, "Janet's Repentance," in *Scenes of Clerical Life*, 237.

75. Gates, "Difference of Native Language," 721.

76. Ibid., 720.

77. Carolyn Williams, "Moving Pictures: George Eliot and Melodrama," in *Compassion: The Culture and Politics of an Emotion*, ed. Lauren Berlant (New York: Routledge, 2004), 133.

78. Simmel, *On Individuality*, 197.

79. Beer, *Darwin's Plots*, 179.

CHAPTER THREE
The Bachelor's Purgatory
Arrested Development and the Progress of Shades

1. Gissing, *Collected Works*, 2:76.

2. John Forster, *Life of Charles Dickens*, vol. 2 (New York: Baker and Taylor, 1872–74; first published, London: Cecil Palmer, 1872–74), 200; G. K. Chesterton, *Charles Dickens* (New York: Schocken Books, 1965; orig. pub. 1906), 229.

3. Gissing, *Collected Works*, 2:54.

4. G. K. Chesterton further described *Little Dorrit* as "so much more subtle and in every way so much more sad than the rest of his work that it bores Dickensians and especially pleases George Gissing" (*Charles Dickens*, 229).

5. Lionel Trilling, "*Little Dorrit*," *Kenyon Review* 15 (1953): 577–90. Reprinted as the introduction to the New Oxford Illustrated Dickens version of *Little Dorrit* (London: Oxford University Press, 1953).

6. John Wain, "*Little Dorrit*," in *Dickens and the Twentieth Century*, ed. J. Gross and G. Pearson (London: Routledge and Kegan Paul, 1966), 175; Dianne Sadoff, "Storytelling and the Figure of the Father in *Little Dorrit*," *PMLA* 95, no. 2 (March 1980): 241. Sadoff also discusses Clennam's lack of visible "work" in the novel—"[W]e never see Clennam working or enjoying his work" (236).

7. Ruth Bernard Yeazell, "Do It or Dorrit," *NOVEL: A Forum on Fiction* 25, no. 1 (Autumn 1991): 43.

8. For a thorough discussion of the preponderance of uncles in Victorian fiction, see Eileen Cleere's *Avuncularism: Capitalism, Patriarchy, and Nineteenth-Century English Culture* (Stanford: Stanford University Press, 2004).

9. Charles Dickens, *Bleak House* (Oxford: Oxford World's Classics, 1998), 64.

10. Charles Dickens, *Great Expectations* (New York: Penguin Books, 2003), 481. The concerns of *Hamlet* pervade *Great Expectations*, with its comic staging of Shakespeare's play, and resonate more broadly throughout Dickens's fiction in which he repeatedly reinvents Hamlet as a tragic prototype for the adult hero who struggles with *having come* of age. Indeed, Hamlet's dilemma would seem to be treated most pointedly in *Little Dorrit* in Clennam's return home after his father's death to investigate—morosely and at length—his suspicion of familial misdeed.

11. As Miller argues in *The Burdens of Perfection*, counterfactual thinking is a constituent part of the novel. I would add that it is a device that appears with greatest frequency in novels featuring mature protagonists. These protagonists are especially prone to retrospection, having been given a longer vista for such backward glances.

12. Gerald Prince, "The Disnarrated," *Style* 22, no. 1 (Spring 1988): 4.

13. Franco Moretti, "Serious Century," in *The Novel*, vol. 1, *History, Geography, and Culture*, ed. Franco Moretti (Princeton: Princeton University Press, 2006), 370.

14. Thomas Hardy, *Tess of the D'Urbervilles* (New York: Norton, 1990), 6.

15. Prince, "The Disnarrated," 5.

16. Elaine Ostry, *Social Dreaming: Dickens and the Fairy Tale* (New York: Routledge, 2002), 65.

17. Despite the history of critical attention devoted to Dickens and the fairy tale tradition, as well as the extensive criticism focused on Amy's story within

a story, the dark source for her tale has gone almost entirely unremarked. It is surprising that cornerstone works on Dickens's use of fairy tales such as Harry Stone's *Dickens and the Invisible World* (London: Macmillan Press, 1979) and Michael Kotzin's *Dickens and the Fairy Tale* (Bowling Green: Bowling Green University Popular Press, 1972) do not mention the Fairy Story's Schlemihlian ancestry. Rachel Bennett's "Hajji and Mermaid in *Little Dorrit*" (*Review of English Studies*, n.s., 46, no. 182 [May 1995]: 174–90) uniquely footnotes the folkloric source for Amy's story, but Bennett's reading of Andersen's influence on Dickens explores how *Little Dorrit* expands upon "The Little Mermaid," rather than "The Shadow." Other studies focusing on Amy as a storyteller and her tale as a narrative, rather than Dickens's fascination with fairy tales per se, likewise tend to omit or pass over the importance of her tale's folkloric sources. For examples, see Nancy Aycock Metz, "The Blighted Tree and the Book of Fate: Female Models of Storytelling in *Little Dorrit*," *Dickens Studies Annual* 18 (1989): 221–41; Julia Swindell, *Victorian Writing and Working Women: The Other Side of Silence* (Minneapolis: University of Minnesota Press, 1985), 87; and Yael Halevi-Wise, "Little Dorrit's Story: A Window into the Novel," *Dickensian* 94, no. 3 (1998): 184–94. In terms of an interest in shadows in *Little Dorrit*, two studies with this focus surprisingly do not mention how her tale recasts shadow folklore: Elaine Showalter's "Guilt, Authority, and the Shadows of *Little Dorrit*," *Nineteenth-Century Fiction* 34, no. 1 (1979): 20–40; and Irene E. Woods's "Charles Dickens, Hans Christian Andersen, and 'The Shadow,'" *Dickens Quarterly* 2, no. 4 (1985): 124–29, which notes the shadow imagery in *Little Dorrit* but does not consider how "The Shadow" is actually retold in the novel by Little Dorrit herself.

18. For the folkloric classification and background of the tale, see the Aarne-Thompson folk index: Antti Amatus Aarne, *The Types of the Folk-Tale: A Classification and Bibliography*, trans. and enlarged by Stith Thompson (New York: B. Franklin, 1928). Also see Victor I. Stoichita, *A Short History of the Shadow* (London: Reaktion Books, 1999).

19. See Adelbert von Chamisso, *Peter Schlemiel*, trans. Peter Wortsman (New York: Fromm International Publishing, 1993; orig. pub. 1814); and Hans Christian Andersen, "The Shadow," in *A Christmas Greeting to My English Friends* (London: Richard Bentley, 1847). The edition quoted later is Maria Tatar's *The Annotated Hans Christian Andersen* (New York: Norton, 2007), 263–79. Dickens was more than aware of Andersen's work, welcoming Andersen to stay at his house as a guest in 1857, while Dickens was completing *Little Dorrit*. Despite their falling out as a result of the visit, the two men acknowledged a continued interest in each other's future projects. For further information on Andersen's visit and their relationship, see Elias Bredsdorff, *Hans Christian Andersen and Charles Dickens:*

A Friendship and Its Dissolution (Copenhagen: Rosenkilde and Bagger, 1956). For Andersen's dedication to Dickens of his *Christmas Greeting* and Dickens's effusive response, see *The Letters of Charles Dickens*, vol. 1, ed. Mamie Dickens and Georgina Hogarth (New York: Scribner, 1880), 242–43.

20. Chamisso, *Peter Schlemiel*, 1.

21. Charles Dickens, *Little Dorrit* (New York: Penguin Books, 1998, first published 1857), 167. Hereafter cited parenthetically in the text with the abbreviation *LD* where necessary for clarification.

22. Stoichita, *Short History*, 153–54.

23. As Shklovsky writes, "The story is, in fact, only material for plot formulation." Viktor Shklovsky, "Sterne's *Tristram Shandy*," in *Russian Formalist Criticism: Four Essays*, ed. and trans. Lee T. Lemon and Marion J. Reis (Lincoln: University of Nebraska Press, 1965), 57.

24. Janice Carlisle, *The Sense of an Audience: Dickens, Thackeray, and George Eliot at Mid-Century* (Athens: University of Georgia Press, 1981), 106.

25. Many readings of *Little Dorrit*'s character doubles overlook that these doubles are often differentiated by age. If Clennam ponders that a "man was certainly not old at forty," then Little Dorrit could be said to demonstrate that a woman was certainly not very young at twenty. Little Dorrit's dual identity as a child and as a woman—and her canny awareness of this double existence—becomes most clear in the chapter "Little Dorrit's Party," in which she feigns being Maggy's daughter to travel through the city at night, as well as to comfort a prostitute contemplating suicide, a task her womanly self finds more difficult to accomplish. Amy both maintains and chafes against this childlike double role, often assigned to her by Clennam, who calls her "my child." Other examples of this age-correlated doubleness in a character include the Patriarch Casby, the Father of the Marshalsea, and Flora, who appears as a hybrid "moral mermaid," acting both her chronological age and her former eighteen-year-old virginal self. Lastly, Fanny and Mrs. Merdle also can be read as age-differentiated doubles.

26. Trilling, "*Little Dorrit*," 590.

27. On Dickens and religion, see Dennis Walder, *Dickens and Religion* (New York: Routledge, 2007); Janet Larson, *Dickens and the Broken Scripture* (Athens: University of Georgia Press, 1985); Andrew Sanders, *Charles Dickens, Resurrectionist* (New York: St. Martin's Press, 1982); and Vincent Newey, *The Scriptures of Charles Dickens: Novels of Ideology, Novels of the Self* (Burlington, VT: Ashgate, 2004).

28. Dickens quoted in Walder, *Dickens and Religion*, 10–11. In a letter dated May 26, 1843, Dickens invoked a speech made by Pusey a few weeks earlier at Christ Church, Oxford, that was regarded as "Dr. Pusey's Public Profession of Roman Catholic Doctrine," as one newspaper reported. In his brief missive on this

occasion, Dickens signed off, "Faithfully Always. Anti Pusey." Charles Dickens, *The Letters of Charles Dickens*, vol. 3, ed. Madeline House and Graham Storey (Oxford: Clarendon Press, 1974).

29. Newman, "Intermediate State," 377. In viewing Ebenezer Scrooge as prefiguring the purgatorial development of Arthur Clennam, my work contributes to a body of scholarship that connects Scrooge with Clennam, though none of these studies has examined the "purgatorial" similarities of their two journeys. Edmund Wilson famously made this comparison in "Charles Dickens: The Two Scrooges," collected in *The Wound and the Bow* (Athens: Ohio University Press, 1997; orig. pub. 1929), and Stone notes, "The rudimentary analysis of Scrooge's childhood, its formative pressure on his adulthood, in *A Christmas Carol* turns into the more careful examination of Clennam's childhood and its consequences in *Little Dorrit*" (*Dickens*, 143). Stone identifies the similarities between Scrooge's and Clennam's childhoods, rather than focusing on the similar narrative features that characterize their development as adults.

30. Some of John Chivery's tombstones can be found on pages 211, 218, and 702–3 of *Little Dorrit*.

31. In *Death and the Future Life*, Michael Wheeler provides one such example in analyzing how the eschatological categories of "Death, Judgment, Hell and Heaven" are instantiated in four different literary case studies. Although he reads Newman's *The Dream of Gerontius* as exemplifying the theologian's ideas about purgatory, Wheeler discusses Dickens's work as portraying "hell on *earth*," (emphasis added) most notably in *Hard Times*. Similarly, Richard K. Fenn insists that Dickens describes America as a hellish "purgatory" in *American Notes for General Circulation*, ignoring the subtleties of Victorian thought that distinguished purgatory, particularly the intermediate state, from the hell he describes. See Fenn, *The Persistence of Purgatory* (New York: Cambridge University Press, 1995). If hell has been well attended to in studies of Dickens and religion, his literary imaginings of purgatory have not received similar attention.

32. Stone, *Dickens*, 41.

33. D. A. Miller, *Narrative and Its Discontents: Problems of Closure in the Traditional Novel* (Princeton: Princeton University Press, 1981), xi. For further examples of studies that discuss how narratives either resist or surpass their conclusions, see Frank Kermode, *The Sense of an Ending* (London: Oxford University Press, 1966); Roland Barthes, *The Pleasure of the Text*, trans. Richard Miller (New York: Hill and Wang, 1975); Barthes, *S/Z: An Essay*, trans. Richard Miller (New York: Hill and Wang, 1975); and Boris Tomashevsky, "Thematics," in *Russian Formalist Criticism: Four Essays*, ed. and trans. Lee T. Lemon and Marion J. Reis (Lincoln: University of Nebraska Press, 1965), 61–95. Brooks's *Reading for the Plot* provides one example

of the latter kind of theory about closure: a death drive that assumes the ease—verging on biological imperative—with which narratives propagate themselves. For James, as for Dickens before him, the doppelganger, or "Nobody" figure, serves as a vehicle for revealing the sensitive gentleman's conundrum: waiting.

34. John Kucich's writing on internalizing conflict in *Repression in Victorian Fiction: Charlotte Brontë, George Eliot, and Charles Dickens* (Berkeley: University of California Press, 1987) extends an interesting possibility for thinking about closure in novels that deploy doppelganger stories, for he shows how "passion" and "repression" are brought together rather than being continually in opposition, a union that *Little Dorrit* enacts by way of the metaphor of a man being reunited with his shadow (or, perhaps one might say, his repressed shady side).

35. Arnold Bennett, *The Evening Standard Years: "Books and Persons," 1926–1931*, ed. A. Mylett (London: Chatto and Windus, 1974), 20.

36. Henry James, "The Altar of the Dead," in *Complete Stories, 1892–1898* (New York: Library of America, 1996; orig. pub. in *Terminations* [London: William Heinemann, 1895]), 452.

37. The religious imagery in this story has garnered the greatest critical interest, often provoking more-extended considerations of James's religious background and position on the afterlife. For example, in "Of Sacred Art and the Artist: Henry James's 'The Altar of the Dead'" (*Christianity and Literature* 51 [2002]: 209–18), Christopher A. Fahy perceives a final reconciliation not simply between Stransom and Acton Hague but also between sacred art and aestheticism, accomplished through James's use of Catholic imagery. See also Edwin Fussell, *The Catholic Side of Henry James* (Cambridge: Cambridge University Press, 1993).

38. James records avidly reading *Little Dorrit* and other works by Charles Dickens in the first part of his autobiography, *A Small Boy and Others* (New York: Charles Scribner's Sons, 1914), 119.

39. James, *Middle Years*, 58.

40. Henry James, *The Ambassadors* (New York: Penguin, 2003; first published by Methuen, 1903). Hereafter cited parenthetically in the text, with the abbreviation *Amb.* where necessary.

41. Henry James, "The Beast in the Jungle," in *Complete Collected Stories, 1898–1910* (New York: Library of America, 1996), 497.

42. The mantra at the crux of the story is this: "He found all things come back to the question of what he personally might have been, how he might have led his life and 'turned out,' if he had not so, at the outset, given it up." Henry James, "The Jolly Corner," in *Complete Collected Stories, 1898–1910* (New York: Library of America, 1996), 704.

43. Herbert F. Tucker, "Epiphany and Browning: Character Made Manifest," *PMLA* 107, no. 5 (October 1992): 1209.

44. The "marked stop in the whirling wheel of life" gives a definition very close to James Joyce's later coinage of *epiphany* as a term to describe "a sudden spiritual manifestation . . . a memorable phrase of the mind itself . . . the most delicate and evanescent of moments" in *Stephen Hero* (reprint, New York: New Directions, 1963), 211.

45. Simmel, *On Individuality*, 198.

46. For a related consideration of James's grammar, see Hisayoshi Watanabe, "Past Perfect Retrospection in the Style of Henry James," *American Literature* 34, no. 2 (1962): 165–81.

47. Henry James, *The Portrait of a Lady* (New York: Norton, 1975).

48. See, for examples, the introduction to *The Ambassadors* by Harry Levin (New York: Penguin, 1986), 17, and Erik Haralson's "Lambert Strether's Excellent Adventure" (in *The Cambridge Companion to Henry James*, ed. Jonathan Freedman [Cambridge: Cambridge University Press, 1998]), 174.

49. As Kevin Kohan notes, "James simply releases Strether from narration, leaving his character where other narrators would not." Kohan, "Rereading the Book in James's *The Ambassadors*," *Nineteenth-Century Literature* 54, no. 3 (December 1999): 400.

CHAPTER FOUR
Odd Women and Eccentric Plotting
Maturity, Modernism, and Woolf's Victorian Retrospection

1. Virginia Woolf, "Modern Fiction," in *The Essays of Virginia Woolf*, vol. 4, 1925–1928, ed. Andrew McNeillie (New York: Harcourt Brace Jovanovich, 1988), 161.

2. Jane Austen, *Emma* (New York: Penguin Books, 2003), 83.

3. Moretti, *Way of the World*; Hugh Kenner, "The Making of the Modernist Canon," *Chicago Review* 34, no. 2 (Spring 1984): 49–61.

4. Henry James, *Washington Square* (New York: Modern Library, 2002), 226.

5. Sylvia Townsend Warner, *Lolly Willowes; or, The Loving Huntsman* (New York: New York Review Books, 1999), 211.

6. Virginia Woolf, "Mr. Bennett and Mrs. Brown," in *Mr. Bennett and Mrs. Brown* (London: Hogarth Press, 1924), 9.

7. Several critics have noted the similarities between "Time Passes" in *To the Lighthouse* and *The Years*. Howard Harper notes, "In the structure of the *oeuvre*, *The Years* could be seen as an expansion of the 'Time Passes' section . . . the heart of darkness which links the mother's edenic domain of 'The Window' with the father's promised land of 'The Lighthouse'" (Harper, *Between Language and Silence:*

The Novels of Virginia Woolf [Baton Rouge: Louisiana State University Press, 1982], 280). Julia Briggs likewise connects *The Years* to the "Time Passes" section in *Reading Virginia Woolf* (Edinburgh: Edinburgh University Press, 2006), 136. Also see Harvena Richter on "duration" in *Virginia Woolf: The Inward Voyage* (Princeton: Princeton University Press, 1970), 175.

8. Virginia Woolf, "A Sketch of the Past," in *Moments of Being: Unpublished Autobiographical Writings*, ed. Jeanne Schulkind (Sussex, UK: Chatto and Windus for Sussex University Press, 1976), 69.

9. *The Letters of Virginia Woolf*, vol. 6, *1936–1941*, ed. Nigel Nicholson and Joanne Trautmann (New York: Harcourt Brace Jovanovich, 1980), 115–16.

10. Pericles Lewis, *Religious Experience and the Modernist Novel* (New York: Cambridge University Press, 2010), 166.

11. This designation of being a "best seller" in the spring of 1937 followed shortly after the publication of Man Ray's famous photos of Woolf for *Time* magazine on April 12, 1937, dual markers of Woolf's popularity with a broad reading audience.

12. July 20, 1933, *The Diary of Virginia Woolf*, vol. 4, *1931–1935*, ed. Anne Olivier Bell, assisted by Andrew McNeillie (New York: Harcourt Brace Jovanovich, 1982), 168.

13. Woolf, "Sketch of the Past," 69.

14. David L. Pike provides one recent example of this long-standing response: "[A]ll went well until *The Years*, when she deserted the poetry to which she fortunately returned in her final work, *Between the Acts*." Pike, *Passage through Hell*, 186.

15. May 28, 1929, *The Diary of Virginia Woolf*, vol. 3, *1925–1930*, ed. Anne Olivier Bell, assisted by Andrew McNeillie (New York: Harcourt Brace Jovanovich, 1980), 229.

16. As Woolf further writes in "Modern Fiction," "So much of the enormous labour of proving the solidity, the likeness to life, of the story is not merely labour thrown away but labour misplaced to the extent of obscuring and blotting out the light of the conception" (160).

17. James's statement about "loose baggy monsters" comes in reference to works by the same authors that Woolf expressed seeking to emulate in *The Years*, notably Thackeray and Tolstoy. See Henry James, "Preface to *The Tragic Muse*," in *The Art of the Novel* (Chicago: University of Chicago Press, 1934; reprint 2011), 84.

18. April 25, 1933, *Diary of Virginia Woolf*, 4:151.

19. November 2, 1932, *Diary of Virginia Woolf*, 4:129.

20. Peter Monro Jack, "Virginia Woolf's Richest Novel," *New York Times*, April 11, 1937.

21. Olga Owens, review of "The Years" (Book Review), by Virginia Woolf, *Boston Transcript*, April 10, 1937.

22. Pamela Transue, *Virginia Woolf and the Politics of Style* (Albany: State University of New York Press, 1986), 164.

23. See three of Jane Marcus's works: "Art and Anger," *Feminist Studies* 4 (1978): 69–98; "Pargeting 'The Pargiters': Notes of an Apprentice Plasterer," *Bulletin of the New York Public Library* 80 (1977): 416–35; and "'No More Horses': Virginia Woolf on Art and Propaganda," *Women's Studies* 4, nos. 2–3 (1977): 265–90. Also see Susan Stanford Friedman, "Lyric Subversion of Narrative in Women's Writing: Virginia Woolf and the Tyranny of Plot," in *Reading Narrative: Form, Ethics, Ideology*, ed. James Phelan (Columbus: Ohio State University Press, 1989), 162–86. In works like that of Friedman, one encounters the common view that Woolf's resistance to story is the unique result of the convergence of feminism and modernism, revealing a tendency to claim narrative lulls as a feminine style in literature.

24. Two critics have given new shape to this debate, probing the tension between a restrictive Victorianism and an allegedly more progressive postwar decentering of plot. Reading *The Years* alongside *The Pargiters*, Christine Froula in *Virginia Woolf and the Bloomsbury Avant-Garde: War, Civilization, Modernity* (New York: Columbia University Press, 2005) and Karen Levenback in *Virginia Woolf and the Great War* (Syracuse: Syracuse University Press, 1999) each discuss what Woolf omitted in transposing the novel-essay into the novel, analyzing the discourses that were submerged as a result. Most interestingly, Froula makes the case that gender and the question of women's sexuality got written out of *The Years*, and she casts the novel as a "repression" of a speech on "the sexual life of women" that Woolf delivered to the London/National Society for Women's Service in 1931. This repression is linked to a latent Victorianism not simply on Woolf's part but also on the part of novel-reading audiences, who crave the satisfaction offered by a more "realistic" approach to storytelling. Levenback uses psychoanalytic language to argue that Woolf "repressed" the "facts" of World War I (facts that Levenback as a historical critic expresses) and gives detailed statistical accounts of civilian losses to show how Woolf captures the illusion of "immunity" felt by civilians (*Virginia Woolf*, 140). Levenback essentially performs a historicist reframing of the counterargument to Froula's position. Instead of linking the novel's uneventful form to the failure of its political vision, Levenback presents *The Years* as a successful act of resistance. The argument that Woolf's resistance to plot amounts to an "anti-authoritarian" form in fiction is often associated with her method of representing history in *Between the Acts* as well.

25. January 5, 1933, *Diary of Virginia Woolf*, 4:142.

26. Brenda Silver, *Woolf's Reading Notebooks* (Princeton: Princeton University Press, 1983), 244.

27. September 24, 1930, *Diary of Virginia Woolf*, 3:320.

28. October 17, 1940, *The Diary of Virginia Woolf*, vol. 5, *1936–1941*, ed. Anne Olivier Bell, assisted by Andrew McNeillie (New York: Harcourt Brace Jovanovich, 1984), 320.

29. August 27, 1934, *Diary of Virginia Woolf*, 4:240. In particular, Woolf records reading *Purgatorio* regularly between 1934 and 1937.

30. Many entries evidence the inseparability for Woolf of reading Dante and writing *The Years*. Here are a few examples, in chronological order: "breaking my back over Dante" (January 10, 1931, *Diary*, 4:5); "If I cant [*sic*] even write here, owing to making up the last scenes, how can I possibly read Dante? Impossible. After 3 days grind, getting back, I am I think floated again" (August 27, 1934, *Diary*, 4:240); "I cant [*sic*] read Dante of a morning after the struggle with fiction. I wish I could find some way of composing my mind—its [*sic*] absurd to let it be ravaged by scenes; when I may not have read all Dante before I—but why harp on death? On the contrary, it is better to pull on my galoshes & go through the gale to lunch off scrambled egg & sausages" (January 11, 1935, *Diary*, 4:274); "I must rinse & freshen my mind, & make it work soberly on something hard: theres [*sic*] my Dante; & Renan. And the horrid winter lap begins; the pale unbecoming days, like an aging woman seen at 11 o'clock" (January 19, 1935, *Diary*, 4:275); "My head is numb today and I can scarcely read Osbert on Brighton, let alone Dante" (March 16, 1935, *Diary*, 4:288); "I cant [*sic*] read Dante after a morning with my novel—too hard" (June 6, 1935, *Diary*, 4:320).

31. April 1, 1935, *Diary of Virginia Woolf*, 4:295.

32. December 2, 1934, *Diary of Virginia Woolf*, 4:264.

33. May 25, 1937, *Diary of Virginia Woolf*, 5:90.

34. Pike considers *Ruff's Guide to the Turf and Sporting Life Annual* as a possibility (*Passage through Hell*, 193).

35. This latter quotation is from one of Woolf's diary entries describing her concept of the "novel-essay": "I have been in such a haze & dream & intoxication, declaiming phrases, seeing scenes, as I walk up Southampton Row that I can hardly say I have been alive at all, since the 10th Oct.... What has happened of course is that after abstaining from the novel of fact all these years—since 1919—& N[ight] & D[ay] indeed, I find myself infinitely delighting in facts for a change, & in possession of quantities beyond counting: though I feel now & then the tug to vision, but resist it. This is the true line, I am sure, after The Waves—The Pargiters—this is what leads naturally on to the next stage—the essay-novel." November 2, 1932, *Diary of Virginia Woolf*, 4:129.

36. Lucio P. Ruotolo concludes that the quotation speaks to "a more mutual sense of human behavior grounded in reciprocity as well as in a loosening of

acquisitive intentions." Ruotolo, *The Interrupted Moment: A View of Virginia Woolf's Novels* (Stanford: Stanford University Press, 1986), 177. Also see Hermione Lee, *The Novels of Virginia Woolf* (New York: Holms and Meier, 1977), 198.

37. Alighieri, *Purgatorio*, Canto XV, lines 61–63, p. 307. Quotations from Dante's *Purgatorio* are taken from the translation by Jean Hollander and Robert Hollander, also used in previous chapters.

38. Ibid., Canto XV, lines 64–66, p. 307.

39. Again, Hermione Lee offers a compelling reading of Dante as a "philosophical centre" for *The Years* in *Novels of Virginia Woolf*, 198.

40. March 27, 1935, *Diary of Virginia Woolf*, 4:291. Also see the entry from March 28, 1935: "Another bridge between P.s [*The Pargiters*] & Dante. But I think I have actually done the Raid this morning."

41. December 1917, *The Diary of Virginia Woolf*, vol. 1, *1915–1919*, ed. Anne Olivier Bell (New York: Harcourt Brace Jovanovich, 1977), 84–85. As Woolf wrote on December 5, "I'm past the middle of *Purgatorio*, but find it stiff, the meaning more than the language, I think," followed immediately by Woolf's entry detailing an air raid on Thursday, December 6, 1917.

42. In *Virginia Woolf's* The Years: *The Evolution of a Novel* (Knoxville: University of Tennessee Press, 1981), Grace Radin mentions that this moment in the text is one that Woolf altered slightly from *The Pargiters*: "[A]fter Eleanor's realization that she is 'a little lightheaded,' the explanation, 'It was the light after the dark; talk after silence, the war, perhaps removing barriers,' has been added (*TY*, 284). Otherwise, the only differences between these page proofs and *The Years* involve matters of punctuation" (137).

43. Woolf to Ethel Smyth, Wednesday, August 26, 1936, *Letters*, 6:67.

44. "In the galleys and page proofs, Sara's suggestion that they drink a toast to the 'New World' is not taken up and repeated by the others, as it is in *The Years*." Radin, *Virginia Woolf's* The Years, 141.

45. This pairing of Eleanor and North parallels that of Septimus and Clarissa in *Mrs. Dalloway*.

46. Virginia Woolf, *The Pargiters* (New York: Harcourt Brace Jovanovich, 1977), 164.

47. Woolf to Stephen Spender, 52 Tavistock Sq., April 30th, 1937, in *Letters*, 6:122.

48. Virginia Woolf, "More Dostoevsky," in *The Essays of Virginia Woolf*, vol. 2, *1912–1918*, ed. Andrew McNeillie (New York: Harcourt Brace Jovanovich, 1987), 85.

49. Scholars such as Radin have noted the Dantean, Platonic, and Sophoclean significance of this move underground in the novel.

Coda: Descent and Tradition

1. Homer, *The Odyssey*, trans. Robert Fagles (New York: Penguin Classics, 1999), 256, lines 254–56.
2. Dickens, *Little Dorrit*, 787.
3. James Joyce, "The Dead," in *Dubliners* (New York: Penguin Modern Classics, 1990), 225.
4. Newman, *Poetry*, 10.
5. Moretti, *Way of the World*, 3–4.
6. James Joyce, *A Portrait of the Artist as a Young Man* (London: Garland Publishing, 1993).

Bibliography

Aarne, Antti Amatus. *The Types of the Folk-Tale: A Classification and Bibliography.* Translated and enlarged by Stith Thompson. New York: B. Franklin, 1928.

Abel, Elizabeth, Marianne Hirsch, and Elizabeth Langland, eds. *The Voyage In: Fictions of Female Development.* Hanover, NH: Dartmouth University Press, 1983.

Ackerman, James S. "Jonah." In *The Literary Guide to the Bible,* edited by Robert Alter and Frank Kermode, 234–44. Cambridge, MA: Belknap Press of Harvard University Press, 1987.

Adams, James Eli. *Dandies and Desert Saints: Styles of Victorian Masculinity.* Ithaca, NY: Cornell University Press, 1995.

Alighieri, Dante. *Inferno.* Translated by Robert Hollander and Jean Hollander. New York: Anchor Books, 2000.

———. *Purgatorio.* Translated by Jean Hollander and Robert Hollander. New York: Anchor Books, 2003.

Andersen, Hans Christian. "The Shadow." In *The Annotated Hans Christian Andersen,* edited by Maria Tatar, 263–79. New York: Norton, 2007.

Andres, Sophia. *The Pre-Raphaelite Art of the Victorian Novel: Narrative Challenges to Visual Gendered Boundaries.* Columbus: Ohio State University Press, 2005.

Arendt, Hannah. *The Human Condition.* Chicago: University of Chicago Press, 1998.

Aristotle. *Poetics.* Translated by Malcolm Heath. New York: Penguin Classics, 1997.

Armstrong, Isobel. *Victorian Poetry: Poetry, Poetics and Politics.* New York: Routledge, 1993.

Auerbach, Erich. *Mimesis: The Representation of Reality in Western Literature.* Princeton: Princeton University Press, 1953.

Auerbach, Nina. "Alluring Vacancies in the Victorian Character." *Kenyon Review,* n.s., 8, no. 3 (Summer 1986): 36–48.

Austen, Jane. *Emma.* New York: Penguin Books, 2003. Originally published 1815.

———. *Persuasion.* New York: W. W. Norton, 2012. Originally published 1818.

Axon, William E. A. "The 'Dream of Gerontius.'" *The Library: A Quarterly Review of Bibliography and Library Lore,* n.s., 6 (1905): 281–87.

———. "On General Gordon's Copy of Newman's *Dream of Gerontius.*" *Manchester Quarterly: A Journal of Literature and Art* 8 (January 1889).

Baker, Joseph Ellis. *The Novel and the Oxford Movement.* Princeton: Princeton University Press, 1932.

Bakhtin, Mikhail. *The Dialogic Imagination.* Austin: University of Texas Press, 1981.

Balzac, Honoré de. *Lost Illusions.* New York: Penguin Classics, 1976.

Barndollar, David, and Susan Schorn. "Revisiting the Serial Format of Dickens's Novel; or, A Little Dorrit Goes a Long Way." In *Functions of Victorian Culture at the Present Time*, edited by Christine L. Krueger, 157–70. Athens: Ohio University Press, 2002.
Barthes, Roland. *The Pleasure of the Text*. Translated by Richard Miller. New York: Hill and Wang, 1975.
———. *S/Z: An Essay*. Translated by Richard Miller. New York: Hill and Wang, 1975.
Baudrillard, Jean. *The System of Objects*. Translated by James Benedict. London: Verso, 2005.
Beckett, Samuel. *More Pricks Than Kicks*. London: Chatto and Windus, 1934.
Beer, Gillian. *Darwin's Plots: Evolutionary Narrative in Darwin, George Eliot and Nineteenth-Century Fiction*. Cambridge: Cambridge University Press, 2000.
———. *George Eliot*. Brighton, UK: Harvester Press, 1986.
Bennett, Arnold. *The Evening Standard Years: "Books and Persons," 1926–1931*. Edited by A. Mylett. London: Chatto and Windus, 1974.
Bennett, Rachel. "Hajji and Mermaid in *Little Dorrit*." Review of English Studies, n.s., 46, no. 182 (May 1995): 174–90.
Bickersteth, Edward Henry. *The Blessed Dead: What Does Scripture Reveal of Their State before the Resurrection?* London: John F. Shaw, 1863.
———. *The Shadowed Home and the Light Beyond*. London: Sampson Low, Marston, Low, and Searle, 1875.
———. *Yesterday, To-day, and Forever, in Twelve Books*. New York: Robert Carter and Brothers, 1875.
Bodenheimer, Rosemarie. "Ambition and Its Audiences: George Eliot's Performing Figures." *Victorian Studies* 34 (Autumn 1990): 7–33.
Bredsdorff, Elias. *Hans Christian Andersen and Charles Dickens: A Friendship and Its Dissolution*. Copenhagen: Rosenkilde and Bagger, 1956.
Briggs, Julia. *Reading Virginia Woolf*. Edinburgh: Edinburgh University Press, 2006.
Brontë, Charlotte. *Villette*. Oxford: Oxford World's Classics, 2008.
Brooks, Peter. *Reading for the Plot: Design and Intention in Narrative*. New York: A. A. Knopf, 1984.
Brown, Kate E. "Loss, Revelry, and the Temporal Measures of *Silas Marner*: Performance, Regret, Recollection." *NOVEL: A Forum on Fiction* 32, no. 2 (1999): 222–49.
Browning, Robert. "Johannes Agricola in Meditation." In *Selected Poems by Robert Browning*, 19. Edited by Daniel Karlin. New York: Penguin, 1989.
Butler, Joseph. *The Analogy of Religion*. New York: Cosimo Classics, 2005. Originally published 1736.

Carlisle, Janice. *The Sense of an Audience: Dickens, Thackeray, and George Eliot at Mid-Century.* Athens: University of Georgia Press, 1981.
Carlyle, Thomas. *On Heroes, Hero-Worship, and the Heroic in History: Six Lectures.* New York: Wiley and Putnam, 1846.
Carpenter, Mary Wilson. *George Eliot and the Landscape of Time: Narrative Form and Protestant Apocalyptic History.* Chapel Hill: University of North Carolina Press, 1986.
Carrington, Hereward. *Psychical Phenomena and the War.* New York: Dodd, Mead, 1919.
Carroll, David. "'Janet's Repentance' and the Myth of the Organic." *Nineteenth-Century Fiction* 35, no. 3 (1980): 331–48.
Caserio, Robert. *Plot, Story and the Novel: From Dickens and Poe to the Modern Period.* Princeton: Princeton University Press, 1979.
Cervantes, Miguel de. *Don Quixote.* Translated by Walter Starkie. New York: Penguin, 2001.
Chamisso, Adelbert von. *Peter Schlemiel.* Translated by Peter Wortsman. New York: Fromm International Publishing, 1993. Originally published 1814.
Chatman, Seymour. *Story and Discourse: Narrative Structure in Fiction and Film.* Ithaca, NY: Cornell University Press, 1978.
Chesterton, G. K. *Charles Dickens.* New York: Schocken Books, 1965. Originally published 1906.
———. *The Victorian Age in Literature.* New York: Henry Holt, 1913.
Cleere, Eileen. *Avuncularism: Capitalism, Patriarchy, and Nineteenth-Century English Culture.* Stanford: Stanford University Press, 2004.
———. "Reproduction and Malthusian Economics: Fat, Fertility, and Family Planning in George Eliot's *Adam Bede*." In *On Your Left: The New Historical Materialism*, edited by Ann Kibbey, Thomas Foster, Carol Siegel, and Ellen Berry, 150–83. New York: New York University Press, 1996.
Cohen, Patricia. *In Our Prime: The Invention of Middle Age.* New York: Scribner, 2012.
Colby, Robert A. "An American Sequel to *Daniel Deronda*." *Nineteenth-Century Fiction* 12, no. 3 (December 1957): 231–35.
Cross, John. *Life of George Eliot.* New York: T. Y. Crowell, 1884.
Culler, Jonathan. *The Pursuit of Signs: Semiotics, Literature, Deconstruction.* Ithaca, NY: Cornell University Press, 1981.
D'Amico, Diane, and David A. Kent. "Rossetti and the Tractarians." *Victorian Poetry* 44, no. 1 (2006): 93–103.
de Certeau, Michel. *The Writing of History.* Translated by Tom Conley. New York: Columbia University Press, 1988.

DiBattista, Maria. *First Love: The Affections of Modern Fiction.* Chicago: University of Chicago Press, 1991.
Dickens, Charles. *American Notes for General Circulation.* New York: Penguin Books, 2000. Originally published 1842.
———. *Bleak House.* Oxford: Oxford World's Classics, 1998.
———. "A Christmas Carol." In *A Christmas Carol and Other Christmas Writings*, 27–118. New York: Penguin Classics, 2003. Originally published 1843.
———. *David Copperfield.* New York: Penguin Classics, 2004.
———. *Great Expectations.* New York: Penguin Books, 2003.
———. *The Letters of Charles Dickens*, vol. 1. Edited by Mamie Dickens and Georgina Hogarth. New York: Scribner, 1880.
———. *The Letters of Charles Dickens*, vol. 3. Edited by Madeline House and Graham Storey. Oxford: Clarendon Press, 1974.
———. *The Life of Our Lord: Written for His Children during the Years 1846 to 1849.* New York: Simon and Schuster, 1999.
———. *Little Dorrit.* New York: Penguin Books, 1998. Originally published 1857.
———. *Our Mutual Friend.* New York: Penguin Books, 1997.
Doyle, Francis Hastings. *Dr. Newman's Dream of Gerontius Lectures Delivered before the University of Oxford, 1868.* London: Macmillan, 1869.
Edelman, Lee. *No Future: Queer Theory and the Death Drive.* Durham, NC: Duke University Press, 2004.
Eliot, George. *Adam Bede.* New York: Penguin Books, 2008. Originally published 1859.
———. "Art and Belles Lettres." *Westminster Review* 66 (1865). New Series, 10 (July and October 1856): 566–82.
———. *Daniel Deronda.* New York: Penguin Classics, 1995.
———. *The George Eliot Letters.* 7 vols. Edited by Gordon S. Haight. New Haven, CT: Yale University Press, 1954–78.
———. "Janet's Repentance." In *Scenes of Clerical Life*, 197–350. New York: Penguin, 1998.
———. "Knowing That Shortly I Must Put Off This Tabernacle." *Christian Observer* (January 1840): 38.
———. *Middlemarch.* New York: W. W. Norton, 1999.
———. *Mill on the Floss.* London: Penguin Classics, 1985.
———. "The Natural History of German Life." In *Selected Essays, Poems and Other Writings*, 107–39. New York: Penguin Books, 1990.
———. Review of *The Progress of the Intellect*, by Robert William Mackay, *Westminster Review* 54 (January 1851): 353–68. Reprinted in *Essays of George Eliot*, edited by Thomas Pinney, 27–45. New York: Columbia University Press, 1963.

———. *Romola*. Oxford: Oxford University Press, 1998.
———. *Scenes of Clerical Life*. New York: Penguin, 1998.
———. *Silas Marner: The Weaver of Raveloe*. New York: Modern Library, 2001.
———. "Worldliness and Other-Worldliness: The Poet Young." In *Essays of George Eliot*, edited by Thomas Pinney, 335–85. New York: Columbia University Press, 1963. Originally published in the *Westminster Review*, January 1857.
Eliot, T. S. *Essays Ancient and Modern*. London: Faber and Faber, 1936.
Esty, Jed. "The Colonial Bildungsroman: *The Story of an African Farm* and the Ghost of Goethe." *Victorian Studies* 49, no. 3 (2007): 407–30.
———. *Unseasonable Youth: Modernism, Colonialism, and the Fiction of Development*. Oxford: Oxford University Press, 2012.
Fahy, Christopher A. "Of Sacred Art and the Artist: Henry James's 'The Altar of the Dead.'" *Christianity and Literature* 51 (2002): 209–18.
Fast, Robin Riley. "Getting to the Ends of *Daniel Deronda*." *Journal of Narrative Technique* 7, no. 3 (Fall 1977): 200–217.
Fenn, Richard K. *The Persistence of Purgatory*. New York: Cambridge University Press, 1995.
Feuerbach, Ludwig. *The Essence of Christianity*. New York: Harper and Brothers, 1957.
Forster, E. M. *Aspects of the Novel*. Orlando, FL: Houghton Mifflin Harvest, 1956.
Forster, John. *Life of Charles Dickens*, vol. 2. New York: Baker and Taylor, 1872–74.
Fraiman, Susan. "*The Mill on the Floss*, the Critics, and the Bildungsroman." *PMLA* 108, no. 1 (January 1993): 136–50.
François, Anne-Lise. *Open Secrets: The Literature of Uncounted Experience*. Stanford: Stanford University Press, 2008.
Friedman, Norman. "Newman, Aristotle, and the New Criticism: On the Modern Element in Newman's Poetics." *PMLA* 81, no. 3 (June 1966): 261–71.
Friedman, Susan Stanford. "Lyric Subversion of Narrative in Women's Writing: Virginia Woolf and the Tyranny of Plot." In *Reading Narrative: Form, Ethics, Ideology*, edited by James Phelan, 162–86 (Columbus: Ohio State University Press, 1989).
Froula, Christine. *Virginia Woolf and the Bloomsbury Avant-Garde: War, Civilization, Modernity*. New York: Columbia University Press, 2005.
Frye, Northrop. "Approaching the Lyric." In *Lyric Poetry: Beyond New Criticism*, edited by Chaviva Hošek and Patricia Parker, 31–37. Ithaca, NY: Cornell University Press, 1985.
Fussell, Edwin. *The Catholic Side of Henry James*. Cambridge: Cambridge University Press, 1993.
Gallagher, Catherine. "Sexing Culture: Malthusian Echoes in George Eliot's Early Fiction." *Feminist Studies in English Literature* 10, no. 2 (2002): 77–96.

Garcha, Amanpal. *From Sketch to Novel: The Development of Victorian Fiction*. Cambridge: Cambridge University Press, 2009.
Gaskell, Elizabeth. *Cranford*. Oxford: Oxford University Press, 2011.
Gates, Sarah. "'A Difference of Native Language': Gender, Genre, and Realism in *Daniel Deronda*." *ELH* 68, no. 3 (2001): 699–724.
Gissing, George. *Collected Works of George Gissing on Charles Dickens*, vol. 2. Edited by Simon J. James. Surrey, UK: Grayswood Press, 2004.
———. *Odd Women*. New York: Penguin Books, 1993.
Goodwin, Gregory H. "Keble and Newman: Tractarian Aesthetics and the Romantic Tradition." *Victorian Studies* 30, no. 4 (Summer 1987): 475–94.
Goslee, David. "New(-)man as Old Man in *The Dream of Gerontius*." *Renascence* 52 (2000): 275–79.
Green, T. H. "Estimate of the Value and Influence of Works of Fiction in Modern Times." In *Works of Thomas Hill Green*, edited by R. L. Nettleship, 3:36. London: Longmans, 1888.
Greenblatt, Stephen. *Hamlet in Purgatory*. Princeton: Princeton University Press, 2001.
Gross, Kenneth. *The Dream of the Moving Statue*. Ithaca, NY: Cornell University Press, 1992.
Grossmith, George, and Weedon Grossmith. *The Diary of a Nobody*. Oxford: Oxford University Press, 1998.
Gwendolen. Boston: Ira Bradley, 1878.
Halevi-Wise, Yael. "Little Dorrit's Story: A Window into the Novel." *Dickensian* 94, no. 3 (1998): 184–94.
Hall, Donald E. "The Private Pleasures of Silas Marner." In *Mapping Male Sexuality: Nineteenth-Century England*, edited by Jay Losey and William D. Brewer, 178–96. Cranbury, NJ: Associated University Presses, 2000.
Hanhart (te Telburg), Karel. "The Intermediate State in the New Testament." PhD dissertation in theology, University of Amsterdam, 1966.
Haralson, Erik. "Lambert Strether's Excellent Adventure." In *The Cambridge Companion to Henry James*, edited by Jonathan Freedman, 169–86. Cambridge: Cambridge University Press, 1998.
Hardy, Thomas. *Tess of the D'Urbervilles*. New York: Norton, 1990.
Harper, Howard. *Between Language and Silence: The Novels of Virginia Woolf*. Baton Rouge: Louisiana State University Press, 1982.
Hayes, Zachary. *Visions of a Future: A Study of Christian Eschatology*. Wilmington, DE: Michael Glazier, 1989.
Heath, Kay. *Aging by the Book: The Emergence of Midlife in Victorian Britain*. Albany: SUNY Press, 2009.
Hennell, Sara Sophia. *Essay on the Sceptical Tendency of Butler's "Analogy."* London: John Chapman, 1859.

Hertz, Neil. "George Eliot's Life-in-Debt." *Diacritics: A Review of Contemporary Criticism* 25, no. 4 (1995): 59–70.

———. *George Eliot's Pulse.* Stanford: Stanford University Press, 2003.

Hill, Alan G. *Callista: A Tale of the Third Century.* South Bend, IN: Notre Dame University Press, 2001.

———. "Three 'Visions' of Judgement: Southey, Byron, and Newman." *Review of English Studies,* n.s., 41, no. 163 (August 1990): 334–50.

Hirsch, Marianne. "Defining Bildungsroman as a Genre." *PMLA* 91, no. 1 (January 1976): 122–23.

Hodgson, Peter C. *The Mystery beneath the Real: Theology in the Fiction of George Eliot.* London: SCM Press, 2001.

Homer. *The Odyssey.* Translated by Robert Fagles. New York: Penguin Classics, 1999.

Hoover, A. J. *God, Britain, and Hitler in World War I: The View of the British Clergy, 1939–1945.* Westport, CT: Praeger, 1999.

Horowitz, Evan. "George Eliot: The Conservative." *Victorian Studies* 49, no. 1 (Autumn 2006): 7–32.

Hutton, R. E. *The Life Beyond: Thoughts on the Intermediate State and the Soul in the Unseen World.* London: Robert Scott Roxburghe House, 1916.

Ince, William. *The Future Life—The Intermediate State—Heaven: Two Sermons Preached in the Cathedral Church of Christ, Oxford, in September, 1895.* London: James Parker, 1895.

James, Henry. "The Altar of the Dead." In *Complete Stories, 1892–1898,* 450–85. New York: Library of America, 1996.

———. *The Ambassadors.* New York: Penguin, 2003. Originally published by Methuen, 1903.

———. *The Art of the Novel.* Reprint, Chicago: University of Chicago Press, 2011. Originally published 1934.

———. "The Beast in the Jungle." In *Complete Collected Stories, 1898–1910,* 496–541. New York: Library of America, 1996.

———. "*Daniel Deronda:* A Conversation." *Atlantic Monthly* 38 (December 1876): 684–94.

———."The Jolly Corner." In *Complete Collected Stories, 1898–1910,* 697–731. New York: Library of America, 1996.

———. *Literary Criticism: French Writers, Other European Writers; The Prefaces to the New York Edition.* New York: Library of America, 1984.

———. *The Middle Years.* New York: C. Scribner's Sons, 1917.

———. *Partial Portraits.* Westport, CT: Greenwood Press, 1970.

———. *The Portrait of a Lady.* New York: Norton, 1975. Originally published 1880–81 in *The Atlantic Monthly* and in 1881 in book form.

---. *A Small Boy and Others.* New York: Charles Scribner's Sons, 1914.
---. *The Turn of the Screw and Other Stories.* Oxford: Oxford University Press, 1998.
---. *Washington Square.* New York: Modern Library, 2002.
Jay, Elisabeth. *The Religion of the Heart: Anglican Evangelicalism and the Nineteenth-Century Novel.* Oxford: Clarendon Press, 1979.
Joyce, James. *Dubliners.* New York: Penguin Modern Classics, 1990.
---. *A Portrait of the Artist as a Young Man.* London: Garland Publishing, 1993.
---. *Stephen Hero.* Reprint, New York: New Directions, 1963.
---. *Ulysses.* New York: Vintage, 1990.
Kenner, Hugh. "The Making of the Modernist Canon." *Chicago Review* 34, no. 2 (Spring 1984): 49–61.
Ker, Ian. *John Henry Newman: A Biography.* Oxford: Oxford University Press, 2009.
Kermode, Frank. *The Sense of an Ending.* London: Oxford University Press, 1966.
King, Amy M. *Bloom: The Botanical Vernacular in the English Novel.* Oxford: Oxford University Press, 2003.
Kingsley, Charles. Review of *The Dream of Gerontius,* by John Henry Newman. *Independent* 24, no. 1214 (March 7, 1872): 3.
---. "The Irrationale of Speech." *Fraser's Magazine* 60 (July 1859): 1–14.
Kingsley, Charles, and Frances Eliza Grenfell Kingsley. *Charles Kingsley: His Letters and Memories of His Life.* New York: Scribner, Armstrong, 1877.
Knight, Mark, and Emma Mason. *Nineteenth-Century Religion and Literature: An Introduction.* Oxford: Oxford University Press, 2006.
Knoepflmacher, U. C. *Religious Humanism and the Victorian Novel: George Eliot, Walter Pater, and Samuel Butler.* Princeton: Princeton University Press, 1965.
Kohan, Kevin. "Rereading the Book in James's *The Ambassadors.*" *Nineteenth-Century Literature* 54, no. 3 (December 1999): 373–400.
Kotzin, Michael. *Dickens and the Fairy Tale.* Bowling Green, KY: Bowling Green University Popular Press, 1972.
Kucich, John. *Repression in Victorian Fiction: Charlotte Brontë, George Eliot, and Charles Dickens.* Berkeley: University of California Press, 1987.
Kurnick, David. *Empty Houses: Theatrical Failure and the Novel.* Princeton: Princeton University Press, 2011.
Larson, Janet. *Dickens and the Broken Scripture.* Athens: University of Georgia Press, 1985.
Lawrence, D. H. *D. H. Lawrence: A Personal Record.* Edited by Jessie Chambers. Cambridge: Cambridge University Press, 1980.
Lee, Hermione. *The Novels of Virginia Woolf.* New York: Holms and Meier, 1977.

Le Goff, Jacques. *The Birth of Purgatory*. Translated by Arthur Goldhammer. Chicago: University of Chicago Press, 1981.

Lessing, G. E. *Laocoön*. Translated by Ellen Frothingham. Boston: Roberts Brothers, 1874.

Levenback, Karen. *Virginia Woolf and the Great War*. Syracuse: Syracuse University Press, 1999.

Levin, Harry. Introduction to *The Ambassadors*, by Henry James, 7–27. New York: Penguin, 1986.

Levine, Caroline. *The Serious Pleasures of Suspense*. Charlottesville: University of Virginia Press, 2003.

Levine, Caroline, and Mario Ortiz-Robles. Introduction to *Narrative Middles: Navigating the Nineteenth-Century British Novel*, edited by Caroline Levine and Mario Ortiz-Robles, 1–23. Columbus: Ohio State University Press, 2011.

Levine, George. *The Boundaries of Fiction*. Princeton: Princeton University Press, 1968.

———. *Darwin and the Novelists*. Cambridge, MA: Harvard University Press, 1988.

———. *The Realistic Imagination*. Chicago: University of Chicago Press, 1981.

Lewis, C. S. *The Great Divorce: A Dream*. San Francisco: Harper San Francisco, 1946.

Lewis, Pericles. *Religious Experience and the Modernist Novel*. New York: Cambridge University Press, 2010.

Lukács, Georg. *The Theory of the Novel*. Translated by Anna Bostock. Cambridge, MA: MIT Press, 1971.

Marcus, Jane. "Art and Anger." *Feminist Studies* 4 (1978): 69–98.

———. "'No More Horses': Virginia Woolf on Art and Propaganda." *Women's Studies* 4, no. 2–3 (1977): 265–90.

———. "Pargeting 'The Pargiters': Notes of an Apprentice Plasterer." *Bulletin of the New York Public Library* 80 (1977): 416–35.

Markovits, Stefanie. "Arthur Hugh Clough, Amours de Voyage, and the Victorian Crisis of Action." *Nineteenth-Century Literature* 55, no. 4 (2001): 445–78.

———. *The Crisis of Action in Nineteenth-Century English Literature*. Columbus: Ohio State University Press, 2006.

———. "George Eliot's Problem with Action." *Studies in English Literature, 1500–1900* 41, no. 4 (2001): 785–803.

Marrin, Albert. *The Last Crusade: The Church of England in the First World War*. Durham, NC: Duke University Press, 1974.

Maurice, F. D. *Theological Essays*. New York: Harper, 1957. Originally published 1853.

McGann, Jerome. "The Religious Poetry of Christina Rossetti." *Critical Inquiry* 10, no. 1 (September 1983): 127–44.
McKeating, Colm. *Eschatology in the Anglican Sermons of John Henry Newman.* Lampeter, UK: Mellen Research University Press, 1992.
Metz, Nancy Aycock. "The Blighted Tree and the Book of Fate: Female Models of Storytelling in *Little Dorrit.*" *Dickens Studies Annual* 18 (1989): 221–41.
Milbank, Alison. *Dante and the Victorians.* Manchester: Manchester University Press, 1998.
Mill, John Stuart. "The Spirit of the Age." In *The Spirit of the Age: Victorian Essays,* 50–90. Edited by Gertrude Himmelfarb. New Haven, CT: Yale University Press, 2007.
Miller, Andrew H. *The Burdens of Perfection: On Ethics and Reading in Nineteenth-Century British Literature.* Ithaca, NY: Cornell University Press, 2010.
Miller, D. A. *Narrative and Its Discontents: Problems of Closure in the Traditional Novel.* Princeton: Princeton University Press, 1981.
———. *The Novel and the Police.* Berkeley: University of California Press, 1988.
Mitchell, W. J. T. *Picture Theory: Essays on Verbal and Visual Representation.* Chicago: University of Chicago Press, 1994.
Moldstad, David. "The Dantean Purgatorial Metaphor in *Daniel Deronda.*" *Papers on Language and Literature: A Journal for Scholars and Critics of Language and Literature* 19, no. 2 (Spring 1983): 183–98.
Moretti, Franco. "Serious Century." In *The Novel,* vol. 1, *History, Geography, and Culture,* ed. Franco Moretti, 364–400. Princeton: Princeton University Press, 2006.
———. *The Way of the World: The Bildungsroman in European Culture.* Translated by Albert Sbragia. New York: Verso, 1987.
Morgan, Monique R. *Narrative Means, Lyrical Ends: Temporality in the Nineteenth-Century British Long Poem.* Columbus: Ohio State University Press, 2009.
Muller, Jill. *Gerard Manley Hopkins and Victorian Catholicism: A Heart in Hiding.* New York: Routledge, 2003.
Neale, Susanna. "The Intermediate State: A Poem, Dedicated (with Permission from Himself) to the Late Author of 'The Christian Year.'" London: Joseph Masters, 1867.
Newey, Vincent. *The Scriptures of Charles Dickens: Novels of Ideology, Novels of the Self.* Burlington, VT: Ashgate, 2004.
Newman, John Henry. *Apologia Pro Vita Sua.* Edited by David J. DeLaura. New York: W. W. Norton, 1968.
———. *The Dream of Gerontius.* London: Burns, Lambert and Oates, 1866.

---. *An Essay on the Development of Christian Doctrine.* South Bend, IN: Notre Dame University Press, 2005.

---. "The Golden Prison." In *Verses on Various Occasions*, 299–300. London: Burns, Oates and Co., 1880.

---. "The Intermediate State." Sermon 25. In *Parochial and Plain Sermons*, 3:367–87. London: J. G. and F. Rivington, 1891.

---. "John Keble." In *Essays Critical and Historical*, vol. 2, 421–53. London: Basil, Montagu, Pickering, 1871.

---. *The Letters and Diaries of John Henry Newman.* Edited at the Birmingham Oratory, Charles Stephen Dessain. London: Thomas Nelson and Sons, 1971.

---. *Poetry with Reference to Aristotle's Poetics.* Edited by Albert S. Cook. Boston: Ginn, 1891.

---. *Tract XC: On Certain Passages in the XXXIX Articles, by Rev. J. H. Newman, B.D., 1841; with a Historical Preface by Rev. E. B. Pusey, D.D., and Catholic Subscription to the XXXIX Articles Considered in Reference to Tract XC by Rev. John Keble, M.A., 1841.* London: Walter Smith, 1866.

The New Oxford Annotated Bible. Edited by Bruce M. Metzger and Roland E. Murphy. New York: Oxford University Press, 1994.

Nicholes, Joseph. "Dorothea in the Moated Grange: Millais's *Mariana* and the *Middlemarch* Window-Scenes." *Victorian Institute Journal* 20 (1992): 93–124.

Nunokawa, Jeff. *The Afterlife of Property: Domestic Security and the Victorian Novel.* Princeton: Princeton University Press, 1994.

Oliphant, Margaret. "A Beleaguered City." In *A Beleaguered City and Other Tales of the Seen and the Unseen*, edited by Jenni Calder, 1–106. Canongate Classics. London: Birlinn, 2000.

---. "The Land of Darkness." In *A Beleaguered City and Other Tales of the Seen and the Unseen*, edited by Jenni Calder, 313–62. Canongate Classics. London: Birlinn, 2000.

Orwell, George. "Inside the Whale." In *George Orwell: A Collection of Essays*, 210–52. New York: Harcourt, 1981.

Ostry, Elaine. *Social Dreaming: Dickens and the Fairy Tale.* New York: Routledge, 2002.

Paris, Bernard. "George Eliot's Religion of Humanity." *ELH* 29, no. 4 (1962): 418–43.

Pater, Walter. *Plato and Platonism: A Series of Lectures.* London: Macmillan, 1895.

Paz, D. G. *Popular Anti-Catholicism in Mid-Victorian England.* Stanford: Stanford University Press, 1992.

Pell, Nancy. "The Fathers' Daughter in *Daniel Deronda*." *Nineteenth-Century Fiction* 36, no. 4 (1982): 424–51.

Pese, Esther R. B. "A Suggested Background for Newman's 'Dream of Gerontius.'" *Modern Philology* 46, no. 2 (November 1949): 108–16.
Pickering, John Thomas. *When a Man Dies Where Does He Go? or, Some Things about the Intermediate State, by a Priest of the Church of England*. London: Skeffington and Son, 1902.
Pike, David Lawrence. *Passage through Hell: Modernist Descents, Medieval Underworlds*. Ithaca, NY: Cornell University Press, 1997.
Pollock, Griselda. *Vision and Difference: Femininity, Feminism, and Histories of Art*. New York: Routledge, 1988.
Prickett, Stephen. *Romanticism and Religion: The Tradition of Coleridge and Wordsworth in the Victorian Church*. Cambridge: Cambridge University Press, 1976.
Prince, Gerald. "The Disnarrated." *Style* 22, no.1 (Spring 1988): 1–8.
Quails, Barry. "George Eliot and Religion." In *The Cambridge Companion to George Eliot*, edited by George Levine, 119–37. Cambridge: Cambridge University Press, 2001.
Radin, Grace. *Virginia Woolf's* The Years: *The Evolution of a Novel*. Knoxville: University of Tennessee Press, 1981.
Richter, Harvena. *Virginia Woolf: The Inward Voyage*. Princeton: Princeton University Press, 1970.
Rischin, Abigail. "Besides the Reclining Statue: Ekphrasis, Narrative, and Desire in *Middlemarch*." *PMLA* 111, no. 5 (1996): 1121–32.
Rossetti, Christina. *The Complete Poems*. Edited by R. W. Crump and Betty S. Flowers. New York: Penguin, 2001.
Rossetti, Dante Gabriel. *The Blessed Damozel*. New York: Thomas Bird Mosher, 1905.
Rowell, Geoffrey. *Hell and the Victorians: A Study of the Nineteenth-Century Theological Controversies Concerning Eternal Punishment and the Future Life*. Oxford Scholarly Classics. Oxford: Clarendon Press, 1974.
Rule, Philip C. *Coleridge and Newman: The Centrality of Conscience*. New York: Fordham University Press, 2004.
Ruotolo, Lucio P. *The Interrupted Moment: A View of Virginia Woolf's Novels*. Stanford: Stanford University Press, 1986.
Sadoff, Dianne. "Storytelling and the Figure of the Father in *Little Dorrit*." *PMLA* 95, no. 2 (March 1980): 234–45.
Saint Catherine of Genoa. *Purgation and Purgatory: The Spiritual Dialogue*. Translated by Serge Hughes. New York: Paulist Press, 1979.
Saint Patrick's Purgatory: A Poem by Marie de France. Translated by Michael J. Curley. Binghamton, NY: Medieval and Renaissance Texts and Studies, 1993.
Sanders, Andrew. *Charles Dickens, Resurrectionist*. New York: St. Martin's Press, 1982.

Sanderson, R. E. *The Life of the Waiting Soul in the Intermediate State.* London: Gardner, Darton, 1896.

Schweitzer, Richard. *The Cross and the Trenches: Religious Faith and Doubt among British and American Great War Soldiers.* Westport, CT: Praeger, 2003.

Scott, Sophia L. *Catholic Views as Held by Our Church in All Ages, on Praying for the Departed Soul in the Intermediate State, and Communion of Saints.* London: James Ivison, Printer, 1876.

Sharrock, Roger. "Newman's Poetry." In *Newman after a Hundred Years,* edited by Ian Ker and Alan G. Hill, 43–61. New York: Oxford University Press, 1990.

Shaw, George Bernard. *Man and Superman: A Comedy and a Philosophy.* New York: Brentano's, 1903.

Sheppard, John. *An Autumn Dream: Thoughts in Verse on the Intermediate State of Happy Spirits; To Which Are Appended, Collections from Various Authors, on the "Separate State," and on the Immateriality of Mind; with a Dissertation on the Opinions Cited Concerning the Mind of the Lower Animals.* London: William Ball, 1837.

Shklovsky, Viktor. "Sterne's *Tristram Shandy.*" In *Russian Formalist Criticism: Four Essays,* edited and translated by Lee T. Lemon and Marion J. Reis, 25–57. Lincoln: University of Nebraska Press, 1965.

Showalter, Elaine. "Guilt, Authority, and the Shadows of *Little Dorrit.*" *Nineteenth-Century Fiction* 34, no. 1 (1979): 20–40.

Shuttleworth, Sally. *George Eliot and Nineteenth-Century Science.* Cambridge: Cambridge University Press, 1984.

Sidenvall, Erik. *After Anti-Catholicism? John Henry Newman and Protestant Britain, 1845–c. 1890.* London: T and T Clark International, 2005.

Silver, Brenda. *Woolf's Reading Notebooks.* Princeton: Princeton University Press, 1983.

Simmel, Georg. *On Individuality and Social Forms.* Chicago: University of Chicago Press, 1971.

Snape, Michael. *God and the British Soldier: Religion and the British Army in the First and Second World Wars.* New York: Routledge, 2005.

Stanford Friedman, Susan. "Lyric Subversion of Narrative in Women's Writing: Virginia Woolf and the Tyranny of Plot." In *Reading Narrative: Form, Ethics, Ideology,* edited by James Phelan, 162–85. Columbus: Ohio State University Press, 1989.

Stendhal. *The Red and the Black.* Translated by Roger Gard. London: Penguin Classics, 2002.

Stevenson, Robert Louis. *The Strange Case of Dr. Jekyll and Mr. Hyde.* London: Penguin Classics, 2003.

Stewart, Susan. *On Longing: Narratives of the Miniature, the Gigantic, the Souvenir, the Collection.* Durham, NC: Duke University Press, 1993.

Stoichita, Victor I. *A Short History of the Shadow.* London: Reaktion Books, 1999.

Stokes, John. "Rachel's 'Terrible Beauty': An Actress among the Novelists." *ELH* 51, no. 4 (Winter 1984): 771–93.

Stone, Harry. *Dickens and the Invisible World.* London: Macmillan Press, 1979.

Swinburne, Algernon Charles. *Miscellanies.* London: Chatto and Windus, 1886.

Swindell, Julia. *Victorian Writing and Working Women: The Other Side of Silence.* Minneapolis: University of Minnesota Press, 1985.

Taylor, Isaac. *Physical Theory of Another Life.* New York: D. Appleton, 1836.

Tennyson, Alfred Lord. *Tennyson: A Selected Edition.* Edited by Christopher Ricks. Berkeley: University of California Press, 1989.

Tennyson, G. B. *Victorian Devotional Poetry: The Tractarian Mode.* Cambridge, MA: Harvard University Press, 1981.

Thackeray, William Makepeace. *Vanity Fair.* New York: Penguin Classics, 2003.

Thompson, Andrew. *George Eliot and Italy: Literary, Cultural, and Political Influences from Dante to the Risorgimento.* New York: St. Martin's Press, 1998.

———. "George Eliot's Borrowings from Dante: A List of Sources." *George Eliot–G. H. Lewes Studies* 44–45 (September 2003): 26–74.

Tidy, Gordon. Introduction to *The Dream of Gerontius.* London: John Lane, Bodley Head, 1916.

Tomashevsky, Boris. "Thematics." In *Russian Formalist Criticism: Four Essays*, edited and translated by Lee T. Lemon and Marion J. Reis, 61–95. Lincoln: University of Nebraska Press, 1965.

Transue, Pamela. *Virginia Woolf and the Politics of Style.* Albany: State University of New York Press, 1986.

Trilling, Lionel. "*Little Dorrit.*" *Kenyon Review* 15 (1953): 577–90.

Trollope, Anthony. *Barchester Towers.* Oxford: Oxford University Press, 2008.

Tucker, Herbert F. "Epiphany and Browning: Character Made Manifest." *PMLA* 107, no. 5 (October 1992): 1208–21.

———. "From Monomania to Monologue: 'St. Simeon Stylites' and the Rise of the Victorian Dramatic Monologue." *Victorian Poetry* 22 (1984): 121–37.

Tudor-Pole, W. *Private Dowding: A Plain Record of the After-Death Experiences of a Soldier Killed in Battle, and Some Questions on World Issues Answered by the Messenger Who Taught Him Wider Truths.* London: J. M. Watkins, 1917.

Viswanathan, Gauri. *Outside the Fold: Conversion, Modernity, and Belief.* Princeton: Princeton University Press, 1998.

Vogeler, Martha S. "George Eliot and the Positivists." *Nineteenth-Century Fiction* 35, no. 3 (1980): 406–31.

Wain, John. "*Little Dorrit.*" In *Dickens and the Twentieth Century*, edited by J. Gross and G. Pearson, 213–25. London: Routledge and Kegan Paul, 1966.
Walder, Dennis. *Dickens and Religion.* New York: Routledge, 2007.
Ward, Wilfrid Phillip. *The Life of John Henry Cardinal Newman*, vol. 2. London: Longmans, Green, 1912.
Warner, Sylvia Townsend. *Lolly Willowes; or, The Loving Huntsman.* New York: New York Review Books, 1999.
Watanabe, Hisayoshi. "Past Perfect Retrospection in the Style of Henry James." *American Literature* 34, no. 2 (1962): 165–81.
Watt, Ian. *The Rise of the Novel: Studies in Defoe, Richardson, and Fielding.* Berkeley: University of California Press, 1957.
Wells, H. G. *Boon.* Vol. 13 of *The Works of H. G. Wells.* London: Unwin, 1925. Originally published 1915.
Whately, Richard. *A View of the Scripture Revelations Concerning a Future State.* Philadelphia: Lindsay and Blakiston, 1856.
Wheeler, Michael. *Death and the Future Life in Victorian Literature and Theology.* Cambridge: Cambridge University Press, 1990.
———. *Heaven, Hell and the Victorians.* Cambridge: Cambridge University Press, 1994.
Wiesenfarth, Joseph, ed. *George Eliot: A Writer's Notebook, 1854–1879.* Charlottesville: University of Virginia Press, 1981.
———. "*Middlemarch:* The Language of Art." *PMLA* 97, no. 3 (1982): 363–77.
Wilde, Oscar. *The Picture of Dorian Gray.* New York: Modern Library, 1998.
Wilkinson, Alan. *The Church of England in the First World War.* London: SCM Press, 1996.
Williams, Carolyn. "Moving Pictures: George Eliot and Melodrama." In *Compassion: The Culture and Politics of an Emotion*, edited by Lauren Berlant, 105–44. New York: Routledge, 2004.
Williamson, Arthur. *The Intermediate State: An Essay upon the Relation of Prayer to a Conscious and Progressive Life in the Intermediate State.* London: Wells Gardner, Darton, 1890.
Wilson, Edmund. *The Wound and the Bow.* Athens: Ohio University Press, 1997. Originally published 1929.
Winnett, Susan. "Coming Unstrung: Women, Men, Narrative, and Principles of Pleasure." *PMLA* 105 (1990): 505–18.
Wiseman, Nicholas. Review of "Loss and Gain." *Dublin Review* 24, no. 47 (March 1848).
Witemeyer, Hugh. *George Eliot and the Visual Arts.* New Haven, CT: Yale University Press, 1979.
Wood, Ellen. *East Lynne.* Oxford: Oxford University Press, 2008.

Woods, Irene E. "Charles Dickens, Hans Christian Andersen, and 'The Shadow.'" *Dickens Quarterly* 2, no. 4 (1985): 124–29.
Woolf, Virginia. *Between the Acts*. New York: Harcourt, 1970.
———. *The Diary of Virginia Woolf*, vol. 1, *1915–1919*. Edited by Anne Olivier Bell. New York: Harcourt Brace Jovanovich, 1977.
———. *The Diary of Virginia Woolf*, vol. 3, *1925–1930*. Edited by Anne Olivier Bell, assisted by Andrew McNeillie. New York: Harcourt Brace Jovanovich, 1980.
———. *The Diary of Virginia Woolf*, vol. 4, *1931–1935*. Edited by Anne Olivier Bell, assisted by Andrew McNeillie. New York: Harcourt Brace Jovanovich, 1982.
———. *The Diary of Virginia Woolf*, vol. 5, *1936–1941*. Edited by Anne Olivier Bell, assisted by Andrew McNeillie. New York: Harcourt Brace, 1984.
———. "George Eliot." *Times Literary Supplement*, November 20, 1919.
———. *The Letters of Virginia Woolf*, vol. 6, *1936–1941*. Edited by Nigel Nicholson and Joanne Trautmann. New York: Harcourt Brace Jovanovich, 1980.
———. "Modern Fiction." In *The Essays of Virginia Woolf*, vol. 4, *1925–1928*, edited by Andrew McNeillie, 157–64. New York: Harcourt Brace Jovanovich, 1994.
———. "More Dostoevsky." In *The Essays of Virginia Woolf*, vol. 2, *1912–1918*, edited by Andrew McNeillie, 83–87. New York: Harcourt Brace Jovanovich, 1987.
———. "Mr. Bennett and Mrs. Brown." In *Mr. Bennett and Mrs. Brown*. London: Hogarth Press, 1924.
———. *Mrs. Dalloway*. Oxford: Oxford University Press, 2000.
———. *The Pargiters*. New York: Harcourt Brace Jovanovich, 1977.
———. "A Sketch of the Past." In *Moments of Being: Unpublished Autobiographical Writings*, edited by Jeanne Schulkind, 61–160. Sussex, UK: Chatto and Windus for Sussex University Press, 1976.
———. *The Waves*. Oxford: Oxford University Press, 1998.
———. *The Years*. New York: Harcourt Brace, 1937.
Wordsworth, William. *The Prelude: The Four Texts (1798, 1799, 1805, 1850)*. New York: Penguin Classics, 1995.
Yeazell, Ruth Bernard. "Do It or Dorrit." *NOVEL: A Forum on Fiction* 25, no. 1 (Autumn 1991): 33–49.

Index

action (concept), 36–39, 73; and acting, 73, 88, 183, 196n8; Dickens's use of, 130, 134, 136; Eliot's use of, 9, 11–12, 34, 58, 67–68, 72–77, 78, 88, 94, 106, 111–12; habitual, 129; inward, 2, 3, 8–9, 12, 20, 48, 67–68, 72–74, 106, 122, 183–85, 189, 193; James's use of, 153–54; Newman on, 34–38, 48; in purgatorial quest stories, 18–19, 35; quotidian, 173–74; in shadow stories, 120, 131, 133; unseen, 9, 75–76, 90, 190; Woolf on, 181–83
Adam Bede (Eliot), 209n7, 213–14n54
adventure stories: and bildungsroman, 61–62; midlife plots in, 12–13, 62–63, 113–15, 150, 154, 155, 191–92; Simmel on, 60–61, 113, 151–52. *See also* specific works
afterlife: action in, 38; another life (concept), 57–58, 81, 84–85, 176, 180, 181, 184–86; consoling model of, 55; gradual conversion in, 25–26; importance to Victorians, 15; maturation in, 16, 19, 26, 29, 31, 33–34, 202n26; Oxford Movement on, 15, 17, 18–19, 30, 32, 65–66, 208n72; soul sleep in, 34–35, 76; in theology, 15–16, 55–57, 62. *See also* eschatology; Judgment; purgatory
"Altar of the Dead, The" (James), 20–21, 146, 147–48, 149
Ambassadors, The (James), 21, 118, 156; delayed beginnings, 148–49; Dickensian tropes, 145–46; epiphanies, 150–54; hoarding, 146–47; in medias res, techniques, 21, 145–46, 148, 154–55
Analogy of Religion, The (Butler), 65
Andersen, Hans Christian: "Shadow, The" 124, 127, 128, 131–33
another life (concept). *See under* afterlife
ante-purgatory, 99–100, 103, 107–8, 216n64
Apologia Pro Vita Sua (Newman), 23, 25, 66
Arendt, Hannah, 38, 204n41
Aristotle: *Poetics*, 18–19, 35–39, 196n8
Armstrong, Isobel: *Victorian Poetry*, 39–40
Arnold, Matthew, 39–40
arrested development, 2–3, 5–6, 20, 67, 72, 118–19, 122, 129, 139–42, 197n20

Aspects of the Novel (Forster), 8
Auerbach, Erich, 16
Austen, Jane, 165, 173; *Emma*, 157; *Persuasion*, 157

bachelors. *See* middle-aged bachelors (character type)
Bakhtin, Mikhail, 7
Balzac, Honoré de, 154; *Lost Illusions*, 9
Barchester Towers (Trollope), 13, 82, 83
Baudrillard, Jean, 69
"Beast in the Jungle, The" (James), 20–21, 129, 146, 148, 156
Beckett, Samuel: *More Pricks than Kicks*, 215–16n63
Beer, Gillian, 15, 67, 113, 114; *Darwin's Plots*, 64
beginnings, 74, 108, 118–19, 145–46, 148, 189, 191, 211n30
"Beleaguered City, A" (Oliphant), 55–56
Between the Acts (Woolf), 224n24
Bennett, Arnold, 145
Bickersteth, E. H., 35; *The Shadowed Home*, 77, 203n36
bildungsroman tradition, 4–6; and adventure stories, 61–62; conversion in, 23; Eliot on, 60, 82–84, 110, 115, 198n21; and midlife narratives, 7–10, 12–13, 119–20, 154–55, 156; and modernity, 191, 197–98n20; use of term, 8; and World War I, 158, 192–93
Blackwood, John, 68
Bleak House (Dickens), 117, 118
"Blessed Damozel, The" (Rossetti), 104–5
botanical imagery, 62, 74–78, 113–14, 210n14
Brontë, Charlotte, 6, 29, 164; *Jane Eyre*, 6, 87; *Villette*, 17, 29, 30, 55, 155, 158, 164
Brooks, Peter, 10; *Reading for the Plot*, 8–9, 198n23, 198n27, 220–21n33
Browning, Robert: "Johannes Agricola in Meditation," 41, 49, 51
Butler, Joseph: *The Analogy of Religion*, 65, 210n17

Carlisle, Janice, 144–45; *The Sense of an Audience*, 130
Carlyle, Thomas: *On Heroes, Hero-Worship, and the Heroic in History*, 97

INDEX

Caserio, Robert, 2, 9, 10, 195n4
Catherine of Genoa, Saint, 202n26
Chamisso, Adelbert von: *Peter Schlemiel*, 123–26, 128, 132
Chesterton, G. K., 116
Christian Observer, The (Eliot), 65
"Christmas Carol, A" (Dickens), 123–24, 138
Clough, Arthur Hugh, 39–40
coincidence, 78–81
collecting, 19, 69, 146
consolation, 19, 28–29, 30, 53, 207n62
conversion, 2–3, 20, 23–25, 29, 32, 48, 174. *See also* maturation
counterfactuals, 18, 120–21, 123, 133–36, 145–46
Cranford (Gaskell), 82, 158
Cross, John, 95
Culler, Jonathan, 46

Daniel Deronda (Eliot): critique of, 5, 59; ekphrasis in, 86; epochs in, 11; futurity in, 64; gradual change in, 59–60, 164; La Pia, use of character, 97–105, 108–9; living statues in, 88–91, 93–94, 111–13; *nostos* in, 114–15; *Purgatorio* citations, 103–10; purgatory metaphor, 17, 62–63, 191; screaming statue in, 85–86, 87, 89; seed cycles, 113–14; unauthorized sequel *Gwendolen*, 59; widows, 81–83, 110, 119
Dante Alighieri, 21, 174–76; *The Divine Comedy*, 17, 68, 96–97, 106–7, 169; *Inferno*, 17, 97, 169; *Paradiso*, 97, 144; *Purgatorio*, 19–20, 30–32, 35, 57–58, 62–63, 66, 68, 83, 95–106, 161, 168, 169, 175–76
Darwin, Charles: *On the Origin of Species*, 67
Darwin's Plots (Beer), 64
David Copperfield (Dickens), 6, 119
"Dead, The" (Joyce), 188–89
descent, 1, 3, 21–22, 79, 144, 162–63, 168, 169–76, 178, 183–87, 188–91
Dickens, Charles, 6, 17, 20, 165, 173, 188
    action, use of, 130, 134, 136
    Bleak House, 117, 118
    "Christmas Carol, A," 123–24, 138
    David Copperfield, 6, 119
    on descent, 190–91
    gradualism, 120–22
    Great Expectations, 7, 139
    "Haunted Man, The," 123–24
    influence on James, 145–46, 147, 149–50
    Life of Our Lord, The, 138
    Little Dorrit, 7, 58; arrested development in, 139–42; counterfactual moments, 120–21, 133–36, 145–46; doppelgangers, 134–35, 145; Judgment in, 17, 136–37, 143; middle-age bachelors in, 20, 116–19, 135–37, 140–45; original title, 131–32; passivity, 2, 73, 129–30, 149–50, 195n6; plot techniques, 117, 119–20, 156; purgatorial motif, 137–39, 144–46; restoration in, 142–45, 150–51; shadow folklore in, 123–30, 144–45; widows in, 82
    marriage plot, use of, 151
    Our Mutual Friend, 117
    plot techniques, 119–20
    religious views, 137–38
    shadow stories, 121–30, 144–45
discourse, use of, 10
Divine Comedy, The (Dante Alighieri), 17, 68, 96–97, 106–7, 169. *See also Inferno* (Dante Alighieri); *Paradiso* (Dante Alighieri); *Purgatorio* (Dante Alighieri)
doppelganger stories, 120, 134–35, 145, 147–48, 219n25
Doré, Gustave, 63, 84; "The Earthly Garden of Bliss," 101; "La Pia of Siena," 98–100, 99; "The Late-Repenters," 102
Dostoevsky, Fyodor, 182, 183
Doyle, Francis Hastings, 27, 28–29, 44, 53–54
drama, 88
Dream of Gerontius, The (Newman), 18–19; as consolation poetry, 28–29, 41, 53–55; disembodied contentment in, 51–52; influence of, 55–58; inward action in, 36, 190; organization of, 42–45; and poetic conciliation, 39–42, 55; popularity of, 26–28; ritualism in, 41, 42–45; salvation in, 49; soliloquies, 39, 41–42, 44, 45–48, 49, 53
Dubliners (Joyce), 176, 188–89

"Earthly Garden of Bliss, The" (Doré), 101
East Lynne (Wood), 6
Edelman, Lee, 212n37
ekphrasis, use of, 84–87, 91, 93–94, 112
Elgar, Edward, 27
Eliot, George, 8, 17, 154
    action, approach to, 9, 11–12, 34, 58, 67–68, 72–77, 78, 88, 94, 106, 111–12
    Adam Bede, 209n7, 213–14n54

246

INDEX

on afterlife, 77–78
another life concept, 81, 84–85
on bildungsroman tradition, 60, 82–84, 110, 115, 198n21
Christian Observer, The, 65
Daniel Deronda: critique of, 5, 59; ekphrasis in, 86; epochs in, 11; futurity in, 64; gradual change in, 59–60, 164; La Pia, use of character, 97–105, 108–9; living statues in, 88–91, 93–94, 111–13; *nostos* in, 114–15; *Purgatorio* citations, 103–10; purgatory metaphor, 17, 62–63, 191; screaming statue in, 85–86, 87, 89; seed cycles, 113–14; unauthorized sequel *Gwendolen*, 59; widows, 81–83, 110, 119
ekphrasis, use of, 84–87, 112
eschatology, 63–67
on futurity, 64–66
on gradualism/maturation, 59–60, 62, 84–85, 86, 110–16
Idea of a Future Life, The, 63, 64
internalized action, use of, 9
"Knowing That Shortly I Must Put Off This Tabernacle," 210n16
and Lessing, 85–92, 105, 112
living statues, use of, 84–85, 88–91, 93–94, 111–12
make-believe beginnings, 73–76
marriage plot, use of, 11–12, 59–60, 83–84, 87, 94–95, 107, 110–11, 114, 115, 118
Middlemarch, 8, 60; epochs in, 11–12; living statues in, 88–89, 91; marriage plot, 83–84, 115; maturity in, 62; memorialization in, 97; middle-aged bachelor in, 118; nature of beauty in, 92–93; storyline, 83
Mill on the Floss, The, 62
narrative hoarding, 68–81
on nature of beauty, 92–93
plot models, 78–81, 110
purgatorial development, 19–20, 62–63, 66, 84, 93, 95, 103–10
Romola, 60, 115
Scenes of Clerical Life, 60, 108
Silas Marner, 19, 60, 64, 67–81, 156; epochs in, 78; hoarding in, 13, 62, 67–72, 75, 79, 123; metamorphosis in, 72–73; middle-aged bachelor in, 118; phantasm of desire in, 74–75; plot model, 78–81; restoration in, 80–81

tableau vivant, 81, 85, 87–90, 94, 112, 153, 213n50
visual arts, use of, 63, 85–87, 93–94, 111–12
Emma (Austen), 157
epiphanies, 150–54, 174, 176
eschatology, 30–35, 210n14; importance to Victorians, 15, 29, 137; maturation in, 16, 36, 65, 85; modern model of, 17, 19, 63; in soliloquies, 45–48. *See also* afterlife; Judgment; purgatory
Evans, Mary Ann. *See* Eliot, George
events (plot unit), 11
evolutionary theory, 15, 33, 64, 65, 66–67

family chronicles, 160, 167–68
female abjection, 85–87, 89, 95
Feuerbach, Ludwig, 64, 65
folklore. *See* shadow stories
Forster, E. M.: *Aspects of the Novel*, 8
Forster, John, 116, 137
François, Anne-Lise, 2
French Revolution, 14–15
Friedman, Susan, 167
Froula, Christine, 224n24
Frye, Northrop, 206n54

Garcha, Amanpal, 10
Gaskell, Elizabeth: *Cranford*, 82, 158
Gates, Sarah, 114
Genette, Gérard, 10
geology, 15, 65
Gissing, George, 5, 116; *The Odd Women*, 157
Goethe, Johann Wolfgang von, 154
Gordon, Charles George, 27, 42–44, 53
Gothic literature, 164
gradualism: in afterlife, 25–26; and doppelgangers, 120; and ekphrasis, 86; and eschatology, 33–34; in family chronicle, 167–68; and historical change, 17–18, 161–62, 168, 185; in maturation, 3, 6, 10, 28–29, 110–16, 191; in narrative lulls, 10, 36, 38, 135–36, 191, 197n13; in poetry, 46; radical, 3, 6, 10, 14–15; vs. stasis, 60; theology on, 15–16, 18, 29, 33–34
Great Divorce, The (Lewis), 56
Great Expectations (Dickens), 7, 139
Greenblatt, Stephen, 31
Gross, Kenneth, 88

Hamlet (Shakespeare), 31–32, 217n10

INDEX

Hardy, Thomas: *Tess of the D'Urbervilles*, 121
"Haunted Man, The" (Dickens), 123–24
heaven, belief in, 57
Hertz, Neil, 64, 78
Hirsch, Marianne, 8
hoarding: economic models of, 62; in *Little Dorrit*, 123, 145; in *Silas Marner*, 13, 67–72, 75, 79, 123
Homer: *The Odyssey*, 4, 21, 184, 188, 189–90

Idea of a Future Life, The (Eliot), 63, 64
Inferno (Dante Alighieri), 17, 97, 169
in medias res, techniques, 18, 21, 145–46, 148, 154–55
In Memoriam (Tennyson), 27, 40–42
inside the whale (concept). *See* Jonah (biblical character)
"Inside the Whale" (Orwell), 1–2
interiority, 4, 8–9, 36, 66, 72–73, 92, 106, 110, 184–85, 189, 193
interludes, 12–13, 19, 80–81, 84, 157, 161–62, 163–64, 183–84
intermediate state, 33–35, 38, 57, 65–67, 68, 76, 78, 106, 108, 115, 138, 143, 216n68

James, Henry, 4, 5, 13, 20–21, 59, 129, 156, 165, 223n17
    "Altar of the Dead, The," 20–21, 146, 147–48, 149
    Ambassadors, The, 21, 118, 156; delayed beginnings, 148–49; Dickensian tropes, 145–46; epiphanies, 150–54; hoarding, 146–47; in medias res, techniques, 21, 145–46, 148, 154–55
    "Beast in the Jungle, The," 20–21, 129, 146, 148, 156
    Dickensian tropes used, 145–46, 147, 149–50
    epiphanies, use of, 150–54
    "Jolly Corner, The," 20–21, 148, 151
    marriage plot, use of, 13, 159
    Middle Years, The, 147, 196n9
    "poor, sensitive gentleman" character, 145–55
    Portrait of a Lady, The, 153
    Washington Square, 158, 159
Jane Eyre (Brontë), 6, 87
"Johannes Agricola in Meditation" (Browning), 41, 49, 51
"Jolly Corner, The" (James), 20–21, 148, 151

Jonah (biblical character), 1–4, 15–16, 79, 149–50, 183–84
Joyce, James, 191–92; "The Dead," 188–89; *Dubliners*, 176, 188–89; *A Portrait of the Artist*, 191–92; *Ulysses*, 21, 192
Judgment: and heaven/hell, 56; purgatorial, 136–42; reconceived model of, 16–17, 19, 31–32; and shadow story, 122; as state of maturation, 25–26, 31, 33–35, 40–41, 65, 67; time in, 35

Keble, John, 28, 54
Kenner, Hugh, 158
King, Amy M., 209n7
Kingsley, Charles, 24–25, 27–28, 53, 55
"Knowing That Shortly I Must Put Off This Tabernacle" (Eliot), 210n16
Kucich, John, 221n34

"Land of Darkness, The" (Oliphant), 55–56
Laocoön (Lessing), 85–86
La Pia de'Tolomei (Rossetti), 100, *103*
La Pia of Siena (literary character), 97–106, *99*, *101–3*
"La Pia of Siena" (Doré), 98–100, *99*
"Late-Repenters, The" (Doré), *102*
Lawrence, D. H., 9
Lee, Hermione, 176, 226n39
Le Goff, Jacques, 31
Lessing, G. E., 85–92, 105, 112; *Laocoön*, 85–86
Levenback, Karen, 224n24
Levine, Caroline, 197n13, 199n33
Levine, George, 10, 15, 24
Lewes, George Henry, 66–67
Lewis, C. S., 55–56; *The Great Divorce*, 56
Lewis, Pericles, 163–64
Life of Our Lord, The (Dickens), 138
Little Dorrit (Dickens), 7, 58; arrested development in, 139–42; counterfactual moments, 120–21, 133–36, 145–46; doppelgangers, 134–35, 145; Judgment in, 17, 136–37, 143; middle-age bachelors in, 20, 116–19, 135–37, 140–45; original title, 131–32; passivity, 2, 73, 129–30, 149–50, 195n6; plot techniques, 117, 119–20, 156; purgatorial motif, 137–39, 144–46; restoration in, 142–45, 150–51; shadow folklore in, 123–30, 144–45; widows in, 82
liturgy, 41–42, 44

INDEX

living statues, use of, 84–85, 88–91, 93–94, 111–13
Lolly Willowes (Warner), 158–59
Loss and Gain (Newman), 23, 25n
Lost Illusions (Balzac), 9
Lukács, Georg, 7

Mackay, Robert William: *The Progress of the Intellect*, 77–78
Marcus, Jane, 167
Mariana (Millais), 84
"Mariana" (Tennyson), 103–4
Markovits, Stefanie, 2, 10, 37
marriage plot: afterlife of, 81–85, 95, 110–11; Austen's use of, 157; critique of, 60, 83–85; Dicken's use of, 151; Eliot's use of, 11–12, 59–60, 83–84, 87, 94–95, 107, 110–11, 114, 115, 118; female development and, 111, 114, 115, 118; James's use of, 13, 159; middle-aged exclusion, 94–95, 118; Trollope's use of, 83; waning use of, 4, 13, 163; Woolf's use of, 157, 162–63, 168
maturation: in afterlife/purgatory, 15, 16–17, 18, 19, 26, 29, 31, 33–34, 57–58; descent/renewal in, 193; gradualism in, 3, 6, 10, 28–29, 110–16, 191; Judgment as, 25–26, 31, 33–35, 40–41, 65, 67; pace of, 11, 12; tropes, 15; unseen, 2; use of term, 196n9
middle age, defined, 15, 196–97n10
middle-aged bachelors (character type), 12–14, 20, 116–18, 145–55
Middlemarch (Eliot), 8, 60; epochs in, 11–12; living statues in, 88–89, 91; marriage plot, 83–84, 115; maturity in, 62; memorialization in, 97; middle-aged bachelor in, 118; nature of beauty in, 92–93; storyline, 83
Middle Years, The (James), 147, 196n9
midlife narratives: adventure stories, 60–63, 150, 192; and bildungsroman tradition, 7–10, 12–13, 119–20, 154–55, 156; events/epochs in, 11–12, 13; historical context, 14–22; marginalization of, 196–97n10; middle-aged character types, 12–14
Milbank, Alison, 106
Mill, John Stuart: *The Spirit of the Age*, 14
Millais, John Everett, 63; *Mariana*, 84
Miller, Andrew, 120, 121, 201n15, 217n11
Miller, Henry, 195n5
Mill on the Floss, The (Eliot), 62

"Modern Fiction" (Woolf), 156, 159, 165, 179
modernism, 56, 168, 197n20, 224n23
moments of non-being, use of term, 173–74, 186
More Pricks than Kicks (Beckett). 215–16n63
Moretti, Franco, 7–8, 121, 154, 155, 158, 192
Morgan, Monique, 40, 46, 206n54
"Mr. Bennett and Mrs. Brown" (Woolf), 159–60
Mrs. Dalloway (Woolf), 181

narrative lulls: and arrested development, 2–3, 5–6; as feminine style, 224n23; as gradual progression, 10, 36, 38, 135–36, 191, 197n13; and introspection, 4, 9, 36, 110, 189; in Jonah story, 1–3; in purgatory visits, 21, 36, 142–43, 189; in Woolf's writings, 166–71, 174
narrative middles, 119, 148, 168, 199n33
Newman, John Henry
on action, 34–38, 48
Apologia Pro Vita Sua, 23, 25, 66
on Aristotle's *Poetics*, 35–39
Dream of Gerontius, The, 18–19; as consolation poetry, 28–29, 41, 53–55; disembodied contentment in, 51–52; influence of, 55–58; inward action in, 36, 190; organization of, 42–45; and poetic conciliation, 39–42, 55; popularity of, 26–28; ritualism in, 41, 42–45; salvation in, 49; soliloquies in, 39, 45–48, 49, 53
on interiority, 190
on Judgment, 16–17, 19, 31
Loss and Gain, 23, 25
on mature conversion, 23–25, 32, 48
on poetry, 37–39
"Poetry with Reference to Aristotle's *Poetics*," 35–39
on purgatory as growth, 16–19, 26, 31–33, 46, 55–56
on purgatory narrative model, 18–19
reacceptance of, 26–27
romantic influences, 200n2, 204n39
Tract 90, 15, 16, 26, 30, 32, 45, 54–55, 65–66, 202n26
nostos, 114–15
novels. *See* family chronicles; Gothic literature; marriage plot; midlife narratives; plot; realism; sensation fiction; specific works

249

INDEX

Odd Women, The (Gissing), 157
odd women/old maids (character type), 21, 156–64, 168
Odyssey, The (Homer), 21, 184, 188, 189–90
Oliphant, Margaret: "A Beleaguered City," 55–56; "The Land of Darkness," 55–56
On Heroes, Hero-Worship, and the Heroic in History (Carlyle), 97
On the Origin of Species (Darwin), 67
Ortiz-Robles, Mario, 199n33
Orwell, George, 1–3; "Inside the Whale," 1–2
Ostry, Elaine, 123
Our Mutual Friend (Dickens), 117
Oxford Movement, 168; on afterlife and purgatory, 15, 17, 18–19, 30, 32, 65–66, 208n72; aftermath of, 26–29, 54, 168; influence of, 57, 137–38

Paradiso (Dante Alighieri), 97, 144
Pargiters, The (Woolf), 166, 167, 224n24
parousia, 34, 38, 76–78
passivity, 2, 38, 73, 79, 132–33, 149–50, 195n6
Pater, Walter, 15
Paul (apostle), 24
Persuasion (Austen), 157
Peter Schlemiel (Chamisso), 123–26, 128, 132
Physical Theory of Another Life (Taylor), 65
Picture of Dorian Gray, The (Wilde), 133
plot: use of term, 10–11; gradual, 4, 8, 11, 164, 167–68, 198n27; of youth, 4–5, 6, 13, 61–62, 113, 119, 160, 191–92. *See also* action (concept); adventure stories; bildungsroman; events; gradualism; marriage plot; midlife narratives; turning points, specific authors; specific works
poena damni, 32
Poetics (Aristotle), 18–19, 35–39, 196n8
poetry: on afterlife, 37–38, 37–39; and conciliation, 41–42, 54–55; devotional, 25–28, 39, 41, 43, 46; dramatic monologue, 39, 40, 41, 45, 46, 49–51, 150; lyric, 27, 40, 41, 46–47, 49, 199n; and narrative theory, 40; and politics, 39–40; purgatorial gradualism in, 46; ritualistic, 36–37, 41–45; solace of, 28–29, 37, 53–55; soliloquy, 39, 41–42, 44, 45–48, 49, 53; theology in, 28, 53–54. *See also* specific works

"Poetry with Reference to Aristotle's *Poetics*" (Newman), 35–39
Portrait of a Lady, The (James), 153
Portrait of the Artist, A (Joyce), 191–92
Pre-Raphaelites, 19–20, 62–63, 84, 87, 89, 95, 98, 100, 103–4
Prickett, Stephen, 24
Prince, Gerald, 120, 121
Progress of the Intellect, The (Mackay), 77–78
Purgatorio (Dante Alighieri), 19–20, 30–32, 35, 57–58, 62–63, 66, 68, 83, 95–106, 161, 168, 169, 175–76
purgatory: as metaphor, 17, 58, 93, 95, 137–39, 145–46, 168, 191; and narrative lulls, 21; as narrative model, 17, 18–19, 95–96, 163; Oxford Movement on, 15, 17, 18–19, 30, 32, 65–66, 208n72; resurgence of belief in, 32; as state of growth, 15, 16–17, 29, 46, 55–56, 58–59; temporality in, 48; in theology, 17–19, 29, 57–58, 63, 106–7, 122; Victorian reinvention of, 30–35, 58. *See also* afterlife; eschatology

radical gradualism. *See under* gradualism
Reading for the Plot (Brooks), 8–9, 198n23, 198n27, 220–21n33
realism, 9–10, 38, 84, 122
Red and the Black, The (Stendhal), 7
Romola (Eliot), 60, 115
Rossetti, Dante Gabriel, 63, 84, 98; "Blessed Damozel, The," 104–5; *La Pia de' Tolomei*, 100, *103*
Rossetti, Christina, 41, 43
Rowell, Geoffrey, 15, 55

Sabbatarian controversy, 138
Scenes of Clerical Life (Eliot), 60, 108
Schlemihl, Peter. *See* shadow stories
Second Coming, 34, 38, 76–78
sensation fiction, 6
Sense of an Audience, The (Carlisle), 130
"Shadow, The" (Andersen), 124, 127, 128, 131–33
Shadowed Home, The (Bickersteth), 77
shadow stories, 18, 20, 69, 123–30, 136, 147–48; and doppelgangers, 134–35; Peter Schlemihl folktale, 120, 122, 123–33, 144–45; and remembrance, 127–28. *See also* specific stories

INDEX

Shakespeare, William: *Hamlet*, 31–32, 217n10; *The Winter's Tale*, 80, 81, 84, 88
Shaw, George Bernard, 207n67
Sheol, 1–3
Short History of the Shadow, A (Stoichita), 127
Silas Marner (Eliot), 19, 60, 64, 67–81, 156; epochs in, 78; hoarding in, 13, 62, 67–72, ; 5, 79, 123; metamorphosis in, 72–73; middle-aged bachelor in, 118; phantasm of desire in, 74–75; plot model, 78–81; restoration in, 80–81
Silver, Brenda, 169
Simmel, Georg, 60–61, 113–14, 151–52, 191
"Sketch of the Past, A" (Woolf), 173
soliloquies, 39, 44, 45–48, 49, 53
soul sleep, 34–35, 76
Southey, Robert, 37
Spirit of the Age, The (Mill), 14
statuary. *See* living statues
Stendhal, 154; *The Red and the Black*, 7
Stevenson, Robert Louis: *The Strange Case of Dr. Jekyll and Mr. Hyde*, 133
Stewart, Susan, 68–69
Stoichita, Victor: *A Short History of the Shadow*, 127
Strange Case of Dr. Jekyll and Mr. Hyde, The (Stevenson), 133
strange introversion, use of term, 25–26, 190
"St. Simeon Stylites" (Tennyson), 41, 49
Swinburne, Algernon Charles, 27

Taylor, Isaac: *Physical Theory of Another Life*, 65
Tennyson, Alfred Lord: *In Memoriam*, 27, 40–42; "Mariana," 103–4; "St. Simeon Stylites," 41, 49
Tennyson, G. B., 28, 53
Tess of the D'Urbervilles (Hardy), 121
Thackeray, William Makepeace: *Vanity Fair*, 6–7, 82, 87
theology: on afterlife, 16, 55–57, 62; on gradual development, 15–16, 18, 29, 33–34; and narrative form, 63–67; in poetry, 28, 53–54; on purgatory, 17–19, 29, 57–58, 63, 106–7, 122. *See also* Newman, John Henry; Oxford Movement
Tieck, Ludwig, 125
Tolstoy, Leo, 165, 173
To the Lighthouse (Woolf), 158–63, 165, 168–69, 181; "Time Passes," 161–62, 164
Tract 90 (Newman), 15, 16, 26, 30, 32, 45, 54–55, 65–66, 202n26

Tractarians, 15, 28, 32, 43, 53, 206–7n62. *See also* Oxford Movement
Trilling, Lionel, 117, 137
Trollope, Anthony, 165, 173; *Barchester Towers*, 13, 82, 83
Tucker, Herbert, 150–51
turning points, 94, 110, 150, 151

Ulysses (Joyce), 21, 192
ut pictura poesis, 85, 89, 92, 212n42

Vanity Fair (Thackeray), 6–7, 82, 87
Victorian Poetry (Armstrong), 39–40
Villette (Brontë), 17, 29, 30, 55, 155, 158, 164

Warner, Sylvia Townsend: *Lolly Willowes*, 158–59
Washington Square (James), 158, 159
Watt, Ian, 9–10
Waves, The (Woolf), 165, 167, 168–69, 181
Wells, H. G., 5
Whately, Richard, 34, 66, 76–77
Wheeler, Michael, 220n31
widows (character type), 81–83, 95–97, 110, 119
Wilde, Oscar, 133–34; *Picture of Dorian Gray*, 133
Williams, Carolyn, 112
Winnett, Susan, 198n27
Winter's Tale, The (Shakespeare), 80, 81, 84, 88
Wiseman, Nicholas, 25
Wood, Ellen: *East Lynne*, 6
Woolf, Virginia, 17–18, 146
  on action, 181–83
  another life concept, 57–58, 176, 180, 181, 184–86
  Between the Acts, 224n24
  character types, 14, 21
  Dante's influence, 169–70, 174–76
  on descent, 189
  on Dostoevsky, 182, 183
  gradualism, 161, 164, 167–68
  and literary interludes, 161–64
  marriage plot, use of, 157, 162–63, 168
  on mature stories, 8, 156
  "Modern Fiction," 156, 159, 165, 179
  on moments of non-being, 173–74, 183, 186
  "Mr. Bennet and Mrs. Brown," 159–60
  Mrs. Dalloway, 181
  narrative lulls, 166–71
  New World concept, 176, 177, 179–81, 184–86, 190
  on novel-essay, 225n35

INDEX

Woolf, Virginia (*cont.*)
    odd women characters, 158–64
    Pargiters, The, 166, 167, 224n24
    plot suspension, 150, 161–62
    purgatorial plotting, 57–58, 163, 168, 169–76
    "Sketch of the Past, A," 173
    To the Lighthouse, 158–63, 165, 168–69, 181; "Time Passes," 161–62, 164
    Victorian novel, use of, 158, 160, 161, 163–69, 170, 172

Waves, The, 165, 167, 168–69, 181
Years, The, 21, 57–58, 158–59, 161–62; as act of resistance, 224n24; air raid scene, 177–87; another life concept, 57–58, 176, 180, 181, 184–86; descent in, 191; early titles, 186; gradualism, 167–68; moments of non-being, 173–74, 183, 186; New World concept, 176, 177, 179–81, 184–86, 190; purgatorial plotting, 169–76; and Victorian novel, 165–69, 172